Gender Education and Equality in a Global Context

What does gender equality mean for young men and women in *poor* communities across different countries?

The Millennium Development Goals aim to achieve basic education for all by 2015. But can such global agendas address national and local gender inequalities and will they empower women through education? New research on gender education makes an important contribution to this global debate.

Shailaja Fennell and Madeleine Arnot have brought together leading international scholars and a new generation of researchers working within development studies, gender studies and education. The result is a thought-provoking book that offers an opportunity to engage critically with existing and emergent conceptual frameworks and methodological approaches. The book is split into three well-defined sections that:

- reconceptualise the definitions of gender equality used by various social scientific disciplines, international organisations and policy makers;
- illustrate the methodologies used to collect the voices of young men and women and their teachers, telling stories of their success in lifting the burdens of poverty and negotiating traditional gender relations through small but significant acts of agency;
- trace the impact of global gender agendas on national education policies, such as citizenship education, poverty reduction strategies, the education of the female citizen and feminist activism around adult women's learning.

Gender Education and Equality in a Global Context is an invaluable introduction to the range of conceptual frameworks and innovative research methods that address contemporary issues of gender education and development.

Shailaja Fennell is a Lecturer in Development Studies and **Madeleine Arnot** is Professor of Sociology of Education at the University of Cambridge, UK.

Gender Education and Equality in a Global Context

Conceptual frameworks and policy perspectives

Edited by Shailaja Fennell and
Madeleine Arnot

Routledge
Taylor & Francis Group

LONDON AND NEW YORK

First published 2008
by Routledge
2 Park Square, Milton Park, Abingdon, Oxon OX14 4RN

Simultaneously published in the USA and Canada
by Routledge
270 Madison Ave, New York, NY 10016

Routledge is an imprint of the Taylor & Francis Group, an informa business

Transferred to Digital Printing 2009

© 2008 Selection and editorial matter, Shailaja Fennell and Madeleine
Arnot; individual chapters, the contributors

Typeset in Galliard by Wearset Ltd, Boldon, Tyne and Wear

British Library Cataloguing in Publication Data
A catalogue record for this book is available from the British Library

Library of Congress Cataloging in Publication Data
Gender education and equality in a global context: conceptual frameworks
and policy perspectives/[edited by] Shailaja Fennell and Madeleine Arnot.
p. cm.
1. Women–Education. 2. Educational equalization. 3. Women in
development. 4. Women in education. 5. Sex discrimination in education.
6. Sex discrimination against women. I. Fennell, Shailaja, 1964– II. Arnot,
Madeleine.
LC1405.G46 2007
371.822–dc22
2007009739

ISBN10: 0-415-41944-1 (hbk)
ISBN10: 0-415-55205-2 (pbk)
ISBN10: 0-203-93959-X (ebk)

ISBN13: 978-0-415-41944-4 (hbk)
ISBN13: 978-0-415-55205-9 (pbk)
ISBN13: 978-0-203-93959-8 (ebk)

Contents

Contributors

Madeleine Arnot is Professor of Sociology of Education, Fellow of Jesus College, Cambridge University and the Academy of Social Sciences. Her primary focus is on gender relations, social equality issues and policies in education and citizenship education. She has been an international consultant for the UNESCO *Gender Monitoring Report*, the Council of Europe and various government gender initiatives in Portugal, Greece, Spain and Argentina. She has directed research programmes on women as citizens; broadening adolescent masculinity; pupil consultation and the education of asylum-seeking and refugee children in the UK. She is currently working on the RECOUP project, focusing on youth, gender and citizenship. Her recent publications include: *Challenging Democracy: international perspectives on gender, education and citizenship* (ed. with J. Dillabough, 2000); *Reproducing Gender? Selected essays on educational theory and feminist politics* (2002); *The RoutledgeFalmer Gender and Education Reader* (ed. with M. Mac an Ghaill, 2006); *Educating the Gendered Citizen* (2007 in press).

Leslie Casely-Hayford is Director of Associates for Change, a research and consulting firm based in Ghana, specialising in education and social development (www.associatesforchange.org). Her research in comparative education and development in Africa and Asia focuses on investigating the barriers to quality education in rural areas of Africa, complementary systems of education, girls' education, social equity and literacy attainment among children. She has consulted for a number of international organisations including: UNESCO, the World Bank, the Canadian Development Agency, and USAID, along with a number of Non-Governmental Agencies. She currently leads the Ghanaian team in the RECOUP project on educational outcomes and poverty. Her publications include: 'The quality dilemma: an ethnographic study of rural education in Northern Ghana' (ed. C. Sunal and K. Mutua, *Forefronts in Education Research*, Info Age Publishing, 2004); 'Reaching educational quality goals in Sub Saharan Africa': A look at Complementary Education Systems (eds C. Sunal and K. Mutua, *The Enterprise of Education*, Info Age Publishing, 2007).

Fatuma Chege is Senior Lecturer and Chair of the Department of Educational Foundations, Kenyatta University, Nairobi, Kenya where she teaches sociology of education and philosophy of education. She is also Chair of Kenya Education Staff Institute and co-founder of Women Educational Researchers of Kenya. Her research focuses on gender, sexuality, HIV/AIDS and life skills education. She has acted as co-regional consultant for the Education Chapter for the UN Secretary-General's *Publication on Violence against Children* (2006). She is currently leading the Kenya team for the RECOUP Educational Outcomes and Poverty Project. Her publications include: *Finding Our Voices: gendered and sexual identities and HIV/AIDS in education* (with R. Pattman, UNICEF, 2003); 'He put his hands between girls' thighs' (in F. Leach and C. Mitchell (eds) *Combating Gender Violence in and around Schools*, Trentham Books, 2006); *Girls' and Women's Education in Kenya: Gender Perspectives and Trends* (with D. Sifuna, 2006).

Christopher Colclough is Professor of the Economics of Education, Professional Fellow of Corpus Christi College and Director of the Centre for Commonwealth Education at Cambridge University. A development economist, he has published extensively on problems of education, human resources and development in low and middle-income countries. He was the founding Director (2002–04) at UNESCO of the *Global Monitoring Report* on 'Education for All', and is presently Director of a five-country Research Consortium on Educational Outcomes and Poverty (RECOUP). Earlier research, as a Professorial Fellow of the Institute of Development Studies, Sussex, included the direction of a multi-country research programme on gender and primary schooling in Africa, work on the linkages between primary education and economic development, on education financing, on development theory and on economic adjustment in Africa. Recent publications include: *Achieving Schooling for All in Africa: Costs, Commitment and Gender* (with S. Al-Samarrai, P. Rose and M. Tembon, Ashgate, 2003).

Shailaja Fennell is a University Lecturer in Development Studies attached to the Department of Land Economy and a Fellow of Jesus College at the University of Cambridge. Her past research has focused on India and China, where she has examined reforms in food production, economic and social mobility of poor agrarian communities and the role of gender norms on the world of work. She has also undertaken research on the provision of infrastructure, particularly housing, education and health in poor urban environments. Her current research centres on forms and financing of educational provision. She is working on the RECOUP project, in the areas of public–private partnerships in education and youth, gender and citizenship. Recent publications include: *Rules, Rubrics and Riches: the relationship between legal reform, institutional change and international development* (2007 in press) and 'The ethics of population control', (in D. Clark, ed., *Elgar Companion to Development Economics*, 2006).

Harriet Marshall is a lecturer in International Education at Bath University where she teaches postgraduate courses on global citizenship education and education in an international context, education research methods and education policy. Her recently completed doctorate at Cambridge focused on sociological interpretations of the global education movement, its pedagogical principles and practice. Her research interests currently concern the relationship between NGOs and schools, and cosmopolitan education. Research publications include chapters and articles on these themes such as: 'The global education terminology debate: exploring some of the issues' (in M. Haydon, J. Levy and J. Thompson (eds) *A Handbook of Research in International Education*, London: Sage, 2007); and 'Global education in perspective: fostering a global dimension in an English secondary school' (*Cambridge Journal of Education*, 2007 37: 3).

Nitya Mohan is a doctoral candidate in the University of Cambridge working with Shailaja Fennell. She holds an MPhil in Development Studies from the University of Cambridge, an MA in Economics and a BSc in Mathematics from Bangalore University, India. She worked with the UNDP (India Country Office) and ILO (Geneva) and taught economics and development theory at Cambridge and Bangalore University. Her research spans economics, political science and development economics, notably topics such as well-being, gender inequality, human development, women's access to health and education and decentralisation of governance. At UNDP, she worked on a best practice manual (*Successful Governance Initiatives and Best Practices: Experiences from across Indian States*) – a critical appraisal of government success stories in education, health and livelihood security, and prepared a summary document of the Karnataka Human Development Report (UNDP, 2005). She will publish 'A Critical Review of the Care Economy' (with V. Bigo, *Cambridge Journal of Economics*, 2007).

Janet Raynor is an independent consultant in education. She is currently working towards a doctorate with Elaine Unterhalter at the University of London Institute of Education on gender, education and capabilities using an inter-generational methodology in a rural area in Bangladesh. Over the last nine years she has worked on a variety of educational programmes in Bangladesh, as well as in other Asian countries, the South Pacific region, Africa and Ecuador. Recent publications include 'The girls' stipend program in Bangladesh' *Journal of Education for International Development* (with K. Wesson, 2006). 'Education and capabilities in Bangladesh' (eds M. Walker and E. Unterhalter, *Sen's Capability Approach and Social Justice in Education*, Palgrave, 2007) and 'Promoting empowerment? Contrasting perspectives on a programme to employ women teachers in Bangladesh, 1996–2005' (with E. Unterhalter in J. Kirk (ed.) *Women Teaching in South Asia*, Sage, 2007). She also contributed to the study of girls' education in South Asia for the Beyond Access Project.

Anju Saigal is currently completing her doctoral studies in education policy at Harvard University in the United States with Wendy Luttrell. Her dissertation, an ethnographic study, examines low-income women's participation in community-based literacy work in Mumbai where she already had several years' experience in grass roots organising in literacy and social development. Her work focuses on mainstreaming out-of-school children in formal schools, developing literacy curricula and training non-formal education teachers. Her research experience and interests lie in the areas of social and political contexts of education, civic participation, and gender and education. She has taught graduate-level courses on globalisation and international education policy at the Harvard Graduate School of Education and Simmons College in Boston, USA.

Nelly P. Stromquist is Professor of Comparative and International Education in the Rossier School of Education at the University of Southern California, USA. She specialises in issues related to international development education and gender, which she examines from a critical sociology perspective. She has considerable experience in formal and non-formal education, particularly in Latin America and West Africa. Her research interests focus on the dynamics among educational policies and practices, gender relations and social change. Three of her most recent books are *Feminist Organizations and Social Transformation in Latin America* (Boulder: Paradigm, 2006), *Género, educación y política en América Latina* (Santillana, 2004) and *Education in a Globalized World: The connectivity of economic power, technology, and knowledge* (Rowman & Littlefield, 2002). She is former president of the Comparative and International Education Society and a 2005–06 Fulbright New Century Scholar.

Malini Sivasubramaniam is a PhD candidate in comparative, international, and development education at the University of Toronto, Canada working with Karen Mundy. Her doctoral research focuses on social capital and gender in mothers' decision making processes and their governance roles in low-cost non-formal primary schools in the slums of Kenya. Her research interests include civil society engagement in gender and education, particularly within sector-wide approaches to education. She has worked as part of a research team on a Canadian International Development Agency (CIDA) cross-case research project examining the role of CSOs in sector-wide approaches to education in Africa and contributed to the final CIDA report *Civil Society Participation and the Governance of Educational Systems in the Context of Sector-Wide Approaches to Basic Education in Kenya* (with K. Mundy, 2006).

Emefa Takyi-Amoako is a doctoral student in the Department of Educational Studies, Oxford University in the UK, working with Ann Childs and David Johnson. Her DPhil thesis, a qualitative study, examines the Ministry of Education donor inter-organisational network of interactions and their influence on policy. Prior to this she obtained a BA degree in English and a Diploma in Education from the University of Cape Coast. She had also completed the Women Studies Programme (MSt) and an Educational Research

Methodology Course (MSc). She has taught graduate-level seminars on the Comparative and International Education Courses and at secondary school level in Ghana. Her research interests include international aid, education, gender, development; postcolonial, feminist and literary theories; and research methodologies. She co-authored a paper with Augustine Agu of UNICEF on 'Partnership Building in Education Management and Development in Ghana'. She is also currently developing and involved in *Attaining the Peak*, an educational enrichment/motivational programme for secondary school students who have the potential to achieve.

Elaine Unterhalter is a Reader in Education and International Development, at the Institute of Education, University of London, UK. She is one of the coordinators of the Beyond Access project, a collaboration between Oxfam, the Institute of Education and a range of policy makers working on questions of gender equality, education and the Millennium Development Goals. She is a member of the Executive Council of the Human Development and Capability Association and coordinates the network on education and the capability approach. She has acted as a consultant on gender and education to UNICEF, the Commonwealth Secretariat, UNESCO and worked on research projects commissioned by the governments of Kenya, South Africa and Bangladesh. Her recent publications include: *Beyond Access: Transforming Policy and Practice for Gender Equality in Education* (ed. with S. Aikman, Oxfam, 2005); *Gender, Schooling and Global Social Justice* (Routledge, 2007), *Amartya Sen's Capability Approach and Social Justice in Education* (ed. with M. Walker, Palgrave, 2007 in press).

Rosie Vaughan is a PhD student at the Faculty of Education, University of Cambridge, UK. Her research interests include the measurement of educational inequalities, education and the capability approach, and the impact of global political and economic change on female education. Having completed a first degree in History, she is currently conducting her doctoral research on the relationship between international organisations and the Indian government in the promotion of girls' education, working with Shailaja Fennell and Madeleine Arnot. She has recently written a paper on 'Measuring capabilities: an example from girls' schooling' (in M. Walker and E. Unterhalter (eds) *Amartya Sen's Capability Approach and Social Justice in Education*, Palgrave, forthcoming 2007).

Anise Waljee is completing her doctoral studies at the University of London, Institute of Education with Dr Anil Khamis, researching the meaning of educational change in Tajikistan, a society in transition. She worked for four years in Tajikistan with an international development agency on helping the Tajik government to reform the education system. She trains educators on organisational change, curriculum development, community participation and project management and education in London, Toronto, Lebanon, Albania and Tajikistan. Her research interests include gender issues in non-Western societies, the education of minority communities, inclusive education and health education. Her work includes anti-racism in education; mapping local knowledge; and, education in the non-formal sector and organisational development. She has taught a module on Muslim education at the Institute of Education and led courses on children's participation in health and development in their communities.

1 (Re)visiting education and development agendas

Contemporary gender research

Madeleine Arnot and Shailaja Fennell

The beginning of the twenty-first century witnessed a profusion of new thinking in gender studies across the social sciences. The philosophical and political conceptualisations of gender equality have been substantially reworked to take into account new social agendas around multiculturalism and diversity while new notions of citizenship and nationhood have required a reconsideration of how to position women in modern society (Benhabib 2002; Yuval Davis 2001). This re-engagement with the theoretical foundations of gender research within the world of academia occurs at a time when gender concerns (particularly around women's empowerment through economic progress and development) have been placed on international agendas (Nussbaum 2000; Sen 2004). The emergence of global equality agendas provides a unique opportunity to bring together the diverse understandings emerging from the different trajectories taken by Western and non-Western traditions of gender research. The possibility of such a confluence has potentially profound implications for an analysis of gender education since, up until now, there has been relatively little interaction between Western and non-Western research.

Gender theorists working in richer Western economies have developed complex systems of monitoring gender inequalities in education, in employment and in civil society. They have also assisted in the development of, for example, anti-discrimination policies, so called 'girl friendly' schooling, anti-sexist pedagogies and extensive programmes to raise teacher awareness (Arnot *et al.* 1999). In contrast, development educationalists concerned about gender have been faced with the imperative of finding resources for mass schooling whilst trying to ensure that the 'girl child' is brought into the educational process. This separation of gender education research within developed and developing nations prevents the conceptual tools used by Western feminists and gender researchers from being challenged by research from developing economies. At the same time in the field of development studies, gender and education projects do not appear to have generated a sufficiently strong identity as a distinctive and progressive line of internationally recognised scholarship. Few such projects address or use theories of gender developed, for example, by Judith Butler, Raewyn Connell and Pierre Bourdieu (see Arnot and Mac an Ghaill 2006) perhaps because they are regarded as emanating from a Western historical and cultural process and political project.[1]

There is therefore a sharp disciplinary divide that cuts through the research on gender, education and development – much of the research on how gender education links to development is located within the subject matter of development studies and relates to educational dilemmas and initiatives in the non-Western world even though there is growing interest in addressing notions of diversity and difference and the pluralities of gender within, for example, the sociology of education and gender studies. A meaningful exchange requires us to consider whether the merging of Western based gender studies and non-Western development studies is feasible or whether it is preferable to ensure that development studies and gender studies maintain their intellectual integrity.

The formation of a global field of gender education research, in effect, implies crossing the bridge from development studies to gender and education studies and vice versa. For some, it means thinking for the first time about the development context, for others it means considering the theoretical and empirical insights of Western gender and educational research, which has developed nationally and internationally since the 1970s. This field could potentially provide students with a wider internationally focused terrain and a larger and potentially more useful range of methodological frameworks. There are already indications of this in the ambitious ethnographic and other, innovative methodologies used by researchers to explore the conditions of gender relations and education – (see Sarangapani's (2003) analysis of classroom learning in an Indian village and Stambach's (2000) study of gender community cultures and schooling in Kenya). In the past, students wishing to enter the field have also had to identify the range of conceptual frameworks for themselves. However, the recent publication of *Practising Gender Analysis in Education* (Leach 2003) and *A Guide to Gender Analysis Frameworks* (March et al. 1999) have helped considerably in this enterprise. Similarly, Unterhalter's (2006) *Schooling and Global Social Justice* for the first time allows the reader to consider simultaneously the Western and development discourses about gender equality and their various intellectual roots, problematics and consequences.

Below, we explore some of these transformations in this field of global gender ducation and introduce the particular approach adopted by authors in this collection and their contribution to this emergent interdisciplinary line of research on gender education and development in a global context.

Global gender goals and gender education

One of the most important catalysts for establishing gender education and development as a new scholarly arena is the increased involvement of international organisations in gender education policy making. This tendency began in the 1990s and was considerably enhanced by the publication of the United Nations Millennium Development Goals (MDGs) in 2000. Such goals focused on the need to ensure development across the globe through a concerted reduction in poverty. They also established the legitimacy of talking about gender equality in relation to education.[2] In conjunction with the Dakar Declaration (2000), which pledged to achieve *Education for All*, the MDGs provided a skeleton framework and devised a set of yardsticks with which to establish the current status of gender educational equality in each nation and assess their progress. Such global gender targets were particularly welcomed in some quarters especially since they identified the scale of the problem and began to demonstrate to national governments the range of factors, variables, forces and constraints associated with gender inequality. However, such universal gender targets also carry with them imperial and colonial legacies of international interference in nation building and national educational systems. Gender equality, although portrayed as a human right, is now also associated with the new demands of neo-liberal economic globalisation, encouraging national regimes and indigenous cultures to move towards Western versions of modernisation.

The global statistics on poverty, inequality and exclusion and, for example, campaigns such as *Making Poverty History* in 2005, now exercise the worlds of policy, academia and civil society. In the summer of 2005, the G8 (the grouping of the world's eight most economically advanced nations, Canada, France, Germany, Italy, Japan, Russia, United Kingdom and United States) met at Gleneagles in the United Kingdom to discuss their role in the reduction of global inequalities. Under review was the proposal for a global fund that could be drawn upon by poor countries to advance towards the MDGs. The G8 has already become somewhat concerned about the limited power of economic growth rates to transform the lives of the majority in national economies. There is a real or perceived failure (or perceived inability) of the field of international development to overcome the inequalities of gender in a world where a third of the population is still mired in poverty.

The promotion of gender equality internationally cannot today easily avoid contemporary debates about the difficulties facing poorer nations in their quest to participate in the global economy. The difficulty of achieving gender equality goals was highlighted by the influential *Global Monitoring Reports* on gender equality (UNESCO, 2003), which found that two-thirds of those reported to be illiterate globally were female and that 54 countries in the world were not likely to achieve gender parity in access and enrolment even in basic schooling by the target date of 2005. Rather than blame girls for their failure to attend school, the thrust of this report and the wealth of associated case study and briefing material alerted governments to the need to 'think through' their educational provision and policy approaches and to begin to establish what used to be called 'gender audits'.[3] The MDG gender equity goals, therefore, represent an important moment for the academic study of gender education, encouraging it to engage critically, theoretically and empirically with gender educational inequalities on a global basis and to articulate and publicise its own voice in international development.

The diversity of forms that gender education takes within different societies, however, makes this educational research work difficult. Take for example the link between education and employment. By the late 1990s, it was already known that regions such as South Asia were resistant to advances in girls' education despite economic growth, while Latin America showed little correlation between literacy and employment (Heward and Bunawaree 1999). These national/local differences in how gender education relates to economic development are increasingly recognised as important – our attention is drawn, for example, to the use of female employment in particular economies, to divergent patriarchal structures found in a wide range of different household and family types, and to the ways in which different religious values, customs and cultural symbolisms are embedded in the category 'woman' (Tinker 1990; Basu 1995). In such contexts also, gender reform has come less through national governments and their education budgets and more from the many interventions into female education from local and international non-government organisations (NGOs and INGOs). Researching and accounting for the processes of gender change is that much more complicated particularly within countries where education is not mainly organised within national welfare systems.

The use of education within gender equality reform movements globally is also patchy. Often the focus of gender reform is outside the school system, working with women and women's organisations in local communities. Gender educational reforms therefore operate unevenly within a country and across countries. The low status of teachers, especially female teachers, makes it unlikely in development contexts that the equivalent form of 'education feminism' found in the UK and other anglophone nations will develop and find expression in published research, school resources and policy documents (Arnot 2002). In less developed economies, without strong empirical educational research traditions and a strong public teacher voice, gender education reform is also expressed through an ideologically diverse group of NGO grass roots activists, projects and initiatives or through government policy statements developed in response to international pressure but with relatively little impact on educational provision. Making sense of these different reform processes and strategies is a challenging task for any gender researcher. Systematic in-depth research on these policies and initiatives not surprisingly is only just emerging.

There is a strong tendency, however, to report rather than research girls' educational initiatives in these settings. Whilst imaginative and politically very important, these initiatives are rarely followed up by in-depth academically based investigations, and, as a result, we do not get clear sight of the significance of the contributions they make to our understanding of pedagogy, teacher training, learning and educational achievement. Even if groundbreaking, the outcomes of these initiatives on girls' and women's identities and lives, whether personal or economic, or their significance on gender relations and dynamics in local communities, are little understood by international academies. Noticeably, the focus of academic papers has often been on advancing gendered estimation of returns to education, enrolment and retention rates (Banerjee *et al.* 2005; Jalan 2002). Thus, despite the extraordinary and rich insights that such initiatives could have offered about the importance of education, and deeper conceptualisations of the educational problems within developing and often poor economies, it is fair to say that they have not made as important a contribution to gender scholarship as they might have.

The time is right to start the process of integrating and moving forward the analytical and empirical frameworks required by gender and educational studies in both Western and non-Western contexts. If 'global' gender scholarship is to take off, then gender education researchers need to be sensitive and attuned to the importance of diverse educational forms that emerge in different national contexts and its implications for gender equality. This will require them to be skilled enough to identify the different discursive frameworks used by policy makers, politicians, teachers, students and communities and their impacts on educational provision, experience and outcomes. The purpose of this book is to identify and assess these conceptual frameworks through the systematic study of gender meanings, practices and actions that are brought into play by inter-national and national gender equality policy agendas and policy initiatives. The conceptual thinking that can be found in this book suggests that these engage-ments are not easily located within one discipline, nor within any one political perspective, or common historical trajectory, even if they are held together by a common pursuit of social justice.

Feminisms and activisms

Notwithstanding such limitations, waves of feminist thinking have informed international and national agendas on gender equality especially since the 1970s – the United Nations International Decade for Women. The earliest gender contribution was termed a *Women in Development* (WID) approach that high-lighted the failure to admit or adequately estimate women's contribution to the national economic effort. Largely overlooked by economic accounting, which focused on industrial production and market based activity, women were recog-nised as an untapped resource who contribute to development. The WID approach used statistical measures to identify the contribution of women to economic production and progress. However this approach was soon overtaken by a more dialectical approach that saw development processes and gender con-struction as mutually constitutive, so that the opportunities for women to con-tribute were moulded or marred by the direction and pattern of economic development. This latter approach, called *Women and Development* (WAD), had a greater allegiance to the types of qualitative research that emerged in the broader field of social science in the 1980s. However its progress was tempered by yet another feminist conceptualisation that regarded *gender* rather than women as the appropriate intellectual focus of any research on development. The so-called *Gender and Development* (GAD) approach offered a new under-standing of the different historical roles that women and men play in society. Gender differences were interpreted as having been shaped by ideological, historical, religious, ethnic, economic and cultural determinants. They were fully 'socialised' in the sense of being understood to be socially constructed by, through, and as a result of developmental processes. Here gender, as power relations and regimes, was the central focus of research on education and development.

Western feminisms have developed their own agenda that has engaged with gender relations within advanced capitalist structures and liberal democratic states. This trajectory has focused particularly on the ways in which gender dualisms, the historic separations of the public and the private, and the formation of multiple gender identities, performances and relational worlds are created. In the last two decades, there has been as strong an interest in the West, particularly in the anglophone traditions, in the social psychology and culture of gender, its normativities, fictions and subjectivities as there has been on its economic determinants. Yet these intellectual engagements, located as they are within the social conditions associated with Western contexts, have been challenged by different parts of the non-Western world. African feminism, Indian feminism and Latin American feminism challenge Western feminist conceptions as exceptional rather than the norm (Mama 1995; Mohanty 1988). These traditions suggest that, as countries have different historical trajectories, they have developed distinctive understandings of gender and gender relations (Momsen and Kinnaird 1993). The privileging of gender relations and patriarchy above other social forms of power (e.g. those of age, rural–urban, caste, ethnicity or race) do not translate easily across societies. Nor do the categories for example of 'woman' and 'man', the concept of the public or the notion of the family since they too are arbitrary cultural formations (e.g. Nnaemeka 1998; Odyoye 2000; Oyewumi 2003). Further, diasporic and migratory contexts rather than stable and embedded cultures shift gender conceptualisations and effect changes in what is possible for men and women (Brah 2002). Western feminisms have not engaged strongly with these conceptual challenges. Not surprisingly, as a result, the imposition of culturally specific Western notions of gender education (transmitted through the MDG goals) through allegedly universal goals of gender equality, has been received critically by some Southern feminist educationalists (Ramphal 2005).

Western feminisms appear to have had difficulty engaging with gendered cultural diversity whether within Western European and North American nations or between nations (see Chapter 8, this volume). Problems have arisen when cultural differences on gender have been taken as a given and, consequently, feminism has found itself acquiescing to gender inequalities within minority groups under the guise of multiculturalism (Okin 1998). The alternative is to explore in more depth the particular, specific contextual conditions in which gender dynamics and patterns work with the society (Stromquist 2002; Jackson and Pearson 1998). The constraints facing women and their emancipation within non-Western contexts can provide exemplary new ways of conceptualising gender equality – the concept of capability is a case in point (see the work of Sen 2004; Robeyns 2005) where capability theory shows education to be a pathway to overcome a deficit in a woman's resources and skills (endowment set) – a deficit that would otherwise prevent her from achieving her own desired goals (i.e. her capabilities) (see Unterhalter's and Raynor's chapters in this volume).

Although these international feminist debates facilitate advances in measuring the contribution of women to economic development, their most important impact lay in the valorisation of the contribution of women beyond the quantitative world of economics (Kabeer 1994). In a sense, feminists have educated international agencies such as the United Nations and World Bank about the patriarchal conditions that shape women's lives (although often the analysis is not couched in this more radical language). They have facilitated the global impact of female knowledge. Women's voices, which speak through research data and through researchers using that data to inform policy makers, are a powerful tool to use when urging change. Voice research – whether by women, or about women, about gender or indeed about male power and masculinity – has the potential to disrupt global agendas and to identify new ones. Voice research urges policy makers to move from the study of (statistical) gender gaps in education, beyond access questions (although not neglecting these) to a study of the social construction of gender inequality and gender dynamics at local levels. Knowledge about the specific sets of gender relations found in these local levels (the micro-politics of gender, rather than macroeconomic theory) generates the intellectual basis for new understandings of gender, education and development.

Educationalists have tried to engage with local contexts to bring girls into the education system. The response has been a string of transnational declarations in the 1980s and 1990s that oscillated between arguments about the needs of the economy for female waged labour and the needs of societies for better educated mothers and hence better educated children (Unterhalter 2000). The breakthrough in terms of conceptualising women's autonomy and rights to education as a human right came in the Beijing Declaration in 1996. By 2003, UNESCO reports had made international gender data that were relevant to these goals internationally available for the first time, and also provided a major resource for educationalists by publishing hitherto unknown case studies of gender change. This new stream of data informs us not just about the gender gaps at all levels of education but also about the severe constraints imposed by limited finance for educational development in poor communities (entailing, restricted curricular resources, too few trained female teachers, a dearth of gender sensitive teacher training and gender-transformative pedagogies and insufficient awareness of the conditions required to promote gender equality etc.). Feminist social scientists have added their call for new and better indicators that go 'beyond access' to reflect the actual level of attainment towards gender equality and more importantly to reflect the relationship of this attainment to women's empowerment and their individual and collective agency (see Aikman and Unterhalter's (2005) score card). This new conceptual thinking forces us to consider the multiple gendered realities that face men and women living in (often rural) poverty both within and across countries and whether schooling itself reproduces the conditions that sustain these realities. The cycles of social reproduction and the ways in which education links to social networks and social capital are now clearly on the agenda. In that sense, the study of gender education and development is moving along lines that parallel the concerns of Western sociologists of education about gender production and reproduction (Arnot 2002), creating the possibility of an important new dialogue globally about the role of schooling in relation to gender justice.

The nature and quality of these debates has brought together a community of scholars who view gender construction as a central social process that directs the impact of education in development contexts. Not only are there continuing contributions by leading international scholars who have been key players in establishing the academic field of gender education and development (for example, Christopher Colclough, Nelly Stromquist and Elaine Unterhalter) but that field is now enriched by valuable additions from young scholars who have undertaken innovative research. They have been attracted to this increasingly important field of international development with its social justice/pro-poor agenda. On the one hand, young scholars have a different global imagination that gives them the motivation to study complex international institutions, agencies, reform agendas, financing, statistical monitoring, etc. On the other hand, new graduates who enter this international community of scholars demonstrate an interest in mixing theory and research, and in moving away from narrowly conceived snapshot quantitative studies and descriptive ethnographies and to more analytic inter-generational and community based socio-cultural projects. It is now not just legitimate to collect the voices of the poor (Narayan 2000) but imperative for gender studies to collect the voices of women (in their diverse roles and at different ages). The unifying theme that emerges from research that now crosses disciplines, links the North and the South, and engages theory with evidence, is the strong desire to promote gender equality even though this may not always be received as the most appropriate foundational concept. The evidence from developing countries indicates that countries that have achieved gender equality in enrolments vary widely in other social and economic characteristics, and this emphatically poses the question as to the meaning of the term itself.

The prospects for gender education and development studies therefore are good. We can already see the impact of this growing field by looking at the role that gender researchers recently played in the UN report on the role of men in promoting gender equality and global peace (Breines *et al.* 2000; UNESCO 2003). The interest in education courses within development studies attest to the attraction of this new field of study.

Redefining gender education research

The aim of this collection is to encourage the reader (whether located within or outside development studies or educational research) to think more sensitively, critically and in a more cautious way about gender education. To this end, we have brought together a range of contemporary examples of research from scholars working across the social sciences on gender education. Whilst some of the contributors have written together, worked on the same project[4] or are familiar with the same literatures, others are new to the field and finding their way in the quagmire of development traditions and educational/social scientific methods of analysis. All the authors themselves are located within the global space of academic research. Their work links together often in quite unexpected ways.

Many of the contributors, for example, point to the important global spaces in which gender can now be found. These global spaces comprise the international agencies and their policy formulations, such as the WID, WAD and GAD approaches we discussed above. The common thread that unites the various contributions is the push for and purpose of *Education for All*. Each piece of conceptual and empirical writing suggests in its own way what would need to be considered relevant to the promotion of such a broad and ambitious goal and how it interacts with notions of gender equality. Where the contributions differ is that often the contributors have explored specific spaces in their own national contexts, throwing light on national/local spaces: those of the rural and urban, the rich and the poor, nation and citizen, and the school spaces of the teacher and pupil, school and community. The manner in which the global and national spaces are traversed by academia, national governments and international organisations differs. There is also an implied presence in many of the contributions of a symbolic space, where changing gender relations are gleaned from the microcosmic steps taken to ensure gender equality of access, treatment or equal citizenship. Here there are acts of everyday resistance, as Saigal called it 'acts of citizenship' (Chapter 9). The power of the symbolic is located in the everyday, and provides a counterpoint to the grander decisions of national governments and international agencies. These small 'gender' acts or performances represent the victories of gender equality that emerge from behind the macro-level statistical measures of gender goals. These tensions, between structure and agency, can be found by reading across the various contributions.

We have divided the book into three parts, opening up debates first on the conceptual terrain, then on research methodologies and approaches and then on gender policy analysis. The first part, titled '(Re)conceptualising gender equality', offers an introduction to a range of past and present theoretical frameworks that can be applied to the study of gender education in the global and national development contexts. These frameworks are not all compatible, but in their different ways they have pointed to important dimensions, conceptual challenges and diverse meanings associated with the notion of gender equality, and they have raised significant research questions. Elaine Unterhalter opens the debate with a focus on the global spaces fashioned by the first and second waves of feminism within which gender equality has been conceived. She distinguishes between *inter-national* and *in/ternational* engagements of global and the national spaces and analyses how they have affected our reading of notions of needs, rights and capabilities and understanding of their usefulness for advancing gender equality. The chapter by Shailaja Fennell follows on from this analysis by re-examining the dominant traditions of human capital theory and gendered labour markets in light of concerns that such traditions fail to address the non-industrial agricultural basis of much development, and the poverty associated with such local contexts. Her analysis offers insights into the different economic agendas around equality and questions whether current state and non-state providers of schooling/education share the same assumptions about gender equality through education. Chapter 4 by Christopher Colclough provides an important insider understanding of the conceptual clarity that was required for global goal setting by international bodies such as the United Nations and its educational arm, UNESCO. He traces the intellectual thinking in international organisations that was behind the announcement of the Millennium Development Goals and the *Education for All* agendas at the turn on the century. The chapter points out that, despite the attention paid to measuring global education goals, problems arise when statistical indicators such as gender parity have not ensured an advancement towards gender equality and there are still obstacles to ensuring adequate financial resources for achieving gender goals in education. The final chapter in this part by Malini Sivasubramaniam suggests that there is much to be gained by using a gendered lens to understand how the notion of social capital can be related to gender equality in education. She distinguishes between neo-liberal and political economy approaches to social capital, indicating that the latter is closer to feminist understandings of gender construction and could provide an avenue to bring the notion of gender equality further into the analysis of education in civil society.

The second part of the book entitled 'Researching agency engagements and empowerment' offers examples of the sorts of research methodologies that have been employed in the study of particular localised gender settings. We have brought together new research in the field that communicates the excitement of engaging in this interdisciplinary project of researching gender education and development. Here the voices of young women and men, the voices of women teachers, and para-teachers speak about everyday gender issues. In this section, the realities of community and family life are brought to bear on the discussion of gender education, questioning how we might interpret the customary traditions and social norms that determine women's everyday life. Chapter 6, by Anise Waljee, for example, takes a strong stand against the imposition of Western interpretations and misinterpretations of the role of religion and traditional customs: misunderstandings that result from an ahistorical and 'outsider' perspective of the relations between economy, society and culture. Her historical analysis of gender and education in a country in transition – Tajikistan – demonstrates the complexity of gender relations within which women and men navigate their way through local economies, political oppressions and international interventions. Fatuma Chege, in Chapter 7, argues equally strongly for the importance of hearing gendered voices and getting behind the surface realities of gender relations. Her chapter reports on the use of group discussions and quite personal individual interviews with boys and girls about the relationship between their own sexuality and the impact of HIV/AIDS in East Africa. The theme of sexuality, violence and gender emerge from her data, challenging mainstream gender policy approaches that marginalise such concerns. Relational worlds are central to the study of gender relations in education. They can, as Leslie Casely-Hayford argues in Chapter 10, affect the ways in which women teachers experience their work and their lives within poor rural communities in Ghana. This chapter uses ethnographic research to examine the gendered experiences of women teachers in rural Ghana, of what it means to be a local teacher as well as a woman alone in an isolated rural area. The integration of such women teachers into community life has major implications for the recruitment of girls into the teaching profession and can impact on girls' educational success. As Janet Raynor shows in her account of her research in Bangladesh, female teachers represent symbols of female agency, breaking away from the expectations of a life spent in domesticity. Chapter 8 offers important insights into the use of inter-generational methodologies that focus on what she calls 'the burdens' women carry in such poor communities. The use of mixed methods to record women's agency is also the subject of Anju Saigal's chapter on women community educators in Mumbai. Her interview data suggest that women can use femininity to engage in 'acts of citizenship', that permit them to create enabling spaces for themselves, and on behalf of the children and communities in which they live and work. The theme of women teachers offering service to their communities comes through a number of chapters and is taken up again in the third part of the book. Global spaces are shown to overlap with these very small, everyday local spaces.

The third part '(Re)defining global equality agendas' explores how such global spaces and local spaces overlap in the context of national policy on education and its relation to the achievement of gender equality. The part begins with a chapter by Harriet Marshall and Madeleine Arnot that examines how the school curriculum has been impacted upon by global agendas and the implications for citizenship – through the complex and contradictory processes of globalisation, through calls for a global citizenship curriculum and global learners. Gender curriculum issues are not marginal to access and equality issues, they are integral to them. Similarly the provision of educational ideals (for example, the ideal woman) is closely linked to concepts of nationhood, and the intervention of international agencies cannot be understood without making such connections particularly in post-colonial contexts. Nitya Mohan and Rosie Vaughan explore this theme in their study of Indian educational policy making since independence and their response to the Millennium Development Goals. Their narratives on female citizenship reveal how the radicalism of the early days of Indian nationalism has been increasingly replaced by the market language of neo-liberal agendas in education. Their analysis highlights successfully the importance of locating gender educational analyses within the politics of citizenship and nation building. A similar conclusion, although not a similar methodology, can be found in Emefa Takyi-Amoako's study of Ghana's poverty reduction strategy that is called for by international financial institutions, but which does not reach far enough into gender inequalities in education to reveal the complex interplay between gender relations, girls' education and poverty alleviation. Global poverty agendas are not sufficient, in her view, to tackle gender inequalities associated paradoxically with globalisation. An alternative approach to gender change is that of feminist non-governmental organisations (NGOs) such as those found in South America. Nelly Stromquist outlines in her chapter the ways in which three leading feminist organisations have found new ways of creating change, focusing as they do on adult learning rather than mass schooling. Her research investigates the methods through which feminists in Latin America organise campaigns through the everyday of the market place, the mass media, women's community groups and their private spheres. Such pedagogies for change are not bound by the conventions of formal educational institutions, and therefore raise the possibility of creating new critical gender consciousness and model alternative strategic approaches to gender equalisation.

The three parts of this book are not mutually exclusive. Each addresses, albeit from different angles and positions, the overlapping of global, local and national spaces within which gender is renegotiated in the educational sphere. The shadow of the new global context of *Education for All* is likely to affect all future gender research. It has set an ambitious overarching agenda that researchers will find difficult to avoid. There is a need to put on that agenda those aspects of gender power, culture and identity that will hold back, if not completely distort, the genuinely powerful and commendable goals of achieving gender equality. Educational systems are again being called into play to reform social inequalities and retrieve gender stability at a time when, paradoxically, the economic and social forces of change are creating further gender divisions. Women's work in particular is being radically reformed by global demands for cheap labour; men's work is being drastically changed in some communities by the reorganisation of economies and the movement of global capital. The role of educational reform linked to social change is still not clearly defined, despite these global ambitions.

The book is very much a beginning rather than an end. It needs to be complemented by many different types and foci of gender and educational research. There is an important place here for research on masculinity, on sexuality, on ethnicity, social class and caste. The scholarly tradition that moves us forward in understanding gender education has benefited immensely from drawing on different disciplines and across many levels. The intention is to sustain a conversation that advances our conceptual frameworks, research techniques and gender equality policy development. The hope is also that this book will further the international dialogue between North and South and bring forth other scholarly contributions in this emergent field of gender education studies in a global context.

Acknowledgements

We would like to thank the organisers of the United Kingdom Forum for International Education and Training (UKFIET) 8th International Conference on Education and Development 2005 for encouraging us to run a strand on

Gender. We would like to acknowledge the time provided to us to develop and complete this book by the Research Consortium on Educational Outcomes and Poverty (RECOUP) project (2005–2010). This project is funded by the Department for International Development of the government of the United Kingdom.

Notes

1 Sociological research on masculinities is an emerging area in South Asia with studies such as the edited volume by Chopra *et al.* (2004) and the study by Osella and Osella (2006).
2 The MDGs did not raise the issue of the contribution of the developed world towards the financing of these gender education goals. This was undertaken in the Dakar Declaration (2000) which stated that no country would be held back on account of financial constraints (see Colclough this volume).
3 Readers new to the field might want to spend time absorbing for themselves some of these new statistical narratives about gender and education and the progress of different world regions and nations towards the goals of gender parity and gender equality. An analysis of these statistical resources and their back-up briefing papers (efareport.unesco.org) present an important opportunity to establish comparative gender and education studies.
4 A number of contributors are currently working on a five year research programme on Educational Outcomes and Poverty (entitled RECOUP) funded by the Department of International Development in the UK. These are Madeleine Arnot, Fatuma Chege, Christopher Colclough, Shailaja Fennell, Leslie Casely-Hayford and others indirectly linked to it, Emefa Amaoko and Rosie Vaughan.

Bibliography

Aikman, S. and Unterhalter, E. (eds) (2005) *Beyond Access: Transforming Policy and Practice for Gender Equality in Education*, Oxford: Oxfam.

Arnot, M. (2002) *Reproducing Gender? Essays on Educational Theory and Feminist Politics*, London: RoutledgeFalmer.

Arnot, M. and Mac an Ghaill, M. (eds) (2006) *The RoutledgeFalmer Gender and Education Reader*, London: RoutledgeFalmer.

Arnot, M. and Weiler, K. (eds) (1993) *Feminism and Social Justice in Education*, London: Falmer Press.

Banerjee, A., Cole, S., Duflo, E. and Linden, L. (2005) 'Remedying Education: Evidence from Two Randomized Experiments in India, December 2005', NBER Working paper 11904.

Basu, A. (ed.) (1995) *The Challenge of Local Feminisms: Women's Movements in a Global Perspective*, Boulder, CO: Westview Press.

Benhabib, S. (2002) *The Claims of Culture: Equality and Diversity in the Global Era*, Princeton: Princeton University Press.

Brah, A. (2002) 'Global Mobilities, Local Predicaments: Globalisation and the Critical Imagination' *Feminist Review*, 70: 30–45.

Breines, I., Connell, R. and Eide, I. (eds) (2000) *Male Roles, Masculinities and Violence: A Culture of Peace Perspective*, Paris: UNESCO.

Chopra, R., Osella, C. and Osella, F. (eds) (2004) *South Asian Masculinities: Contexts of Change, Sites of Continuity*, New Delhi: Women Unlimited/Kali for Women.

Colclough, C., Al Samarrai, S., Rose, P. and Tembon, M. (2004) *Achieving Schooling for All in Africa: Costs, Commitment and Gender*, Aldershot: Ashgate.

Davies, L. (1998) *Gender and Management Issues in Education: An International Perspective*, Stoke on Trent: Trentham.

Elson, D. (ed.) (1995) *Male Bias in the Development Process* (2nd edn) Manchester: Manchester University Press.

Elson, D. (2002) 'Gender justice, human rights and neo-liberal economic policies' in M. Molyneux and S. Razavi (eds) *Gender, Justice, Development and Rights*, Oxford: Oxford University Press.

Hart, G. (2002) *Disabling Globalization: Places of Power in Post-Apartheid South Africa*, Pietermaritzburg: University of California Press and University of Natal Press.

Heward, C. and Bunawaree, S. (ed.) (1999) *Gender, Education and Development*, London: Zed Books.

Jalan, J. (2002) 'Small Bang for Big bucks? An Evaluation of a Primary School Intervention in India' (with Elena Glinskaya), mimeo, the World Bank.

Jackson, C. and Pearson, R. (1998) *Feminist Visions of Development*, New York: Routledge.

Kabeer, N. (1994) *Reversed Realities: Gender Hierarchies in Development Thought*, London: Verso.

Kabeer, N. (1999) 'Resources, Agency, Achievements: Reflections on the Measurement of Women's Empowerment' *Development and Change*, 30: 435–464.

Leach, F. (2003) *Practising Gender Analysis in Education*, Oxford: Oxfam.

Mama, A. (1995) *Beyond the Masks: Race, Gender and Subjectivity*, London: Routledge.

March, C., Smyth, I. and Mukhopadhyay, M. (1999) *A Guide to Gender-analysis Frameworks*, Oxford: Oxfam.

Mohanty, C. (1988) 'Under Western Eyes: Feminist Scholarship and Colonial Discourses' *Feminist Review*, 30: 61–88.

Momsen, J. and Kinnaird, V. (eds) (1993) *Different Places, Different Voices: Gender and Development in Africa, Asia, and Latin America*, London: New York: Routledge.

Narayan, D. (2000) *Voices of the Poor, Volume 1: Can Anyone Hear Us?*, Oxford: Oxford University Press (for the World Bank).

Narayan, U. (1997) *Dislocating Cultures: Third World Feminism and the Politics of Knowledge*, New York: Routledge.

Nnaemeka, O. (ed.) (1998) *Sisterhood, Feminisms and Power: From Africa to Diaspora*, Trenton, NJ: Africa World Press.

Nussbaum, M. (2000) *Women and Human Development: the Capability Approach*, Cambridge: Cambridge University Press.

Nussbaum, M. (2004) 'Women's Education: A Global Challenge' *Signs*, 29: 325–355

Odyoye, M.A. (2000) *Daughters of Anowa African Women and Patriarchy* Maryknoll, NY: Orbis.

Osella, C. and Osella, F. (2006) *Men and Masculinities in South India*, London: Anthem Press.

Oyewumi, O. (2003) *The Invention of Women: Making an African Sense of Western Gender Discourses*, Minneapolis: University of Minnesota Press.

Okin, S. (1998) 'Is multiculturalism bad for women?' in J. Cohen and M. Howard (eds) *Is Multiculturalism Bad for Women?* Princeton: Princeton University Press.

Ramphal, A. (2005) 'Quality and Equality in Education: Gendered Politics of Institutional Change'. Online, available at: www.ioewebserver.ioe.ac.uk/ioe/cms/get.asp?cid=7746&7746_0=10872 – 17k – (accessed 10 December 2006).

Rao, N. and Smyth, I. (eds) (2005) *Partnerships for Girls' Education*, Oxford: Oxfam.

Robeyns, I. (2005) 'Three Models of Education: Rights, Capabilities and Human Capital'. Online, available at: www.ingridrobeyns.nl/Downloads/TRE.pdf. Downloaded on 18 January 2007.

Sarangapani, P. (2003) *Constructing School Knowledge: An Ethnography of Learning in an Indian Village*, New Delhi: Sage.

Sen, A. (2004) *Development as Freedom*, Oxford: Oxford University Press.

Stambach, A. (2000) *Lessons from Mount Kilimanjaro: Schooling, Community, and Gender in East Africa*, New York: Routledge.

Stromquist, N.P. (1997) *Literacy for Citizenship. Gender and Grassroots Dynamics in Brazil*, New York: State University of New York Press.

Stromquist, N. (2000) 'Voice, harmony and fuge in global feminism' *Gender and Education*, 12, 4: 419–434.

Stromquist, N. (2002) *Education in a Globalized World: the Connectivity of Economic Power, Technology and Knowledge*, Lanham, MD: Rowan and Littlefield.

Subrahmanian, R. (2005) 'Education exclusion and the development state' in R. Chopra and P. Jeffrey (eds) *Education Regimes in Contemporary India*, Delhi: Sage.

Tinker, I. (ed.) (1990) *Persistant Inequalities: Women and World Development*, Oxford: Oxford University Press.

UNESCO (2003) *Gender and Education for All: the leap to equality EFA monitoring report*, Paris: UNESCO.

Unterhalter, E. (2000) 'Transnational visions of the 1990s: contrasting views of women, education and citizenship' in M. Arnot and J-A. Dillabough (eds) *Challenging Democracy: International Perspectives on Gender, Education and Citizenship*, London: Routledge.

Unterhalter, E. (2006) *Gender, Schooling and Global Social Justice*, London: Routledge.

Yuval-Davis, N. (1994) 'Women, ethnicity and empowerment' *Feminism and Psychology*, special issue 4, 1: 179–198.

Yuval-Davis, N. (2001) 'Nationalism, feminism and gender relations' in J. Hutchinson and M. Guibernau (eds) *Understanding Nationalism*, Cambridge: Polity Press, pp. 120–141.

Part I

(Re)conceptualising gender equality

2 Global values and gender equality in education

Needs, rights and capabilities[1]

Elaine Unterhalter

In the mid 1960s less than 50 per cent of girls of primary school age were in school in South Asia, Africa and the Arab states compared much higher proportions of boys. By the beginning of the twenty-first century, although there had been huge increases in primary and secondary enrolments for girls and boys worldwide, nearly one billion adults and children still had little or no education. Girls and women comprised 62 per cent of this huge population (Unterhalter 2007a: xii, 157). Global concerns at these grave injustices have drawn on different values to consider the nature of gender inequalities in education and appropriate remedial actions. Needs, rights and capabilities have been given different emphases by different players at different times to ground policies and actions.

This chapter delineates how these shifts relate to changing configurations of global interactions between governments, multilateral institutions and civil society. In the first section, I consider the ways in which value shifts in what I call 'global space' have linked to changing demands and concerns about gender equality in education. In the second section, I focus more specifically on three framings of global values – needs, rights and capabilities – and their changing dynamic within the two periods. I show that there are concurrent debates about these values, which are also often deployed differently by multilateral institutions, governments and global civil society. The changing nature of global space has a bearing on these different vocabularies and the significance of the demands and forms of action they highlight.

'Global space' and gender equality in education

There appears to be two waves of thinking about 'global space' and gender equality in education. The first runs from approximately 1970 to 1992, and the second from 1993 to the present. The first, which I shall call *inter-national*, is associated with the primacy of states in 'global space' and is constituted by nation states interacting with each other. The space of the global and the national are distinct and formally connected, with the global conceived as 'above' the national. The second wave, which I call *in/ternational*, is associated with networks, sometimes of states, civil society, corporations, sometimes of combinations of these. Here, the global, the national and the local become intermixed, forming and reforming each other without the sharp distinctions of the previous era. Thus the global is mixed in with the national as much as the reverse is true. While formal distinctions remain, there are also informal crossings of boundaries between local, national and global.

Inter-national gender values (1970 to 1992)

The first wave begins in the 1970s and runs to the early 1990s. It is associated with what, at the time, appeared immutable features of the global order. Nation states delimited not only who was and was not a citizen, but also drew the boundaries of economies. Thus gender as a set of social relations was powerfully framed by citizenship and nationality in ways that were not generally considered problematic at the time. The world was divided between capitalist and communist blocs, with an amorphous 'third world' comprising countries whose histories and contemporary political economies were heavily marked by colonialism. The content and organisation of schooling was often explicitly associated with aspirations concerning national identity, national economic growth and values associated with prevailing understandings of capitalism, communism or responses to colonialism.

From the early years of the twentieth century, in many countries, feminism was a feature of women's struggles for the vote and the transformation of social policy, engagements with socialism, anti-fascist movements and national liberation. Much of this early feminism focused on women gaining access to specific political, economic and cultural settings. During the 1960s, feminism took on a wider range of concerns shifting the locus of political action to consider, for example, aspects of sexuality, violence against women, the politics of the family, and processes of education and artistic representation. While most of this activity took place within the boundaries of nation states women began to make connections with each other across borders on the basis of shared interests in forms of gender inequality and mutual concern with developing new visions and values relating to gender equality and difference (Tinker 1990; Staudt 2003; Winslow 1995). The first World Conference on International Women's Year held in Mexico City in 1975 was one site where these inter-national connections began to be made.

In this period at least two meanings of gender equality were being advanced. The first, emerging out of 'first wave' feminism was concerned with the inclusion of women and girls and the development of social policies that broke down the barriers that had kept them out of schools, jobs and political participation. Here gender equality meant sameness between men and women in relation to their opportunities to participate in society and the respect they were accorded. In development policy and practice these ideas of gender equality linked with *Women in Development* (WID) and aimed to expand access to education (Unterhalter 2005). A much more amorphous meaning of gender equality was associated with 'second wave' feminism in the West. Some strands were concerned with affirming women's difference from men stressing the importance of acknowledging separate ways of talking, interacting and conceptualising political and social relations (Nicholson 1997). Hence gender equality was a matter of bestowing equal concern and recognition on these different spheres of interest. Another strand was concerned with breaking down essentialising concepts concerning women and men and recognising multiplicity, complexity and diversity (Ahmed 1998; Weedon 1997). In this latter approach, there was a recognition that gender equality could not be separated out from other intersecting aspirations concerned with race, ethnicity or class, and a transformation of the wider social structures that formed these inequalities (Skeggs 1997; Bhavnani 2001). Aspects of this second strand connected with the theorisation of gender and development (GAD) as a critique of WID. In education, GAD theorists drew attention to unequal gendered relations in schools, families and political economy (Unterhalter 2005).

Grave upheaval in the global economy followed from the oil shocks of the early 1970s. The debt crises that ensued were associated with an erosion of confidence in nationally managed economies and a new economic orthodoxy stressed how growth would be achieved through freeing markets and reducing the place of the state in the social sector. In many third world countries, high levels of debt forced them to accept structural adjustment policies that meant the introduction of school fees, the end of free medical treatment and a radical reduction of jobs in the public sector (Rai 2002).

Against this background of strongly differentiated national education systems, contested meanings of gender equality and wide fluctuations in economic fortunes, global space was understood primarily in terms of a bargaining table, somewhat in the shape of the large table in the Hall of Mirrors at Versailles in 1918 at which the leaders of the world and their national delegations had carved out a global order of states. 'Global space' was thus a negotiation in relation to national sovereignty and had implications primarily for citizens. The most powerful demand in relation to gender equality was for the equal recognition of all citizens. Thus gender equality in education entailed equal recognition of girls and boys in access to school, progression and completion. All those who fell outside the boundaries of citizenship, either because their state had no official standing, or they had no standing within it, were considered 'problems' generally addressed in an ad hoc way. Part of this partial and often neglectful treatment of those without citizenship entailed inadequate concern with education and gender issues (Werbner and Yuval Davis 1999).

'Global space' and the in/ternational (1993 to the present)

From the early 1990s, the notion of a world primarily made up of citizens of nation states began to disintegrate. A new vision of 'global space' began to form, where notions of the intermixing of national, regional, local and global gained currency. The emergence of hybrid affiliations across diverse sectors concerned with political economy, social and cultural processes I have termed in/ternational, although other writers highlight the significance of globalisation, cosmopolitanism and global cultural flows (Held and McGrew, 2003; Appadurai 1997; Appiah 2006). This second wave reshaped thinking about gender equality in education in fundamental ways.

This second wave is generally associated with globalisation and the reframing of the concerns of nation states in relation to a new political, economic and cultural formation of the global order (Held and McGrew 2002; Castells 2000). Economic growth came to be understood not as the outcome of actions in the domain of the state or the market, but rather the outcome of the complex interplay with some powerful states regulating global machineries concerned with trade, information, communication, debt and a wide range of resource transfers ranging from aid to knowledge (Stiglitz 2002). But while certain governments have been key actors in relation to this aspiration for a regulated global economy, others have been minor players with little to bargain over and very limited ability to support their citizens in relation to education, health or socio-economic development. The period therefore has been associated with widening gaps between the richest and poorest countries and peoples (UNDP 2005).

The large country blocs of the first period, loosely organised for some member states around an articulation of values concerned with capitalism, communism or anti-colonialism came to be replaced by new regional formations (the EU, NAFTA, SAARC, the African Union) where a common expression of values has often been fiercely contested. New clubs for global decision making have also emerged, for example the G8, the OECD, the WTO, working side-by-side, but sometimes at odds with the older machinery of the UN. In these new clubs, it is power and influence rather than values (real or rhetorical) that shape who is inside and who is outside decision making circles (Stiglitz 2002; Rose 2005).

The effects of these shifts in the global political economy on education and gender equality are complex. On the one hand, countries become concerned with national education attainment, which is seen to be a proxy for the national capacity to compete and thrive in the new knowledge economies. Thus, where countries score on the Programme for International Student Assessment (PISA), or other league tables that rank universities, is a matter of considerable national anxiety. This stress on attainment of excellence in certain areas of education goes together with, but is often in tension with, concerns to promote national identity – linguistically, through stress on particular values, or in certain evocations of history. On the other hand, these national education projects are accompanied by processes by which, to varying degrees, schools and higher education have opened up to students, teachers, expertise, learning materials and forms of assessment from beyond national boundaries. However these processes are generally highly contested and controversial. On the whole, it is elites that travel between education systems (Odin and Manicas 2004; Colclough 2006) and there has only been limited formal articulation of higher education in selected countries. But the effects of poverty, war and large-scale labour migration mean that it is by no means only the most advantaged who move around the world reshaping schooling and higher education. Mobility across education systems takes diverse forms and has differential effects.

In this second wave feminism has, on the one hand, become more institutionalised. Policies to 'mainstream' gender and strengthen national gender machineries have been implemented in many countries and in multilateral and regional organisations (Rai 2003). The mainstreaming project received considerable attention in education within some governments and UN organisations (Subrahmanian 2005; Leo-Rhynie 2000). The accession of a large number of countries to the Convention on the Elimination of Discrimination against Women (CEDAW) led to significant reforms in the law on issues ranging from ownership of property to reproductive rights (Antrobus 2005). A further feature of mainstreaming has been the large numbers of women who have entered the primary labour market and had access to social benefits from work (Unifem 2005). Teaching has been an important area for women's employment (Kirk 2007 forthcoming; UNESCO 2000; Gaskell and Mullen 2006). These have all been achievements of feminist projects to include women in education, politics and work. But feminism has not been limited to this terrain. It has become enormously diverse as, worldwide, thousands of groups concerned with different aspects of gender and women's lives flourish and network across national boundaries. The Fourth World Conference on Women held in Beijing in 1995 was attended by 50,000 and 180 governments participated in drafting the Platform for Action. This became a symbol of this diversity because of the range of groups concerned with women and gender who attended and the multiplicity of issues raised (Antrobus 2005; Staudt 2003).

In contrast, the second period was marked by financial instabilities and considerable uncertainty in relation to many national political issues and associated foreign policy. The period also saw the emergence of widespread activity by global civil society, which has come to define itself politically not just as a sphere of social and political action outside the state, but as a network of associations concerned with developing a counterhegemonic argument on global poverty, environmental degradation, and gendered, racialised and ethnicised exclusions from social policy (Eade and O'Byrne 2005; Mundy and Murphy 2001).

In contemporary 'global space', there is no set table with one chair for each nation state. The notion of 'global space' in this period can now be depicted as a series of shifting café conversations. Some take place in well appointed surroundings, where places are set, only those invited attend and meetings follow particular agendas. But others are hasty stand-up exchanges amongst incongruous or shifting groups with a very wide range of interests. Some take place in virtual space through internet cafés. 'Global space' is thus diffuse and, at certain moments, openings occur for particular groups, but may just as quickly close. People come to these different kinds of café tables as representatives of citizens, or of civil society, or of locales or peoples, not citizens, defined by ethnicity, 'culture', race, gender or sexuality. Here the form of the demand for gender equality in education is not set, but is amorphous and contested, sometimes taking the form of the tropes of the Beijing Declaration and Platform of Action and sometimes taking a very different character when concerned with sexualities, religious differences, nostalgic localism or individuated consumerism.

These two waves of thinking about gender equality and education in relation to understandings of 'global space' mean that the value connotations that underpin global concerns with the question of gender in education have shifted considerably as one period gives way to another. Below I explore these value shifts in the concept of gender equality.

The value basis of gender equality in education

In the inter-national phase, concern with gender equality in education drew on *needs, rights* and *capabilities* as terms of value. However the explicit or implicit assumption was that the obligation to respond rested primarily with nation states and the proper sphere of 'the global' was primarily coordinating or monitoring. In the in/ternational phase, the language of needs, rights and capabilities recurred but the primacy of states in relation to obligations to respond receded somewhat or came to be placed in conjunction with other forms of obligation, raising the question of the nature of principles of global justice more sharply.

The language of needs, rights and capabilities

In the inter-national phase, the meaning attributed to gender tended to be either a noun or an adjective (Unterhalter 2007a: 3). As a noun, gender tended to mean 'girls' and in this guise signalled something about the ways in which the social construction of sexual difference had a bearing on how girls were treated in families and classrooms. Gender was also construed as an adjective and applied to social structures, such as the legal system, the curriculum, and to social practices and identities. Thus it signalled the ways in which gendered forms of institutions, practices and identities generally acted in exclusionary and discriminatory ways. This was the sense in which gender came to be used in the Jomtein Declaration, which launched the Education for All (EFA) movement in 1990. The declaration asserts that:

> The most urgent priority is to ensure access to, and improve the quality of, education for girls and women, and to remove every obstacle that hampers their active participation. All gender stereotyping in education should be eliminated.
>
> (WDEFA, 1990)

In this passage, gender identifies a group that is being left out of quality education – girls and women – and describes aspects of the obstacles, such as the nature of textbook images, which explain this exclusion. The assumption was that equality (and gender equality specifically) entailed equal numbers of girls and boys accessing school and progressing through different levels. The use of gender as a noun did not signal difference. A second assumption was that gender equality enjoined equal regard for all within particular spheres, for example in the depiction of children in textbooks or the employment of women and men as teachers (Unterhalter 2007b). Thus an aim of policy was to take away the connotations of discrimination and subordination from the adjectival use of gender.

The values associated with needs, rights and capabilities came to be deployed both academically and in the language of policy to support these slightly different projects for equality during the first phase. The view of education as a basic need and the implication that gender equality in education entailed an opportunity for all to have such basic needs met emerged in the 1970s when some development economists critiqued the assumptions of modernisation that poverty would be eradicated by economic growth, the expansion of employment, higher incomes and the trickle-down effects of successful capitalism (Streeten *et al.* 1981; Stewart 1985). The *basic needs approach* to social policy stressed one should not focus on particular outcomes or on humans as a means to social, economic or political ends. This latter focus was widespread in writing on education where concern with rates of return and building human capital was deeply entrenched (Psacharopoulos 1973; Becker 1993). Basic needs theorists stressed it was important to consider those who might never be economically productive and never increase human capital. Some people might have important preferences that could not be satisfied on the same terms as everyone else, such as the old, the very young, those with disabilities or those who were excluded from political or economic participation because of historically located forms of discrimination on the grounds of gender, race or ethnicity. Wiggins (1985) highlighted that there was a normative basis to need. The argument he developed was that the importance of needs was that they expressed aspects of a condition of human flourishing. Failure to ensure a certain level of human flourishing – meeting basic needs – would constitute harm. Stewart (1985: 6) showed that provision of education and health were intimately connected with a minimal provision of a good life, below the threshold of which harm would result.

A number of feminist commentators distinguished between the practical and strategic needs of women, with practical gender needs linked to issues of immediate survival – food, shelter, water – and strategic needs associated with political struggles to transform gendered relations (Moser 1993; Molyneux 1985). The distinction was later amplified when the realm of the strategic came to be associated with the term 'interests' and later rights (Molyneux 1998; Molyneux and Razavi 2002). Education can be both a practical gender need and a strategic gender interest. Assessing this may depend on the context and the content of that education. Gender equality in education associated with 'practical gender needs' might entail paying particular attention to provision of education, taking account of the social relations that prevent access to learning, participation and achievement. These social relations were found in the household economy and the ways in which women and girls internalised a view that they did not deserve education and their basic needs could be met with minimal education provision (Ames 2005; Leggatt 2005). Equality is thus an aspect of equal regard as much as equal resources to address need.

However the policy language associated with basic needs did not explore or even fully express the difficulties of how need was defined in particular contexts, how need linked with rights and whether education was part of the threshold of need. Basic needs came increasingly to be associated with a commodity that could meet that need, generally viewed as four or five years in school. Torres (2000) shows how the concept of EFA shrank from concern with education for all, to concern with the schooling of children; from universalising basic education to universalising access to primary education; and from supporting basic learning needs that would facilitate a deepening of future learning to providing for minimum learning needs, i.e. a minimal number of years in school. (In monitoring education systems the commodity of a set number of years of schooling came to stand for the notion that basic learning needs had been met.) While the Jomtien Declaration (1990) tried to associate basic learning needs with a broad range of ideas about how such needs would be satisfied, the forms of policy monitoring used by the governments and UNESCO tracked whether five years of schooling had been achieved for girls and boys (WDEFA 1990; UNESCO 2000). The implication was that gender equality entailed assessing whether girls or boys had the requisite numbers of years of schooling, that these amounts were equivalent and nothing more. Global space generally denoted a sphere where cross-national monitoring of these amounts took place. Although the Jomtien conference had tried to establish the conditions for the political alliances that might shape a richer notion of global discussion and dialogue, the conference was dominated by the agendas of large UN organisations; more diverse voices struggled to be heard and assessment of EFA became measurements of commodities for provision (Chabbott 1998; Shotton 1998; Torres 2000).

The language of *rights* was not linked with commodities, but was constrained in a different way by notions about the state. In this period, rights were associated with legal documents and generally evoked the notion of citizenship. It was through association with a state that a person had a right to education similar to rights held by other citizens regardless of gender or race. But formal legal provision gave very little attention to context. The injustices of gendered settings, feminist lawyers remarked, generally made it very difficult to realise rights in practice (Charlesworth 1995). Feminist critiques of international declarations such as the Universal Declaration on Human Rights (1948) and the Convention on the Rights of the Child (1989) highlighted how their rather bland statements about gender equality failed to note the specific abuses women experienced, the discrimination entailed in separating women's rights from human rights and the omissions entailed by not looking closely at gendered relations in the family (Bunch 1990). The attempt to use international law to secure gender equality through the CEDAW (1979) had had mixed results as many countries used the reservation clauses to exempt themselves on the grounds of religion or culture from those clauses dealing with equalities in marriage, inheritance and work (Stamatopoulou 1995: 38). Much feminist discussion of rights stressed the particular forms of violence women faced, focused on respecting negative freedoms for women and the obligations of the state to protect women from gender based violence. In this context the global women's movement gave little attention to women's rights to education (Friedman 1995).

These discussions of rights made equality and gender equality in education particularly problematic. For Carole Pateman (1988) equal rights that have been granted, such as in education, do not become realised partly because ideas of social contract that had underpinned the emergence of democracy had never considered women as equal partners to the political bargain that established the state. Iris Young (1990) remarked that it was essential to challenge faces of oppression, such as exploitation, marginalisation, violence, powerlessness and cultural imperialism. The persistence of these meant that the equal distribution of resources such as rights to education did not deliver the aspirations invested in them. The collusion of schools with these forms of oppression made them uneasy spaces in which to look for a realisation of rights (Eisenberg 2006). The feminist critique of rights and justice in the first phase was that particular contexts – such as the forms of international treaties or institutions grounded in citizenship – made rights an uncertain vehicle through which substantive gender equality could be delivered. Nonetheless the aspiration expressed through CEDAW was that states could and should deliver gender equality and that gender equality in education was one indication that this promise was being fulfilled. The global realm of discussion and debate was used to advance the demand for the recognition of women's rights as human rights and argue against the ways in which the reservation clauses of CEDAW were applied.

The capability approach, formulated in the inter/national period in the writings of Amartya Sen, initially expressed some sharp differences with the concept of basic needs and ideas about group rights, that were sometimes associated with advocates of women's rights. Sen argued that the notion of basic needs failed to take account of personal differences, so that one child with particular learning needs might require a different form of education from another; needs, in his view, implied passivity on the part of the needy and the concept was unable to encapsulate a wider view of development (Sen 1984: 513–515). Rights, in Sen's view were often used in ways that did not clearly enough distinguish the importance of process freedoms, such as freedoms to participate in discussions concerning rights and education, and outcomes, for example the content and level of education achieved. Sen argued for the importance of a term of value, such as capability, that could distinguish these different processes and signal a terrain that was not simply contoured by legal relationships. A capability is defined as 'a person's ability to do valuable acts or reach valuable states of being; [it] represents the alternative combinations of things a person is able to do or be' (Sen 1993: 30). Thus capabilities are opportunities or freedoms to achieve what an individual reflectively considers valuable. When evaluating learning, education or schooling, it is therefore important to assess not how much money nor happiness an individual derives, but what the range of valued opportunities are, and the freedoms that will support the connection between valued opportunities and outcomes or capabilities and functionings.

Sen was concerned that gendered relations inside and outside the household supported each other and helped form the perceptions of women, that they did not deserve benefits from joint family enterprises or that they could not articulate their preferences; for example, the wish to be educated (Sen 1990). In a household negotiating about a woman taking time off household chores and childcare to attend a literacy class, the woman may accept that she should not attend, because she considers she does not deserve to be educated, or that her failure to contribute money to the household means she cannot 'take time' for her literacy class. Sen argued that it was important to evaluate equality not with regard to preferences, what the woman said she wanted, nor to satisfaction in the family, that there was not conflict over her wish to attend a class. Equality should be considered in relation to capabilities, that is the range of valued beings and doings she had available.

The complex ideas Sen explored on gender and the capability approach took a somewhat different form when he began to link these to an intervention in policy and practice. His collaboration with Mahbub ul Haq on the Human Development Index (HDI), first published in 1990, focused on particular amounts of education that might comprise a dimension of human development and act as a proxy for expanding capabilities (Sen 2003; ul Haq 1995). In the Gender Development Index (GDI) of 1995, there was a simple incorporation into the HDI of gender differences assessed in terms of number of years lived, education acquired and income earned (Anand and Sen 1995). Thus, in the GDI, the project of expanding capabilities for women did not look very different from satisfying needs. The stress in the HDI and the GDI on ranking country performance highlighted the ways in which the project for gender equality in education was to be articulated through the notion of a global social justice that involved encouraging states to improve their GDI or HDI rankings.

In the first period, it can be seen that there was some disjuncture between the axiological discussions of needs, rights and capabilities, and policy formulated to put these values into practice that tended to overlook the concerns with gendered sites of power and the relationship of private and public that was animating feminist discussion. The emphasis on the obligation of states to deliver policy entailed a rather limited notion of the global, conceived primarily as a space to monitor the effectiveness of policy with regard to citizens, and not itself an area for contesting ideas or generating values.

Agency, solidarity and global obligations

This emphasis was to change considerably in the in/ternational period, when needs, rights and capabilities came to focus more on agency, with the consequence that thinking about gender equality in education came to mean not just equal resources and equal regard, but something thicker associated with active engagement in expressing aspects of solidarity, formulating ideas about equality or facilitating the freedoms that might allow for a project in gender equality in education to emerge. In this context global space was not simply a realm for concluding international agreements or monitoring international benchmarks, but became associated with negotiating political demands and recalibrating global institutions. The site of policy now no longer rests only with governments, but takes in a wide range of spaces framed, for instance, by civil society, the family, language and culture. In this changing political climate, although the policy vocabulary for gender equality and education still deploys terms concerned with needs, rights and capabilities, they signal wider spheres of action and different normative concepts.

In this second wave, needs theorists have argued that key features of needs were neglected in the pragmatic ways the basic needs approach was put into practice. Hamilton (2003), for example, has distinguished three categories of needs: *vital needs* are necessary conditions for human existence, but these needs cannot be 'simply' reduced to biological needs, as in the basic needs approach (Hamilton 2003: 28–29). Vital needs exist whether or not a person experiences them as needs. *Social needs* are very broadly formulated as the 'interpretative framework within which actual individuals and groups interpret their own everyday needs' and these include public provision for needs and needs that emerge from production and consumption. *Agency needs* are 'general ethical and political objectives that relate to human functionings and the performance of valued human tasks. Agency needs are developed and met, and in the process they help enable full human functioning' (Hamilton 2003: 35).

Hamilton's three categories of needs provide a different foundation for gender equality in education from the basic needs approach. If vital needs are not biological, education up to certain levels can be understood as a vital need, necessary for human existence in contemporary times where essential information is transmitted through written text, the labour market is organised in relation to levels of schooling and school facilitates inclusion in social and political associations. Education in a much broader sense than schooling may also be a social need, providing the language through which political, social and economic demands are made. However, education cannot be limited to what is formally taught in school, but must take in a wide rage of education settings in which social interactions take place. Education is the precondition for and the outcome of agency needs.

Soron Reader (2006) argues that needs can be specified locally and claims of need may be very diverse. In education, for example, responding to needs does not necessarily imply supplying only four (or ten) years of schooling as came to be the practice in implementing the basic needs approach. Need only implies passivity if it is assumed that needs can only be met by someone else.

The argument for gender equality based in rights in the in/ternational period has been particularly concerned with rights as positive freedoms associated with the provision of education, health, housing and welfare, not primarily with rights and negative freedoms from violence, which comprised a major component of work in the previous period. Rights are seen as multidimensional, concerned not just with civic and political rights, but also economic and social rights and the conditions in which all those who suffer forms of discrimination and injustice can secure rights (Vizard 2006; Molyneux and Razavi 2002). In this guise, the language of rights that gender campaigners used tactically from the 1990s to gain access to global decision-making bodies has come to offer a rich notion through which civil society organisations engaged in local campaigns have sought to hold states accountable, for example for delivery on promises of rights to education or health (Unterhalter 2007a; Mundy and Murphy 2001). Sen has formulated the idea of rights as ethical obligations expressing links not only between states and citizens but a wide range of social actors animated not just by legal duties but also concerned with care and compassion (Sen 2004). The language of rights to education used in policy documents may sometimes sound rhetorical and often emphasises the existence of international agreements as the reasons individuals have rights rather than substantive notions concerned with human dignity and equality. However, such language suggests steps through which gender campaigners have sought to institutionalise processes to affect gender equality in education (Robeyns 2006; Unterhalter 2007a). Some local studies show how the language of rights contained in policy is much contested and imperfectly understood by development workers who are employed on projects concerned with gender, education and rights (Greany 2006; Page 2005), other studies indicate how, in the context of educational denial, the language of rights has been used to gain redress through the courts or other legal processes (Tomasevski 2003; Subrahmanian 2002). This suggests that the language of rights offers some potential to broaden ideas concerning gender equality in education to encompass a wider range of entitlements, not just those secured through international treaties or policy documents. Many global organisations are struggling to realise their commitment to rights as ethical obligations in relation to the financing of education, campaigning in relation to HIV or planning for the effects of climate change (Unterhalter 2007a; Aikman and Unterhalter 2007).

In this in/ternational period, the concept of capabilities has come to be understood as important not just in its own right, but as a useful contributory notion to underpin some of the ethical notions associated with rights (Sen 2005; Brighouse 2004; Robeyns 2006; Nussbaum 2006). Notions of human dignity, freedoms, agency and reflection on what one has reason to value, are all associated with the notion of capabilities, and these help undergird the notion of rights with normative ideas that orient this language away from 'simple' legalistic frameworks. Gender equality in education understood in terms of the capability approach entails considering the interplay of obligations between individuals, states and civil society in order to secure the freedoms to expand a capability set and give all women and men equal conditions to reflect on and achieve dimensions of learning, education and schooling they have reason to value (Unterhalter 2007a; Walker 2007; Unterhalter 2007b).

Equality is no longer a matter of equal amounts, but a more substantive idea associated with solidarities and confronting injustice. This is an ambitious project not yet fully realised intellectually, institutionally or in the interactions of global civil society, but it is an idea that seeks to imbue the in/ternational period not just with dialogues across difference but also a notion of the principles that might underpin that process.

Conclusions

Gender inequalities in schooling have been a concern since the 1970s, but shifting global relations have meant that the terms of value that address these injustices have changed. The initial focus on providing a set amount of schooling through states addressing basic needs in the most minimal way has shifted to expanded notions of needs, rights and capabilities where obligations are held by governments, civil society and organisations. While many continue to see the achievement of gender equality simply in securing equal numbers of girls and boys the same amount of schooling, much wider notions of gender equality in education as a substantive idea of deep obligations between people are emerging. These ethical ideas jostle to be realised through policy that is deeply compromised by the inequalities of economic and political power and the appalling consequences of wars, but paradoxically the ways in which global, national and local have become intertwined in contemporary times seems to open the way for a deeper consideration not just of practices and processes for gender equality in education, but of the principles that might generate deeper understanding and action for justice.

Note

1 Versions of this paper were presented at the Philosophy of Education seminar at the Institute of Education, University of London in May 2005, the HDCA conference in Paris and UKFIET conference in Oxford in September 2005. I am indebted to students in the Capability Approach Reading Group at the Institute of Education in Autumn 2006 for searching questions. My thanks to Des Gasper, Harry Brighouse and Lorella Terzi for some critical commentary, to Madeleine Arnot and Shailaja Fennell for guidance and suggestions on revision, and to Rosa Crawford for research assistance.

References

Ahmed, S. (1998) *Differences that Matter: Feminist Theory and Postmodernism*, Cambridge: Cambridge University Press.

Aikman, S. and Unterhalter, E. (2007) *Practising Gender Equality in Education*, Oxford: Oxfam.

Ames, P. (2005) 'When access is not enough: educational exclusion of rural girls in Peru' in S. Aikman and E. Unterhalter (eds) *Beyond Access. Transforming Policy and Practice for Gender Equality in Education*, Oxford: Oxfam, pp. 149–165.

Anand, S. and Sen, A. (2003) 'Gender inequality and human development: theories and measurement' in S. Fukuda-Parr and A.K. Shiva Kumar (eds) (2003) *Readings in Human Development: Concepts, Measures and Policies for a Development Paradigm*, New Delhi: Oxford: Oxford University Press.

Antrobus, P. (2005) *The Global Women's Movement: Issues and Strategies for the New Century*, London: Zed Books.

Appadurai, A. (1997) *Modernity at Large: Cultural Dimensions in Globalization*, Minnesota: University of Minnesota Press.

Appiah, A. (2006) *Cosmopolitanism: Ethics in a World of Strangers*, London: W.W. Norton.

Becker, G. (1993) *Human Capital* (3rd edn; 1st edn 1964), Chicago: University of Chicago Press.

Bhavnani, K. (2001) *Feminism and 'Race'*, Oxford: Oxford University Press.

Brighouse, H. (2004) *Justice*, Cambridge: Polity Press.

Bunch, C. (1990) 'Women's rights as human rights: towards a re-vision of human rights', *Human Rights Quarterly*, 12: 486–498.

Castells, M. (2000) *The Rise of the Network Society: The Information Age*, Oxford: Blackwell Publishers.

Chabbott, Colette (1998) 'Constructing educational consensus: international development professionals and the World Conference on Education for All', *International Journal of Educational Development*, 18, 3: 207–208.

Chabbott, C. (2003) *Constructing Education for Development: International Organisations and Education for All*, London: Routledge.

Charlesworth, H. (1995) 'Human rights as women's rights' in J. Peters and A. Wolper (eds) *Women's Rights, Human Rights*, New York: Routledge, pp. 103–113.

Colclough, C. (2006) 'Wider picture: globalisation and higher education', paper delivered at Case-Study Symposium on African Development: The Case of North Kenya, City University, London, 31 October 2006.

Eade, J. and O'Byrne, D. (2005) *Global Ethics and Civil Society*, Aldershot: Ashgate.

Eisenberg, A. (2006) 'Education and the politics of difference: Iris Young and the politics of education', *Educational Philosophy and Theory*, 38, 1: 7–23.

Friedman, E. (1995) 'Women's human rights: the emergence of a movemenet' in J. Peters and A. Wolper (eds) *Women's Rights, Human Rights: International Feminist Perspectives*, London and New York: Routledge.

Gaskell, J. and Mullen, A. (2006) 'Women in teaching: participation, power and possibility' in C. Skelton, B. Francis and L. Smulyan (eds) *The Sage Handbook of Gender and Education*, London: Sage, pp. 453–468.

Greany, K. (2006) 'Rhetoric versus realities: an exploration of the challenges of addressing gender equity through a rights based approach to education in Niger', unpublished MA dissertation, Institute of Education, University of London.

Hamilton, L. (2003) *The Political Philosophy of Needs*, Cambridge: Cambridge University Press.

Held, D. and McGrew, A. (eds) (2002) *Governing Globalization*, Cambridge: Polity Press.

Held, D. and McGrew, A. (eds) (2003) *The Global Transformations Reader: An Introduction to the Globalization Debate*, Cambridge: Polity Press.

Kirk, J. (ed.) (2007 forthcoming) *Women Teachers in South Asia*, New Delhi: Sage.

Leggett, I. (2005) 'Learning to improve policy for pastoralists in Kenya' in S. Aikman and E. Unterhalter (eds) *Beyond Access. Transforming Policy and Practice for Gender Equality in Education*, Oxford: Oxfam, pp. 128–138.

Leo-Rhynie, E. (2000) *Gender Mainstreaming in Education: A Reference Manual for Governments and Other Stakeholders*, London: Commonwealth Secretariat.

Molyneux, M. (1985) 'Mobilisation without emancipation? Women's interests and the state and revolution in Nicaragua', *Feminist Studies*, 11, 227–254.

Molyneux, M. (1998) 'Analysing women's movements' in C. Jackson and R. Pearson (eds) *Feminist Visions of Development*, London: Routledge, pp. 65–87.

Molyneux, M. and Razavi, S. (2002) 'Introduction' in M. Molyneux and S. Razavi *Gender Justice, Development, and Rights*, Oxford: Oxford University Press, pp. 1–42.

Moser, C. (1993) *Gender Planning and Development*, London: Routledge.

Mundy, K. and Murphy, L. (2001) 'Transnational advocacy, global civil society? Emerging evidence from the field of education', *Comparative Education Review*, 45, 1: 85–126.

Nicholson, L. (ed.) (1997) *The Second Wave*, London: Routledge.

Nussbaum, M. (2006) *Frontiers of Justice*, Cambridge, MA: Harvard University Press.

Odin, J.K. and Manicas, P.T. (eds) (2004) *Globalization and Higher Education*, Honolulu: University of Hawaii Press.

Page, E. (2005) 'Gender and the construction of identities in Indian elementary education', unpublished PhD thesis, Institute of Education, University of London.

Pateman, C. (1988) *The Sexual Contract*, Cambridge: Polity Press.

Psacharopoulos, G. (1973) *Returns to Education. An International Comparison*, Oxford: Elsevier.

Rai, S. (2002) *Gender and the Political Economy of Development*, Cambridge: Polity Press.

Rai, S. (ed.) (2003) *Mainstreaming Gender, Democratizing the State?* Manchester: Manchester University Press.

Reader, S. (2006) 'Does a basic needs approach need capabilities?' *Journal of Political Philosophy*. 14, 3: 337–350.

Robeyns, I. (2006) 'Three modes of education: rights, capabilities and human capital', *Theory and Research in Education*, 4, 1: 69–84.

Rose, P. (2005) 'Is there a "fast track" to achieving education for all?' *International Journal of Educational Development*, 25, 4: 381–394.

Sen, A. (1984) *Resources, Values and Development*, Oxford: Blackwell.

Sen, A. (1990) 'Gender and cooperative conflicts' in I. Tinker (ed.) *Persistent Inequalities*, New York: Oxford University Press, pp. 123–149.

Sen, A. (1992) *Inequality Re-examined*, Oxford: Clarendon Press.

Sen, A. (1993) 'Capability and well-being' in M. Nussbaum and A. Sen (eds) *Quality of Life*, Oxford: Oxford University Press.

Sen, A. (2002) 'Processes, liberty and rights' in A. Sen (ed.) *Rationality and Freedom*, Cambridge: Harvard University Press, pp. 623–658.

Sen, A. (2003) 'Foreword' in S. Fukuda-Parr and A. Shiva-Kumar (eds) *Readings in Human Development*, New Delhi: Oxford University Press, pp vii–xiii.

Sen, A. (2004) 'Elements of a theory of human rights', *Philosophy and Public Affairs*, 32: 4 pp.

Sen, A. (2005) 'Human rights and capabilities', *Journal of Human Development*, 6, 2: 151–166.

Shotton, J. (1998) *Learning and Freedom: Policy and Paradigms in Indian Education and Schooling*, New Delhi: Sage.

Skeggs, B. (1997) *Formations of Class and Gender: Becoming Respectable*, London: Sage.

Stamatopoulou, E. (1995) 'Women's rights and the United Nations' in J. Peters and A. Wolper (eds) *Women's Rights, Human Rights*, New York: Routledge, pp. 36–49.

Staudt, K. (2003) 'Gender mainstreaming: conceptual links to institutional machineries' in S. Rai (ed.) *Mainstreaming Gender, Democratizing the State?* Manchester: Manchester University Press, pp. 40–66.

Stiglitz, J. (2002) *Globalization and its Discontents*, London: Allen Lane.

Stewart, F. (1985) *Planning to Meet Basic Needs*, London: Macmillan.

Streeten, P., Burki, S.J., ul Haq, M., Hicks, N. and Stewart, F. (1981) *First Things*

First – Meeting Basic Human Needs in Developing Countries, New York: Oxford University Press.

Subrahmanian, R. (2002) 'Engendering education: prospects for a rights based approach to female education deprivation in India' in M. Molyneux and S. Razavi (eds) *Gender Justice, Development, and Rights*, Oxford: Oxford University Press, pp. 204–238.

Subrahmanian, R. (2005) 'Gender equality in education: definitions and measurements', *International Journal of Educational Development*, 25, 4: 395–407.

Tinker, I. (ed.) (1990) *Persistent Inequalities*, New York: Oxford University Press.

Tomasevski, K. (2003) *Education Denied*, London: Zed Books.

Torres, R.M. (2000) *One Decade of Education for All: The Challenge Ahead*, Buenos Aires: International Institute for Education Planning.

ul Haq, M. (1995) *Reflections on Human Development*, Oxford: Oxford University Press.

UNDP (2005) *Human Development Report*, New York: Oxford University Press.

UNESCO (2000) *Investing in Education: Analysis of the World Education Indicators Programme*, Paris: Unesco.

Unifem (2005) 'Progress of the World's Women 2005: Women, Work & Poverty', available online at: www1.bpcd.net/cgi-bin/nph-proxy.cgi/000000A/http/www.unifem. org/attachments/products/PoWW2005_eng.pdf.

Unterhalter, E. (2005) 'Fragmented frameworks? Researching women, gender, education and development' in S. Aikman and E. Unterhalter (eds) *Beyond Access: Developing Gender Equality in Education*, Oxford: Oxfam Publishing, pp. 15–35.

Unterhalter, E. (2007a) *Gender, Schooling and Global Social Justice*, London: Routledge.

Unterhalter, E. (2007b forthcoming) 'Gender equality, education and the capability approach' in M. Walker, and E. Unterhalter (eds) *Amartya Sen's Capability Approach and Social Justice in Education*, New York: Palgrave.

Vizard, P. (2006) *Poverty and Human Rights*, Oxford: Oxford University Press.

Walker, M. (2007 forthcoming) 'South African girls' lives and capabilities' in M. Walker and E. Unterhalter (eds) *Amartya Sen's Capability Approach and Social Justice in Education*, New York: Palgrave.

WDEFA (1990) 'World Declaration on Education for All' in UNESCO (2000) *The Dakar Framework for Action*, Paris, UNESCO Publishing.

Weedon, C. (1997) *Feminist Practice and Poststructuralist Theory*, Oxford: Blackwell.

Werbner, P. and Yuval Davis, N. (1999) *Women, Citizenship and Difference*, London: Zed Books.

Wiggins, D. (1985) 'Claims of need' in T. Honderich (ed.) *Morality and Objectivity*, London: Routledge.

Winslow, A. (ed.) (1995) *Women, Politics and the United Nations*, Westport CT: Greenwood Press.

Young, I.M. (1990) *Justice and the Politics of Difference*, Princeton: Princeton University Press.

3 Contested gender frameworks

Economic models and provider perspectives on education

Shailaja Fennell

Economic models have focused on the individual benefits of acquiring education in terms of economic mobility with little regard to gendered or social impacts. Studies of poor agricultural economies emphasise the multiple burdens that are faced by women and men in the world of work that limit the socially transformative role of education and the empowerment of women. In response to these conceptual frameworks, feminist critiques have called for a broader terrain that explicitly recognises the social construction of gender through the adoption of an expanded social science framework. The agendas of current providers of education are uncertain and there are concerns regarding the impact of different types of provision on gender equality. This chapter sets out the nature of this contestation with the aim of bringing the perspectives of educational providers to bear upon national and international goals of gender access and equality.

In this chapter, I begin with an examination of the key role of human capital theory in economic models of the provision of education, emphasising the investment dimension of the provision of education with its large returns in relation to individual achievement. Feminist economists have called for a move away from regarding women as merely contributors to the economic process, whilst ignoring the gender constraints within households and labour markets. They argue for a much broader societal framework. The second section explores the relationship between gender, work and education using the lens of development. National provision of education arguably has to recognise the gender dynamics of agricultural economies, which are shaped by both traditional gender cultures and the uneven gender impacts of globalisation on national economies. The economic transformations of developing economies not only challenge the assumptions within mainstream economic theory but also pose a complex gender politics for educationalists. In the third section, I suggest a new research agenda for educational research within the new contours of a national market for education drawn by a global neo-liberal agenda. The conceptual models adopted by new providers of education are potentially very important for the provision of mass compulsory education of the sort envisaged by Education for All. It is not clear that these non-state providers, working within development contexts, have the same or equivalent understandings of the complex link between schooling and the economy, and importantly the ways in which gender relations shape that relationship. In conclusion I argue that there is a need to embed the findings of the feminist critique more thoroughly in our understanding of educational provision to ensure that present providers are able to work more effectively with regard to educational goals in the national and international spheres.

Contested economic approaches to gender and education

Human capital theory made a huge impact on both academic and policy circles at national and international levels between the 1950s and the 1980s (Sweetland 1996). Central to this theory was the importance of education in economic growth. The main premise of human capital theory is that the investments made by human beings in on-the-job training, education at primary, secondary and tertiary levels, informal learning and vocational training, should be regarded as a form of capital accumulation. This notion was regarded as radical, if not unacceptable, as it seemed to equate human beings with machines and consequently inanimate objects thereby raising moral and philosophical concerns among economists (Schultz 1961). Maximising human skills through education provided the key to labour's contribution to economic growth in the capitalist world, and possibly exceeding that provided by physical capital through the twentieth century. The power of this conceptual approach emanates from equating investment in labour skills with the power of technology, where human capital has the ability to drive economic growth in the same way as do the ideas of the entrepreneur or the improvements in machines. Human capital theory shifted the focus from the manual contribution of labour to the skill contribution through 'activities that influence future real income through the embedding of resources in people' (Becker 1962: 9).

The gains to both the individual and society from the wide range of opportunities for improving economic mobility through education became the subject of much research through the 1960s in the United States with the burgeoning of a literature on returns to education. The focus of these theoretical studies was to calculate the additional private income that would accrue from the decision to invest in education (Schultz 1961; Becker 1962). The effect of additional years of education on individual earnings emerged as a rich area for empirical research (Mincer 1958). Calculations of the share of human capital to growth rates also emerged as a research area with estimates of contributions amounting to 43 per cent of the growth in the US economy during the time period of 1929–1957 (Dennison 1962). Another important area of the empirical literature was the calculation of the returns to college education to establish whether they were lower than returns to physical/tangible capital, in which case there would be an underinvestment in education that needed to be resolved (Becker 1962). Early theoretical work argued that the returns to investment in developing countries would be even higher than in the West, as investment in human capital would be able to remedy the much greater deficit of capital faced by these societies and therefore holding a much greater potential for economic growth (Schultz 1962). These theoretical propositions were supported by econometric results from studies in 32 countries (Psacharpoulos 1973), which indicated that returns to education were higher in developing countries, with a far greater gap between returns to human and physical capital. Additionally, the returns were the highest in primary education, while the costs of tertiary education were far higher in developing than in developed countries. The implication for developing countries was that they should embark on a large and sustained programme of investment in education to ensure a high rate of national economic growth.

The popularity of human capital theory as the most appropriate conceptual framework for educational provision also contributed to the establishment of the field of economics of education in the 1960s in the United States and Western Europe. It encouraged a coalescence of the fields of labour economics, public economics, economic growth theory and development economics (Sweetland 1996). The theory of human capital provided a strong rationale for expanding education across capitalist and developing countries through public provision of education that would be accessed by private individuals who freely chose to enhance their skills to ensure economic mobility through employment in the labour market. The legacy of human capital theory within the field of the economics of education was that of a simple but powerful tool of regarding the role of education as a crucial input that contributed to economic output.

This simple yet compelling conceptual approach of the theory of human capital made it very attractive for ensuring high levels of economic growth in advanced capitalist countries in the West. As well as that, it was heralded as the harbinger of growth for developing countries across Asia, Africa and Latin America. However the large-scale investment in education that was undertaken in the 1950s and the 1960s in developing countries provided mixed results and, by the 1970s, doubts were raised about the accuracy of the approach (Blaug 1978). The high cost of providing education resulted in a demand for education that far exceeded the available supply. Also the much higher cost of tertiary and secondary education over primary education left meagre funds for the latter resulting in high drop-out rates by fourth and fifth grade (Sobel 1978). The relative neglect of the financing of the provision of education within the theory of human capital, as well as an absence of a theory of demand for education, came in for considerable flack. At one point the model was termed a 'research program' that could only be relevant if conducted in the United States where there was no possibility of supply exceeding demand (Blaug 1978).

There is still considerable concern about the implications of the human capital approach for those wishing to make a case for state provision of education. There are serious questions regarding whether the returns to education provide robust results across all groups and societies and whether these results are neutral in relation to income and social class. Also the difference in returns to education between men and women at primary, secondary and tertiary level showed that the returns for women were the highest at primary level while that for men was at secondary and tertiary level (Barro 2001). It would also appear that, while human capital theory emphasises the economic benefit of education to the individual and the economy, it downplays the fact that the *social returns* to education are very difficult to estimate (Bennell 2002) and ignores the impact of social class, religion or 'race' on the opportunity to invest in education. It is not clear what might be the necessary and sufficient conditions to overcome these social markers (Schulz 1961; Becker 1962). Consequently the model lacks an understanding of the role which social class plays in facilitating or impairing the effectiveness of human capital when individuals attempt to secure a foothold in the labour market (Bowles and Gintis 1975). The focus of this approach rests on the ability of the individual to choose to invest in human capital by 'entering', i.e. using, the existing market for education.

Where educational choices have to be made for children who are not independent economic agents, it is clear that it is the family rather than the individual that makes the choice of investing in education on behalf of the child. As a result, the human capital model needed to be extended so as to recognise the unit of the family in the decisions about educating children as well as about events such as marriage and divorce that also affect the investment decisions of the household (Becker 1981). In *A Treatise on the Family*, Becker assumes that members of a family would cooperate to ensure that their decisions regarding investment, labour and consumption jointly maximise the economic returns of the household (ibid.). Where adults are making decisions regarding the investment in children's education, it is presumed that altruism rather than competition guides the family.

The differential pattern of investment for men and women that has consequences for their education cannot be discounted. As human capital theory regards all members of a household as rational, it assumes that if women work as homemakers, rather than in the labour market after marriage, they must have lower returns to education than that of their husbands. If the returns to education for women were higher than for their prospective partners, then it would not be rational for women to forgo family income by exiting the market (ibid.). Consequently the lesser presence of women in the labour market is regarded as the result of a cooperative decision jointly taken by an 'economically rational' husband and wife to maximise their joint outcome. This model of the household is termed the so-called New Household Economics (NHE). The proposition that women and men choose between the labour market and the home based on their individual choice presumes that women and men are treated identically in both arenas. In such a world, the decisions that women and men take regarding investment in human capital will be guided by their particular skills, or comparative advantage, so as to achieve maximal gain in the labour market.

The division of labour between men and women in a society has been the subject of feminist critiques since the 1960s. The traditional social science position, that the processes of capitalism and modernisation would draw both men and women into the labour market in an identical fashion, was repudiated by evidence that the division of labour historically undervalued women's contribution as well as pushing their work out of the public sphere and into the private sphere of the household (Scott 1989; Pateman 1988). Gendered patterns of the division of labour have been identified dating from centuries before the industrial revolution (Pahl 1987). The era of industrial revolutions in Europe to a large extent broke down the traditional gender division of labour in agricultural and proto-industrial activities. The Enclosure Acts in eighteenth century England, for example, put an end to women's labour activities such as *gleaning* (the picking of grain after the harvest had been removed from the field) and *estover* (the gathering of the hay after harvesting). Women were increasingly pushed back into the household while men left the field to work in the factory (Humphries 1990).

Western feminist scholarship in the 1970s saw this shift in the location of women's work as a consequence of industrialisation and was strongly influenced by the Marxist critiques of capitalism which represented it as an exploitative and alienating system within which women were subordinated in the home and excluded from the world of work. The gender division of labour provided a strong basis for confronting the NHE with evidence of power and hierarchy within the household. Feminist economists have shown that household should not be regarded as a harmonious unit but a site of gender conflict and exploitation (Wooley 1988). There has consequently been a shift away from examining how education would affect *inter-household* differences for both women and men to the manner in which investment decisions affect members with the household, that is the *intra-household* processes that determine what resources and opportunities, such as for education, are available to individual male and female members.

The focus of the Western feminist critique on the relationship between industrialisation, the world of work and the gender division of labour drew responses across the developing world. The casting of women's employment into an industrial world is inappropriate for countries where agriculture still provides the largest sectoral contribution to national income and the contribution of women to this sector would be even less visible (Mohanty and Alexander 1997). The considerable importance of agriculture as a basis for the gender division of labour within historical processes and institutions outside the West indicated that the gender division of labour needed to be examined from *within* those societies (Bray 1997).

The conceptualisation of gender and education in development

The relationship between the gender division of labour and economic development was the subject of path-breaking work by Ester Boserup in the 1970s. Her research drew on the experiences of developed and developing countries and argued that gender roles in agriculture are principally determined by the *system of production*, the *economic status* of the household and the *level of technology*. The *type of production system* in agriculture, whether settled agriculture of the intensive or extensive type, or pastoral or of a mixed-use nature, composed of both crop production and livestock herding, affects the labour demand within the sector (Boserup 1965, 1981). Where there is a relative scarcity of labour in relation to the availability of land within a system of high labour demand, there would be a compelling need for *all* members of the family to participate in agriculture. The gender division of labour in this scenario demands that women work outside the home and are also major contributors to the labour requirements of the household. There are, however, very clear norms about what constitutes women's work and men's work that are affected by the economic status of the household and ownership patterns. The work that falls to men and women in households indicates that there are hierarchies of age and gender that result in the younger and female members of the household expending the longest hours in the most repetitive and low-value work. Where there is a combination of subsistence crop, or production for consumption, and cash crop produced, women tend to work on subsistence production and men on cash crops.

The *economic status* of the household has a major impact on the gender division of labour. In situations where households are able to undertake commercial crop production resulting in greater wealth accruing to the household, there is often concomitant withdrawal of women from the labour force and their replacement by contract male labour (Sen 1981a, b). Wealth accumulation by a household therefore does not automatically result in greater leisure for women members but a return to the confines of the home. These shifts between the farm and the home in the labour contribution of women are couched in the language of economic mobility, 'our women do not need to work' or cultural norms, 'our women do not work'. Behind these economic and cultural explanations, there is evidence often of patrilineal inheritance patterns that imposed restrictions on women's mobility outside the home (Boserup 1989).

The re-conceptualisation of the work patterns of men and women in agriculture affected the analysis of the relationship between gender and economic development during the 1970s and 1980s. Subsequent research indicates that economic development might even exacerbate the gender asymmetries imposed on women in the field and the household (Moser 1983). The impact of economic development on men and women's work in a modernising agricultural world has raised questions about the increasing demands of women to bear the *triple burden* of contributing labour, the bearing of children and the caring for the family, i.e. production, reproduction and care (Beneria 1979; Dixon-Mueller 1981). There are serious concerns that the nature of capitalist development across developing countries has resulted in a re-designation of women and men's work through the period of neo-liberal economic reforms in the 1980s that has led to severe contraction of areas of male employment (such as the traditional factory sector) and increased employment for young women in export-oriented multinational units (Beneria 1985; Beneria and Roldan 1987).

The close relationship between women's work, the increasing pressure of the *triple burden* and the imposition of social norms from the surrounding local culture brings out very sharply the high level of drudgery in women's work that exists in the agricultural sector. The role of education as a possible catalyst to catapult women out of the domestic sphere and into the labour market therefore provides a very different trajectory from the relationship between gender and education that was introduced by human capital theory.

Contemporary education research is using the theory of capabilities and entitlements with its new emphasis on the power of education through the enhancement of the individual's negotiatory skills and set of choices within a contested site (Sen 1999; Robeyns 2006; Unterhalter 2002). Such theory highlights the 'freedom enhancing' aspect of education created by the improved access to resources and markets within a framework of capabilities facilitating the measurement of different dimensions of women's empowerment and agency (Nussbaum 2000). New research on gender, education and development draws on these measures of women's empowerment to examine their everyday lives in poor agricultural communities and in urban slums and its relationship to their aspirations (Raynor this volume). This conceptual framework redresses the tendency in economic debates on education to emphasise the returns to education with the emphasis on income. The capabilities approach replaces this focus on the 'instrumental value' of education, i.e. the consequences of women's education solely in terms of their contribution to economic development, with a direct emphasis on the importance of the socially transformative and catalytic aspects of education, i.e. the 'intrinsic value' of the educational process, which are not so readily translatable into monetary values.

Contemporary difficulties in charting any simple or direct causal relationship between gender, education and development can be seen most clearly in the decade-long debate about the relationship between education, development and female fertility. The early studies in economic demography saw the fall in fertility rather as evidence of a 'demographic transition', the shift from a high-fertility high-mortality regime to a low-fertility low-mortality regime in developing countries (Dyson 1996). The associated falls in infant mortality and maternal mortality were applauded as an indication of reduction in the reproductive burden imposed on women by traditional agriculture and were also seen as a way out of drudgery and poverty for poor households. Economic demography since the 1980s has pointed to a negative correlation between the educational level of women and female fertility. In the 1990s, microeconomic studies on women's education and female fertility show how female fertility has fallen – pointing to the fact that reproductive decision making still eludes the women or couples concerned and resides with others in the household (such as the mother-in-law). It thus highlights the difficulties of inferring women's autonomy from educational achievement (Basu 1993; Jeffery and Jeffery 1997).

Our understanding of the relationship between women's education, fertility and economic development also owes a considerable debt to the international feminist concerns enunciated, for example, at the International Convention on Population and Development (ICPD) in Cairo in 1994, where calls were made for a shift in the focus from looking at women as passive recipients of economic and educational policy to a socially transformative approach that directly addresses the relationship between sexual and reproductive health and rights (Fennell 2006b) and away from such a macro-level, instrumental approach. Significantly, this global shift facilitated a move away from household models that assumed informed choice regarding the optimal number of children, to considerations regarding the reproductive rights of women (Kabeer 1994). The nexus between education and fertility is informed by the knowledge that the relationships of women within their household and community are a complex combination of familial and personal choices. Notions of modernity and human capital investment sit very uneasily with these complex local realities.

Today, reduced growth of the formal manufacturing sector has gone hand in hand with an increase of short-term and self-employment in the informal sector. There is a distinct preference for female workers in their teens and twenties within the informal sector as they are regarded as more amenable to discipline and less likely to object to the long hours and difficult conditions of work (Davin 2004; Sen 1999). The consequences of this huge shift in the gender division of labour, with a reduction of opportunities for men in the labour market, has given rise to *hyper-masculinities* in the social and cultural spheres, such as the playing out of macho behaviour by middle-aged unemployed working class men in Mexico to counterbalance the loss of status in the tradi-tional sphere (Beneria and Roldan 1987). In national labour markets where there has been a rising demand for young women as factory employees in export factories, there is growing evidence of *excessive femininities*, with young women devoting more time and money to grooming and dressing in a increas-ingly feminine manner to signal submissive behaviour within the home so as to counteract their increased presence in the labour market (Jacka 1997). The opposing tendency that is witnessed between upward mobility in the labour market and social status in the household and community indicates that there is no easy relationship that is discernable between the spheres of production, reproduction and care for both men and women. The case of female labour in export-processing industries in Latin America indicates that where there have been increases in women's autonomy and bargaining power, there has been a subsequent rise in discriminatory practices against them, both at the work place and in the community (Beneria 1999). The new and more fluid and fragile types of employment have often exacerbated the triple burden on women in the urban sector as well as resulting in the unravelling of the traditional safety nets for women in the rural economy (Leach 1994; Aggarwal 1995).

In these poverty-riddled environments, the notion that education will provide a panacea for releasing women from the drudgery of rural work and protect them from the fluctuating fortunes of urban livelihoods in a global economy appears to be far-fetched. Indeed the reality of the triple burden on women means that increasing the supply of education to ensure an increased enrolment of girls from poor families is very unlikely to succeed. Indian evid-ence shows that local initiatives evaluating the access enhancement strategies that were set up under the District Primary Education Programme (DPEP) in the 1990s have perversely resulted in a relative pushing-out of girls and mar-ginal groups, creating 'hierarchies of access', as they did not take account of local power structures in relation to caste, race and gender in the local community (Ramachandran 2002). Equally, research on marginalised groups indicates the presence of specific mechanisms that militate against the inclusion of *dalits* and *adivasi* groups in India (Balagopalan and Subrahmaniam 2003).[1]

The state has been the major but not necessarily the sole provider of educa-tion in the last half century of development in the non-Western world. In many countries there is a range of non-government providers, such as the private (for-profit) provider and the non-profit NGO (non-governmental organisation) as well as the religious and community based schools. In the last section I will try and open up this new and growing area of gender analysis through examining the mode of operation adopted by each type of provider. The analysis is a pre-liminary exploration of how providers might be brought into the field of gender, education and development.

Provider perspectives on education and consequences for gender and development

The impact of government as well as non-government providers – ranging from the private for-profit provider, the NGO and the religious provider such as the private (for-profit) provider and the non-profit NGO as well as the religious and community based schools – on goals of gender equality, is a matter of consider-able interest (Fennell 2006b). There is evidence that government and non-government, non-profit programmes can help advance gender goals in education. Vietnam provides an example of a strong state sectoral programme in education that has have been able to pursue universal primary education (UPE) in a relatively autonomous manner. In contrast, in Indonesia, the state education system is supported by religious as well as private *madrasahs* (community schools). The consequence of targeted interventions by non-government and government initiatives at the local level has been an accelera-tion in achieving the goal of gender parity, such as in the *Cheli-Beti* programme in Nepal and the Malaysian government's strategy of homing in on existing gender based social networks to improve girls' enrolment and retention levels at primary and secondary levels respectively (ibid.). Despite these recent initiatives, there is little or no analysis of how providers perceive education, i.e. the type of 'good' that they are providing, or how this perception of the nature of educa-tion will impact gender concerns. In Table 3.1, I to set out a tentative typology of current providers, against their mode of operation, with a view to linking perceptions of the educational 'good' and to the goal of gender equality.

The first provider entered in the grid is *government*, which has had a long history of provision spanning over the colonial as well as post-independence eras. Education has traditionally been regarded as a *public good* that lacks the properties of exclusivity and rivalry, implying it should be provided by a single monopolist for production to be financially viable (Case 2001). This view has

Table 3.1 Provider approaches and the consequences for gender

Provider	Mode of operation	Nature of good	Gender concerns
Government	Trickle-down	Public monopoly	Gender-neutral/blind
For-profit	Input	Reputational good	Social reproduction of gender
Faith/community	Identity	Club good	Operates within gender norms
NGO	Catalytic	Merit good	Gender inclusion

been upheld by national governments, which have tended to be exclusive monopoly providers of education. However, monopoly pricing of education has negative consequences as it discriminates against the poor. It also lacks a conceptual space to analyse how the social construction of gender constrains the ability of poor families to send their girls to school and is therefore 'gender-blind'.[2]

The next three categories in Table 3.1 all refer to non-government providers. The second category I have called the *for-profit providers*, who tend to view the entry into the educational sector as an opportunity for 'marketisation' of education and focus on maximising returns from private investment for each school. This model has a strong ability to ensure that there are schools providing high quality education at the top end of the income ladder supported by the vociferous demand of upwardly mobile middle classes. The emphasis of this model is likely to result in social reproduction rather than transformation, given its association with elite schooling rather than mass schooling. The goal here could well be one of trying to ensure a greater pool of high quality technically and professionally skilled employees using the 'reputational effect' of private allegedly high quality schooling. A new aspect in such provision is the creation of 'brands' of education through the replication of successful schools in different national and international locations.[3] The weakness of such a model of educational provision from a gender perspective is that it does not take into account any notion of *externality*, or financial spillovers/synergies between projects that might reduce the cost of each schooling project, nor does it take note of the potential socially beneficial aspects of financial investment in the community such as increased value attached to schooling with the establishment of a local community school. There also appears to be little or no attempt by such private education providers to influence the world of work, or the role of men and women within it, and consequently these examples of private educational provisions are likely to operate within existing patterns of gendering in the spheres of production and reproduction. Such a mode of operation may well replicate existing gender relations in static economies and might even accentuate the extreme type of *masculinities* and *femininities* that emerge in volatile economies in a globalising world.

The third category listed in Table 3.1 is that of the *faith/community* providers of education. The educational models currently undertaken by the faith/community provider of education suggest a different emphasis from those above. Here the focus appears to be on the 'identity' aspect of education. This model underlines the pressing need of poor, marginalised or minority groups to make up for severe deficits in human capital. It looks to provide education that would enhance community notions of 'identity', such as in teaching in the vernacular or working with religious constructs of schooling, and thereby drawing in the more vulnerable sections into the heart of the community. In rural Pakistan, for example, families prefer to send their daughters to *madrasahs* in the village – as it is regarded as a 'safe space' – rather than the state school that is often located outside the village. This emphasis on the notion of community also imbues an element of 'exclusivity' to a public good so that it begins to resemble a comfortable club rather than a free-for-all, what we might call *a club good*. These initiatives provide a degree of gender freedom arising from working within the local community norms. They can therefore open up access to education for girls but do not necessarily have positive consequences for more Western notions of empowerment (see Waljee this volume).

In the colonial period, the emergence of the non-governmental approach to education was closely related to the work of the churches and associated missionary activities in the educational sector. In the post-independence period, there has been a rise of a new category of providers, the NGO sector, emerging from civil society movements and motivated by social and cultural aims. The *community/faith* provider and the *NGO* provider have not only emerged at different historical junctures within countries in the non-Western world but also suggest that different methods of operation are in use in the provision of education. The common conceptual base of such providers appears to be the view that economic aims are secondary to cultural, civic, religious aims.

At first glance, these two groups of *non-governmental non-profit* providers appear to recognise 'difference' as the key to maximising educational access. Both providers tend to see their provision in terms of a political project, often framed in terms of social justice goals although, in recent decades, they have begun to recognise the importance of the economic impacts of the labour market of the political project. Given the evidence that returns from education are high, particularly at primary and junior secondary levels, the economic case for such NGO involvement in the provision of schooling is relatively easy to make.

The fourth category provided in the table is that of the *non-governmental* provider. Interventions have a strong catalytic dimension in the grounded reality of power relations in the local sphere and draw on the markers of gender, 'race' and caste. Operating within the model of 'inclusion', some educational NGOs confront and change local gender norms that are inimical to the advancement of gender equality. It would appear that their view of education is one of providing a 'merit' good, i.e. one that has benefits to all and therefore must be maximally provided by overcoming local specificity and discrimination.[4]

The exploratory mapping I offer in Table 3.1 at the very least indicates that the current modes of operation might be taken as an indicator of the nature of the educational 'good' being provided and suggests the different relationship of such providers to the economics of education and the role of investment in school provision. It also permits us to ask questions regarding the implications of such providers for the future of gender access and equality in the field of education and development. It would be appropriate to note that if governments continue to maintain a monopolist approach to education and do not engage with such non-government providers, they will have to be content with what economists call a *trickle-down* effect – where economic growth *slowly shifts educational levels and hence the lives* of men and women. This approach will manifestly fail to address the differential manner in which education affects men and women in the household, labour market and the community. Where the catalytic approach of the *NGO* innovative interventions is brought in, there is the possibility of advancing the empowerment of women, but such innovative interventions may put too much of the onus of economic and social change on women themselves (Ramachandran 2002). In cases where there is an expansion of the *profit* provider with a narrow view of the returns from education to individual investment, a considerable input will be required from feminist researchers to understand the gender implications of underlining existing social differences such as gender. The contribution of *community/faith* providers working with the fractured identity of the poor and dispossessed can bolster group solidarity and raise social capital (see Sivasubramaniam this volume) but they too can be problematic as they operate within existing community norms that may be inimical to individual autonomy, thus hindering the attainment of national and international goals of gender equality.

This section, whilst offering only a preliminary analysis of different types of educational providers within the development context, begs important questions about the range of conceptualisations of 'the educational good' that are implied by the diverse models of state and non-government educational provision. It also suggests that we do not yet know how these educational investments impact on the social construction of gender and gender relations within and across other social divisions. The current lack of clarity about the types of provider and their impact on gender goals arguably distorts international debates about the feasibility and the likelihood of promoting gender equality within increasingly marketised and diversified educational systems.

Conclusion

A contemporary analysis of the three types of political economy of education described in this chapter suggests that the hope of using education as a catalyst in the field of gender and economic and socio-cultural development rests on its ability to understand the gendered division of labour as well as the gender implications of government and non-governmental educational provision within those gender divided societies.

One of the most important keys to understanding the transformative, if not catalytic power of education is in gauging its impact on the world of work. In countries where a majority of the population live and work in the rural economy, the way forward lies in understanding that men's and women's work are constructed within the household and strongly directed by local social norms. The likelihood of education releasing women from the triple burden of work is dependent on their ability to make individual choices to access education, whether this is for themselves or on behalf of their daughters. Any mass education programme must be constructed with regard to the social and cultural practices, including those that relate to the construction of local *masculinities* and *femininities* as much as in the provision of schools in the local community if it is to make headway in moving towards parity of access for girls and boys.[5]

The ability to discern the asymmetric impact of educational policies on particular groups has been considerably advanced by the study of gender. The consequences of the present activities of providers have noteworthy if sometimes disturbing implications for gender goals. There is a need to develop this initial analysis of provision in relation to gender goals in education so as to gain a thorough understanding the promises and challenges that such provision holds for the field of gender, education and development.

The changing national contexts and growing range of national initiatives within which we are examining the relationship between gender, education and the global agendas of human development point to the critical need to bring together feminist critiques and economic theories regarding development and education. This is important if we are to engage with international debates on gender equality. The success of girls' education is intricately related to the economic demands on their labour and their contribution to the livelihood opportunities of the family. Any policy to attain the goal of 'Education for All' must recognise that gender provides a lens with which to identify the inequalities that are present in society.

Notes

1 *Dalits* are those who were previously classified are 'untouchables' and representing the lowest rung of the caste system. *Adivasi* is the term used for tribal/indigenous populations in India.

2 Since 2002, I have researched new forms of educational provision that have emerged in Central and South Asia with a view to constructing a typology of providers and engaging with the implications for domestic finance, international donors and educational aid programmes.

3 The term 'gender-blind' is used in the feminist economic literature to connote a macroeconomic policy that regards men and women as being identical in relation to economic opportunities (Elson 1991).

4 The Delhi Public School, first set up as a single school at Mathura Road, New Delhi in the 1950s, today has six independent schools each with its own management under that name in Delhi alone. They have also set up schools by this name in other key cities in India, such as Mumbai, and abroad, in Singapore and Dubai.

5 Mahila Samakhya in India is an excellent illustration of the benefit of a social network for transforming gender relations by providing 'accelerated learning' programmes for girls and their mothers in poor communities.

Bibliography

Aggarwal, B. (1994) *A Field of One's Own: Gender and Land Rights in South Asia*, Cambridge: Cambridge University Press.

Balagopalan, S. and Subrahmaniam, R. (2003) '*Dalit* and *Adivasi* children in schools: some preliminary research themes and findings', *IDS Bulletin*, 34, 1. Brighton: Institute of Development Studies.

Barro, J. (2001) 'Human Capital and Growth', *American Economic Review*, 91, 2: 12–17.

Basu, A. (1993) *Culture, the Status of Women, and Demographic Behaviour: Illustrated with the Case of India*, United States: Oxford University Press.

Becker, G.S. (1962) 'Investment in Human Capital: A Theoretical Analysis', *Journal of Political Economy*, 70, 5: 9–49.

Becker, G.S. (1981) *A Treatise on the Family*, Cambridge, MA: Harvard University Press.

Benavot, A. (1981) 'Education, Gender and Economic Development: A Cross National Study', *Sociology of Education*, 62, January: 14–32.

Beneria, L. (1979) 'Reproduction, Production and the Sexual Division of Labour', *Cambridge Journal of Economics*, 3, 3: 203–225.

Beneria, L. (1985) *Women and Development: The Sexual Division of Labor in Rural Societies*, Westport, CT: Praeger.

Beneria, L. (1999) 'Globalization, gender and the Davos Man', *Feminist Economics*, 5, 3: 61–83.

Beneria, L. (2003) *Gender, Development and Globalization: Economics as if People Mattered*, London: Routledge.

Beneria, L. and Feldman, S. (eds) (1992) *Unequal Burden:Economic Crises, Persistent Poverty, and Women's Work*, Westview Press Inc.

Beneria, L. and Roldan, M. (1987) *The Crossroads of Class and Gender: Industrial Homework, Subcontracting, and Household Dynamics in Mexico City*, Chicago: University of Chicago Press.

Bennell, P. (1996) 'Rates of return to education: does the conventional pattern prevail in Sub-Saharan Africa', *World Development*, 24: 183–199.

Bennell, P. (2002) 'Hitting the Target: Doubling Primary School Enrolments in Sub-Saharan Africa by 2015', *World Development*, 30, 7: 1172–1194.

Blaug, M. (1962) *Economic Theory in Retrospect*, Cambridge: Cambridge University Press.

Blaug, M. (3rd edn, 1978) *The Economics of Education: A Selected Annotated Bibliography*, Oxford: Pergamon Books.

Boserup, E. (1965) *The Conditions of Agricultural Growth: The Economics of Agrarian Change under Population Pressure*, London: G. Allen and Unwin.

Boserup, E. (1970) *Women's Role in Economic Development*, New York: St Martin's Press.

Boserup, E. (1981) *Population and Technological Change*, Chicago: University of Chicago Press.

Boserup, E. (1989) 'Population, the Status of Women, and Rural Development', *Population and Development Review*, 15 (supplement: Rural Development and Population: Institutions and Policy): 45–60.

Bowles, S. and Gintis, H. (1975) *Schooling in Capitalist America*, New York: Basic Books.

Bray, F. (1997) *Technology and Gender: Fabrics of Power in Late Imperial China*, Berkeley and Los Angeles: University of California Press.

Case, A. (2001) 'The primacy of education', Working Paper in the Research Program in Development Studies, Princeton University, June.

Davin, D. (2004) 'The impact of export-oriented manufacturing on the welfare entitlements of Chinese women workers' in S. Razavi, R. Pearson and D. Danloy (eds) *Globalisation, Export-oriented Employment and Social Policy: Gendered Connections*, UNRISD: Palgrave, pp. 67–90.

Dennison, E. (1962) *The Sources of Economic Growth in the United States*, New York: Committee for Economic Development.

Dixon-Mueller, R. (1981) *Women's Work in Third World Agriculture: Concepts and Indicators*, Geneva: International Labour Office.

Dyson, T. (1996) *Population and Food: Global Trends and Future Prospects*, London: Routledge.

Easterly, W. (2001) 'The middle class consensus and economic development', *Journal of Economic Growth*, 6, 4: 317–335.

Fennell, S. (2006a) 'The ethics of population control' in D. Clark (ed.) *The Elgar Companion to Development Studies*, London: Edward Elgar.

Fennell, S. (2006b) 'Future policy choices for the education sector in Asia', paper presented at the Asia 2015 conference, 'Promoting Growth, Ending Poverty', DFID. Available online at: www.asia2015conference.org/pdfs/fennell.pdf.

Fennell, S. (2007) forthcoming. 'Tilting at windmills: public–private partnerships in Indian education today', *Educational Dialogue*.

Humphries, J. (1990) 'Enclosures, Common Rights and Women: The Proletarianization of Families in late Eighteenth and early Nineteenth Century Britain', *Journal of Economic History*, L, 1: 17–42.

Jacka, T. (1997) *Women's Work in Rural China: Change and Continuity in an Era of Reform*, Cambridge: Cambridge University Press.

Jeffery, R. and Jeffery, P. (1997) *Population, Gender, and Politics: Demographic Change in Rural North India*, Cambridge: Cambridge University Press.

Kabeer, N. (1994) *Reversed Realities: Gender Hierarchies in Development Theory*, London: Verso.

Leach, M. (1994) *Rainforest Relations: Gender and Resource Use among the Mende of Gola, Sierra Leone*, Edinburgh: Edinburgh University Press.

Mincer, J. (1958) 'Investment in Human Capital and Personal Income Distribution', *Journal of Political Economy*, 66, 4: 281–302.

Mohanty, C. and Alexander, M. (ed.) (1997) *Feminist Genealogies, Colonial Legacies, Democratic Futures*, New York: Routledge.

Moser, C. (1983) *Gender Planning and Development: Theory, Practice and Training*, London: Routledge.

Nussbaum, M. (2000) *Women and Human Development: The Capabilities Approach*, Cambridge: Cambridge University Press.

Pahl, R. (1984) *Divisions of Labour*, Oxford: Blackwell.

Pateman, C. (1988) *The Sexual Contract*, Stanford: Stanford University Press.

Pritchett, L. (1996) 'Where has all the education gone?' World Bank Policy Research, Working Paper No. 1581.

Pritchett, L. (2004) 'Towards a new consensus for addressing the global challenge of the lack of education', Working Paper 43, available online at: www.cgdev.org/content/publications/detail/2746.

Psacharopoulos, G. (1973) *Returns to Education: An International Comparison*, Amsterdam: Elsevier.

Psacharopoulos, G. and Patrinos, H. (2004) 'Returns to investment in education: a further update', *Education Economics*, 12, 2: 111–134.

Ramachandran, V. (2002) *Gender and Social Equity in Primary Education: Hierarchies of Access*, New Delhi: European Commission.

Robeyns, I. (2006) 'Three models of education', *Theory and Research in Education*, 4, 1: 69–84.

Roldan, M. (1985) 'Renegotiating the marital contract: intra-household patterns of money allocation and women's subordination among domestic outworks in Mexico City' in D. Dwyer and J. Bruce (eds) *A Home Divided: Women and Income in the Third World*, Stanford: Stanford University Press.

Rowbotham, S. (1974) *Woman's Conciousness, Man's World*, London: Penguin.

Schultz, T. (1961) 'Investments in human capital', *American Economic Review*, 51, 1: 1–17.

Scott, J. (1989) *Gender and the Politics of History*, New York: Columbia University Press.

Sen, A. (1981a) 'Market Failure and Control of Labour Power: Towards an Explanation of "Structure" and Change in Indian Agriculture: part 1', *Cambridge Journal of Economics*, 5, 4: 327–350.

Sen, A. (1981b) 'Market Failure and Control of Labour Power: Towards an Explanation of "Structure" and Change in Indian Agriculture: part 2', *Cambridge Journal of Economics*, 5, 3: 201–228.

Sen, A. (1999) *Development as Freedom*, London: Oxford University Press.

Sianesi, B. and Van Reenen, J. (2000) 'The returns to education: a review of the macro-economic literature', CEE Discussion Papers 0006, Centre for the Economics of Education, London School of Economics.

Sobel, I. (1978) 'The Human Capital Revolution in Economic Development: Its Current History and Status', *Comparative Education Review*, 22, 2: 278–308.

Sweetland, S.R. (1996) 'Human Capital Theory: Foundations of a Field of Inquiry', *Review of Educational Research*, 66, 3: 341–359.

Unterhalter, E. (2002) 'The Capabilities Approach and Gendered Education: An Examination of South African Complexities', *Theory and Research in Education*, 1, 1: 7–22.

Wooley, J. (1988) 'A non-cooperative model of family decision making', Discussion paper No. TIDI 125, London School of Economics.

4 Global gender goals and the construction of equality

Conceptual dilemmas and policy practice*

Christopher Colclough[1]

The Millennium Declaration, issued in the year 2000, committed the nations of the world to promoting gender equality and women's empowerment, as part of a set of wide-ranging measures to halve the incidence of poverty over the first 15 years of the new century. The commitments made to tackle gender inequality in education are specific and time-bound, and appear to provide a clear agenda for action and policy change. In this chapter, I first examine the process by which these gender goals became established. I then attempt to disentangle the meanings, and the theoretical underpinning of their various formulations. In the final section, I assess the feasibility of their attainment and the actual/potential roles of the international community in this process

The place of gender in international development goals

The basis for a global commitment to gender equality in education has been built in some detail over the past 35 years. This has had two 'arms'. First, a series of international human rights treaties has been adopted and ratified by the great majority of countries, which requires states to make education universally available, and to pursue educational policies that do not discriminate on the grounds of gender.[2]

Notwithstanding this apparent global near-consensus, the simple ratification of these treaties by governments does not imply that the necessary rights obligations will be observed. To help secure such observance, a reporting procedure is in place that is meant to allow the relevant UN treaty organisations to be informed of progress made. In recent years, however, about one-third of the ratifying states have not submitted such reports (Tomasevski 2003). This prevents reliable international assessments of progress being made, and the treaty obligations are widely ignored in many of these cases.

Partly in response to this patchy implementation, a second 'arm' has comprised a series of international declarations issued under the auspices of the United Nations. These, as summarised in Table 4.1, have followed from the World Conferences on Education for All (1990), on Population and Development (1994), on Women (1995) and on Social Development (1995) and

Table 4.1 Evolution of development goals in education – from Jomtien to the MDGs

Date	Event	Goal	Target date
1990	WCEFA	UPE	2000
1994	ICPD	UPE	before 2015
		Primary gender parity	before 2015
1995	FWCW	UPE	2015
		Primary gender parity	2005
1995	WSSD	Prim/sec gender parity	2005
2000	WEF	UPE	2015
		Prim/sec gender parity	2005
		Gender equality in education	2015
2000	UN Summit	UPE	2015
		Prim/sec gender parity	2005
		All levels gender parity	2015

Notes

Acronyms represent the following events:

WCEFA – World Conference on Education for All, Jomtien, Thailand;

ICPD – International Conference on Population and Development, Cairo, Egypt;

FWCW – Fourth World Conference on Women, Beijing, China;

WSSD – World Summit for Social Development, Copenhagen, Denmark;

WEF – World Education Forum, Dakar, Senegal;

UN Summit – UN Millennium Summit, New York, USA.

provide separate commitments on the part of all signatories, to provide universal education and to protect and promote the rights of women in education and throughout society.[3]

Some of these commitments were brought together by the Development Assistance Committee (DAC) of the Organisation for Economic Cooperation and Development (OECD) in 1996 as part of a broader attempt to set up targets for international development. In May of that year, the DAC adopted a new development strategy[4] for global progress that embraced many of the development targets – including those on education and on gender equality – which had emerged from the UN summits earlier in the decade. As part of this strategy a limited number of indicators were proposed for monitoring progress towards the targets. Subsequently, many donors incorporated these principles into their aid policies, and many also began to see the International Development Targets (IDTs) as crucial objectives for the assessment of development success.

This process was further formalised at the 2000 UN Millennium Summit, when world leaders, from rich and poor countries alike, adopted a set of eight time-bound goals that, when achieved, were expected to halve poverty world-wide by 2015.[5] The first seven of these goals gave commitments to cut the incidence of poverty and hunger, get every child into school, empower women, reduce child mortality, improve maternal health, combat HIV/AIDS, malaria, and other diseases, and ensure environmental sustainability. The eighth goal recognised that to achieve the first seven goals, significantly more – and more effective – aid, sustainable debt relief and fairer trade rules would be required throughout the 15-year period to 2015. Targets for education were specifically incorporated within two of these eight goals: the second expressed a commitment to achieve universal primary education (UPE) by 2015 (defined in terms of the completion of a 'full course of primary schooling'); the third goal, which is concerned with achieving gender equality and women's empowerment, included a specific target for the elimination of gender disparities in education over the same period.

By the turn of the century, therefore, a broadly based consensus promoting the Millennium Development Goals (MDGs) as objectives for development policy appeared to have been established amongst the group of nations, organisations and agencies that are often collectively referred to as 'the international community'. Formally, this 'community' might be taken to comprise representatives of the 200 or so member states of the United Nations and their dependent territories. In fact, however, representatives of a small group of richer nations, and in particular of the G8 countries, have always had a major influence on the formation and application of development policy orthodoxy. Such influence stems mainly from their economic power, their consequentially dominant voices in international trade and debt negotiations, and their roles as main providers of international aid for development purposes. They control appointments to the leadership of many of the multilateral development agencies, in particular the World Bank and the International Monetary Fund (IMF), and much of the economic and social research that informs their position on development policy is conducted by residents of these countries. Notions of what comprises 'good' development policy have changed over the past half century, from preoccupations with maximising growth via various forms of state intervention, to a much greater concern with the alleviation of poverty in the context of more liberal economic policy regimes. These shifts in policy emphasis have, in turn, reflected the main changes in economic orthodoxy within industrialised countries – away from the Keynesian state-interventionist models of the 1960s and 1970s, to more neo-liberal, market-oriented forms of economic management in recent years. State actions are now encouraged (quintessentially by the MDGs) to focus more upon the provision of basic services, and aid agencies have been willing to support those endeavours, where 'sound' economic management of the broader economy is in place.

In this context, the appeal of the MDGs from the perspective of aid providers was that they provided a checklist of quantifiable objectives for state action, and a set of shorthand criteria for assessing whether major progress with poverty reduction is being made. It appeared that the efficacy of policy reform in developing countries was to be judged in their terms. If it could be shown that national development policies – including those affecting gender equality – were designed to deliver the 2015 goals, they would, by implication, attract sufficient support from aid agencies to help them be secured. Such expectations, however, are as yet far from being met.

The Dakar EFA goals: a crucial addendum to the MDGs

Also in 2000, a World Education Forum was convened by UNESCO in Dakar, Senegal, with the objectives of reviewing and extending the global commitments for educational progress. The meeting agreed on six 'Education for All' (EFA) goals, which were considered not only essential, but also attainable and affordable, given the presence of the necessary international resolve. The resulting 'Dakar Framework for Action' declared that, by 2015, all children of primary-school age would participate in free schooling of acceptable quality, that adult illiteracy would be halved, that progress would be made in providing early childhood care and education, and that learning opportunities for youth and adults and all aspects of education quality would be improved. One of these 'Dakar' goals also committed the nations of the world to 'eliminating gender disparities in primary and secondary education by 2005, and achieving gender equality in education by 2015, with a focus on ensuring girls' full and equal access to and achievement in basic education of good quality' (UNESCO 2000a: paragraph 7). The Dakar conference resolution even went so far as to promise that 'no countries seriously committed to education for all will be thwarted in their achievement of this goal by a lack of resources' (UNESCO 2000a). Thus, industrialised countries seemed to be saying, for the first time, that resources for achieving EFA – mediated by the MDG goals – would be available to all those who needed them. Subsequent progress, however, has been modest. For example, between 2000 and 2004, aid to basic education in developing countries increased by around two-thirds, from $2.6 billion to around $4.4 billion.[6] Although this might seem substantial, it compares poorly with an *additional* $6 billion annual aid that was estimated to be needed for all children to be enrolled in primary school over the years to 2015.[7] Accordingly, in the first few years after the MDG/Dakar conferences, aid to basic education increased by less than one-third of the annual amount required to meet the UPE and gender goals. More recent estimates now put the size of the gap at around $9–10 billion (in 2005 prices) from 2005 onwards, mainly reflecting the slow start to increased aid flows since the start of the new century (DFID/HM Treasury 2005). Notwithstanding the new enthusiasm demonstrated by G8 representatives at the Gleneagles meetings in 2006, it is unlikely that such resources will be forthcoming either in a timely fashion, or using modalities appropriate to the scale of actions required. This partly stems from the immense practical difficulties involved in rapidly scaling up aid programmes. In addition, however, the 'sound economic management' conditionalities required by aid agencies, mentioned earlier, themselves explain why some of the most needy states – being also the most 'unsoundly' managed – will not be early recipients of the aid resources they require.

Towards gender equality in education: concepts and feasibility[8]

Both the Dakar gender goal and the MDG gender target aimed to achieve parity in primary and secondary enrolments by 2005. Yet when these goals were agreed, in 2000, it was already clear that that objective could simply not be achieved. In order to do so, over the five intervening years, large numbers of out-of-school girls would have needed to enrol in (or rejoin) classes at levels well beyond primary grade one. Such 'mid-career' enrolment would have been extensively required if secondary enrolment parity were to have been achieved within a five-year period, at least in those many school systems in which male pupils significantly outnumbered girls at all grade levels. This kind of enrolment behaviour would have been unsustainable over the medium term and, in most countries, it would not have been feasible in the first place.

The international community has made a habit of setting unrealistic target dates for the achievement of its educational goals. From Table 4.1, it can be seen that each of the targets set for 2000 or 2005 envisaged an impossibly rapid reform agenda: achieving universal primary education over ten years from 1990, or gender parity of enrolments over five to ten years from 1995 or from 2000 were infeasible tasks. It had, for example, taken 30 years for primary enrolments in developing countries to increase from half to three-quarters of all children of primary-school age by 1990. Enrolments would have had to double in Sub-Saharan Africa, and to triple in many countries in the region, if all children were to be enrolled by the century's end.[9]

Similarly, it had taken almost two decades for female enrolments to increase from 79 per cent to 84 per cent of those of males by the late 1990s.[10] Progress towards gender parity in enrolments can be represented by a 'gender parity index' (GPI). This simply expresses the gross (or net) enrolment ratio (GER) for girls at any given level of the education system, as a proportion of the same ratio for boys. Thus, if the primary GER for girls is 95 and that for boys is 100, the primary-level GPI would be 0.95. It follows that gender parity is indicated by a GPI value of 1.0. Figure 4.1 shows those countries where changes in GPIs exceeded five percentage points over the decade 1990–2000. Although good progress towards parity was made in a significant number of cases, in only 16 countries was there an improvement in the GPI of greater than ten percentage points over the decade. Yet, by the year 2000, 38 countries still had primary GPIs of less than 0.90. Twenty-two of these were in Sub-Saharan Africa, where gender inequality of enrolments remained extreme in many cases – half of them having GPI values of less than 0.70. Accordingly, a universal move to gender parity over a five-year period from 2000 would be impossible to achieve in the face of these historical and regional trends.

Thus, it was predictable that both the enrolment and the gender goals would not be achieved within the time frames chosen. Only those set for 2015 appeared to allow sufficient time to be achievable, although even that would depend upon sustained national effort and international aid over the 15-year

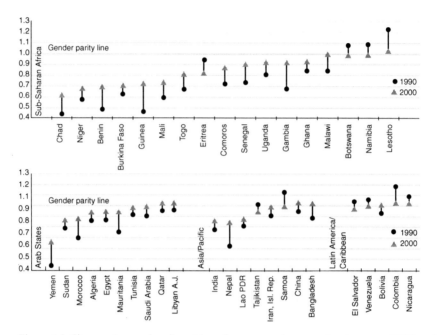

Figure 4.1 Changes in gender disparities of gross enrolment ratios between 1990 and 2000 (countries with changes of five percentage points or more, in increasing order of GPI in 2000) (source: UNESCO 2003: 54).

period. It could, of course, be argued that failure to achieve the first of the MDGs, which happened in 2005, would provide an incentive to marshal further support and try harder, and that, thus, there was deliberate over-optimism built into the goal-setting process. Yet such intentional subtlety seemed, in the event, denied by the nature of the discussions at the UN Special Assembly on the Millennium Goals, held in New York in September 2005. These scarcely alluded to the world's failure to achieve the gender target in that year – preferring, instead, to concentrate attention on the ways and means of reaching those set for 2015.

Notwithstanding these circumstances, differences in the wording of the Millennium and Dakar goals imply that the question of what is meant by equality is central to an assessment of whether or not it can be achieved (see Table 4.2). The third MDG commits signatories to 'promote gender equality and empower women'. This undertaking, therefore, gives a generalised commitment to the promotion of equality – one that extends well beyond the framework of education. Somewhat surprisingly, however, the operational target by which this goal was to be achieved and monitored was to 'eliminate gender disparity in primary and secondary education, preferably by 2005, and to all levels of education no later than 2015' (UN 2001). This target is often misleadingly taken as being synonymous with the gender goal itself, whereas it was, at the time, simply

Table 4.2 Gender goals compared

EFA Dakar gender goal

Eliminate gender disparities in primary and secondary education by 2005 and achieve gender equality in education by 2015, with a focus on ensuring girls' full and equal access to, and achievement in, basic education of good quality.

Millennium gender goal

Goal 3. Promote gender equality and empower women

Target 4. Eliminate gender disparity in primary and secondary education, preferably by 2005, and to all levels of education no later than 2015.

Sources: UNESCO 2000a; UN 2000.

judged to be one of the clearest ways of monitoring the progress being made towards equality and women's empowerment.[11]

The MDG target makes no mention of equality, but only of the need to achieve enrolment parity – i.e. equal numbers (or proportions) of boys and girls attending school, college or university. This notion of parity is a quantitative, static concept. However, since progress towards gender parity in enrolments suggests a weakening of the structures that privilege men in society, it can suggest progress towards achieving equality in a broader sense. Nevertheless, such progress may be made whilst, at the same time, enrolment declines for boys, girls or both, were recorded. This happened during the 1990s in Africa, where the impact of recession and adjustment brought a reduction of primary enrolments in many countries – more strongly so for boys than for girls.[12] Here, then, an apparent move towards gender parity was secured in a highly undesirable way. Thus, account needs to be taken of the trajectory being made towards gender parity: it is not merely the quantitative balances themselves that are important but also the processes by which they are secured.

The wording of the Dakar goal moves us beyond gender parity to take on the more ambitious agenda of achieving gender equality in education by 2015. Although definitions vary, full equality would seem to require the achievement of equality of opportunities to participate in education, of equality in learning processes whilst at school, of equality of outcomes – such that learning achievements would not differ by gender – and, finally, of equality of external results – such that job opportunities and earnings for men and women with similar qualifications would be equal. These are demanding conditions,[13] which imply that the gender parity indicator alone provides an inadequate proxy for the achievement of equality in education in this broader sense. Identifying the true nature of the global agenda is thus not straightforward. Even to achieve enrolment parity will require social and economic changes that go beyond the purview of ministers of education. Achieving full equality in education, as envisaged by Dakar, is much more ambitious.

The extent to which either of these goals can be achieved in poor states is dependent, usually, upon an approach to policy reform that is deeply rooted, and that embraces a sophisticated understanding of the causes of existing inequalities. In that context, since the early 1970s, there has been a bifurcation between descriptive, or developmentalist work on gender issues (often referred to as 'women in development' (WID) approaches), and more structural and analytic ('gender and development' (GAD)) approaches to understanding discrimination and female subordination. Writers in the former tradition were initially concerned with emphasising the crucial roles played by women in the traditional economy, and the costs to growth if, on being displaced by industrialisation, they were not reabsorbed into the wage economy. Women and men were characterised as having equal productive capacities, yet very unequal access to education and other resources. Social and market imperfections that created women's exclusion needed to be addressed. This 'efficiency' argument for the equal treatment of men and women lay at the heart of the WID case: if women were excluded from contributing to development, potential output was lost, and there was a clear case for directing resources towards them.[14]

A major omission from many of these early writings was any serious attempt to analyse the position of women in society in relation to that of men. Treating women as the only focus for analysis was ultimately misleading. Feminist analysts began to argue that the constraints faced by women could not be understood without examining the nature, basis and reproduction of male power. As the centrality of relations between women and men became acknowledged in accounting for their unequal roles in development, the key category for analysis shifted from 'women' towards 'gender'.[15] With this shift towards a 'gender and development' paradigm, came a view that departed radically from the WID tradition; that relations between the sexes are not necessarily non-conflictual – indeed that socially constructed gender relations may be characterised by opposition and conflict (Whitehead 1979). It is not the physical and biological differences between men and women, so much as the socially differentiated aspects of gender that lead to the different ways in which women and men are constrained during their lives. Emphasis shifted towards analysing gender relations in the household, which were seen as being the main source of subsequent inequality. Gender roles that appear natural in most cultures have in fact emerged from long-standing past practice, which ascribes them with normative significance (Connell 1987). Gender reforms in the wider society become constrained by this history, which gives men, and some women, a deeply personal stake in the maintenance of the status quo, and makes it unlikely that the state will be able to initiate significant social change (Stromquist 1989: 171; Kabeer 1994: 36–37).

Perhaps, not surprisingly, the language of international policy documentation has traditionally been informed mainly by the stance of WID analysts, who take a more liberal and optimistic view of the prospects for gender reform. State forces are seen by such writers to be at least tractable – if not benevolent. Advice, evidence and argument are judged capable of influencing governments to ensure women's rights to education and other social goods, and to the labour market and economic reforms that such outcomes require. Arguably the vocabularies of both the MDGs and of the Dakar goals, are in this tradition. These goals urge the world to move towards equality in education by achieving parity of enrolments – implying, however, that this can be simply done by moving available policy levers to bring outcomes that will have positive or neutral, rather than negative, effects for sections of important elite groups.

Nonetheless, some recent publications from international agencies have analysed prospects for their better attainment more subtly than the initial formulation of the goals seemed to imply. Unterhalter (2005: 23–24) points out that the 2003/4 *EFA Global Monitoring Report* (UNESCO 2003), which focuses upon the ways in which the gender and education goals may be achieved, is in the GAD rather than the WID tradition. It recognises the deeply embedded constraints both in education and, particularly, in society at large, which act to frustrate piecemeal attempts at reform. A similar stance is taken by the report on progress towards the gender goal from the MDG Task Force 3 (UN Millennium Project 2005). There are, of course, contradictions, in that both of these documents also include (but do not limit themselves to) familiar policy agendas as ways forward. Although the need for profound social and economic change as a means to achieving gender equality is a recurring theme of their analyses, for pragmatic reasons many of their proposals need to entertain a more gradualist approach to reform. What is different in these recent international documents, however, is a clear recognition that action is needed across a wide array of sectors and interests, extending well beyond education itself, if the goal of gender equality in education is to be achieved.

Reducing gaps between targets and action

Assuming that adequate policy change is indeed within reach, what can be done by the UN, or by the international community more broadly, to hold countries to their promises? It is obvious that, in matters of social and economic policy, if national governments choose to ignore the commitments that they have publicly espoused there is no easy sanction available to make them change their behaviour. As suggested earlier, adding the political commitments made in UN declarations to the legal undertakings embedded in UN human rights treaties can be expected to increase the likelihood that governments will take their own pledges seriously. But it certainly does not ensure that that will be so, as the continued substantial inequalities between male and female school enrolments in more than 90 countries demonstrate.[16] However, there are two main ways in which the international community can bring pressure to bear: first, periodic reporting of progress towards the EFA goals at the national level provides some accountability of governments and international agencies for actions taken or missed. Second, negotiated partnership arrangements – notably between governments and international agencies via the international aid process – provide a means of leverage to secure 'better' education policies in exchange for the provision of financial and technical aid resources over the medium term.

Although both of these pressure lines may, even in principle, have only limited power to influence action, there is an important question as to whether the established machinery is best suited to the tasks in hand. In that regard, UNESCO was assigned a central role by the World Education Forum. The organisation was mandated to take a leadership role in sustaining international support for EFA and to promote better global coordination of such efforts. Although it has had some success as regards informing the global debate and providing a key means of increasing the accountability of national and inter-national EFA actors, it has been less clearly successful in leading and coordinating increased international support for EFA. This is partly because it is difficult for an agency that does not, itself, have access to significant resources, to influence the decisions of those who do have such access, and to mobilise new aid monies for EFA.

Two major developments attended UNESCO's enhanced role. First the Director General convened annually (from 2001) a small and flexible 'High Level Group' that would meet to discuss detailed progress towards EFA and to design strategies for its improvement. The group comprises ministers of educa-tion or their representatives from 10–15 countries, bilateral and multilateral development agencies (usually represented by the heads of their education divi-sion) and directors of a set of international and national NGOs that are active in education, or judged to be articulate in matters of educational aid and policy. The membership of the group – particularly the countries represented – has changed somewhat from year to year. A communiqué is issued, based upon its deliberations, which is variously reported by the international press. It is intended that its content should influence national and international educa-tional policy and that it would inform public opinion on matters of EFA.

The second development was the establishment of a new annual publication – an EFA *Global Monitoring Report* (*GMR*) – which was intended to provide an independent and high quality assessment of the world's progress towards EFA, and which would directly inform the deliberations of the High Level Group. This publication has been produced annually since 2002 by a team that is based in UNESCO, but which remains independent of it in terms of its professional stance and editorial policy. The report has been well resourced by a group of bilateral agencies. It provides both a global statistical overview of education systems, in all their detail, and of aid to education, drawing upon the resources of the UNESCO Institute of Statistics in Montreal, and of the OECD DAC database in Paris. It also gives substantial analysis of key challenges for educa-tion and aid policies, informed by a large body of research commissioned and/or synthesised by the report team. Annual issues since 2002 have covered financing EFA, gender equality, the quality of education, literacy, and early childhood care and education, respectively. The *GMR* has achieved wide inter-national currency and influence. A recent evaluation of the first three reports, commissioned by the international community, finds it to be 'a high quality, authoritative document that has become a flagship for UNESCO' (UNIVER-SALIA 2006: 8). It has improved both the flow of information and the quality of analysis of the issues, so that the policy-making process at the international level is better-informed than before.

On the other hand, its influence upon opinion and policy has been neither linear nor uncontentious. As an example of this it is worth considering the impact of the Education for all Development Index (EDI), which was first published in the 2003/4 *GMR*, and has subsequently been updated annually.[17] This index aims to provide a summary statistic that indicates the progress that countries are making towards EFA, in such a way that they can be compared and ranked, one with another. Its constituents reflect four of the six Dakar goals, one indicator being included as a proxy measure for each of them.[18] Rather like the Human Development Index, which is not necessarily strongly correlated with the usual indicators of development success, the EDI reveals that some relatively well-off and successful countries (such as South Africa, Saudi Arabia, Guatemala) are in fact strongly lagging on EFA-progress measures, whereas some low income countries (such as Cuba, China, Tajikistan) have very high EDI scores. These kinds of comparison serve to show that many of the countries with low levels of educational provision could – given greater political commitment – sharply improve their relative positions. In other words, much more could be done by these countries to live up to their agreed EFA commitments.

There is, almost always, a range of technical issues to overcome in the construction of an index. For example, in the case of the UNDP's Human Development Index, there is a problem as to how to add together, or even compare the relative importance of, its selected constituents – life expectancy at birth, the adult literacy rate, the gross enrolment ratio and GDP per capita – within the same index. Even where measurement problems do not impose incommensurability, there is a real question as to how the different elements in an index should be weighted. In that case, value judgements are inescapable, which can strongly affect national index values and country rankings.[19] However, in the case of the EDI, the technical problems are relatively absent – all constituents of the index can be expressed in percentages and each of them provides a reasonably direct proxy measure for the relevant Dakar goal. Moreover, since the Dakar Framework document does not assign greater importance to the achievement of some goals rather than others, there is no obvious need to weight any of the constituents of the index with values other than unity. Thus the index is calculated as a simple average of the percentage values for each of the four indicators of progress towards EFA.

Notwithstanding its relatively uncomplicated design, the index at first proved controversial, mainly because it provided a transparent instrument for making simple comparisons and, sometimes, for delivering unpalatable messages. Representatives of some countries with low values for the EDI objected to its methods of calculation, and to the reliability of the data it utilised. They pointed to the time lag of two or three years between the collection of the data and their publication internationally, thereby implying that the reliability, or currency, of the messages they contained could be questioned. This aspect of securing accountability proved to be one of the more contentious aspects of the *GMR*'s impact.

Since the gender goal was represented, in the index, by the average gender parity values for primary and secondary education and for adult literacy, broader measures of equality were thereby assumed to be correlated with the progress being made towards gender parity. As argued earlier, although there is a reasonable case for this (and, in any event, measurement problems militate against the use of more complex measures over the short term), a shift to gender equality would in fact require changes along a much broader front than mere enrolment indicators. Thus, although the simple enrolment comparisons implied by the use of the gender indices track only some of the easier aspects of progress towards gender equality, even these proved controversial. In the case of China, for example, increases in the private costs of attending primary schools had led, during the late 1990s, to enrolment declines for both girls and boys, particularly in the poorer rural counties. Reporting of these facts for the 2003/4 Global Monitoring Report (UNESCO 2003) initially led to extensive correspondence between members of the report team and Chinese colleagues, who argued that the data used must be erroneous and that the relevant conclusions could not properly be drawn.

On the other hand, by the second and third years of its use, a number of countries had accepted the power of the index and were beginning to use it as a criterion for their own success: the new Indian administration, for example, announced at the High Level Group (HLG) meeting in Brasilia in 2004 that they had adopted a target for India being substantially higher in the index ranking by 2010. Furthermore, the press in most countries seized on the index as an excellent means of producing attention-grabbing copy, and it allowed a straightforward way for lobbyists to call government ministers to account for their country's present position on EFA, and to commit themselves to improving it.

The claim that the data were too old (or inaccurate) to be dependable was not a tactic used only by those developing countries who were embarrassed by their position in the national rank order of EFA progress. It was also used by some of the international agencies who found themselves compared unfavourably with others who were allocating more substantial resources to securing EFA objectives (generally via support to basic education and primary schooling). Such agency representatives typically argued that their policies had changed and that data for the most recent year (rather than the preceding one) would show a better picture of their aid programme. The fact that the discussion topics at HLG were only rarely formally revisited the following year meant that the subject – and the particular nature of the protest – may escape re-inspection when the data became available.[20]

This circumstance reveals a more fundamental flaw with the current processes of international coordination of EFA. The machinery, such as it is, is mainly contingent. The High Level Group itself has no formal role and its outcome does not extend beyond a communiqué that has no formal status on the international stage. Although the communiqué is issued for publication, and it may achieve some coverage in the international press, its proposals for action do not get translated upwards either within the UN bureaucracy or in a parallel international political process. The impact of the communiqué is not monitored, nor yet formally revisited, in successive HLG meetings. Its messages disappear into the ether, and their longevity tends to be more affected by the quality of the *Global Monitoring Report* document, and by the extent of its distribution, than by the formal discussions of it at HLG itself.

Conclusion

The aim of achieving gender equality in education – and more broadly so in society – has become established, along with a small number of other discrete poverty-focused policy objectives, at the very top of the international development agenda during the course of the last decade. Whilst it might be thought that a concern to promote greater equality should in any case be implied by any emphasis on poverty, the specific identification of gender equality as an important target for anti-poverty action was a new departure. Its inclusion implies that the impact of gender theory and evidence upon our understanding of the causes of poverty has now attained high-profile operational significance.

The international community has espoused the MDGs primarily because they define policy objectives in terms of outcomes and because they allow the performance of nations, and of agencies, to be assessed and compared. This chapter has shown, however, that gender equality in education is not easy to monitor as an outcome of policy change. The main indicator adopted as an interim target – the achievement of gender parity in enrolments – risks being too reductionist. The obvious possibility of greater gender parity being promoted by enrolment declines for both boys and girls indicates that achieving static outcome targets is not always a good guide to policy success.

More generally, there has been a latent tension between some of the practical 'can do' presuppositions of the MDGs that were historically informed by gender theory in the WID tradition, and more fundamental structural reforms that would be implied by a GAD framework. Although there is recent evidence from UN documentation that these traditions can each generate complementary insights for policy, the more radical feminists are likely to point to their contradictions, and to remain pessimistic that present agendas will deliver equality.

However, the outcome indicators associated with the MDGs are increasingly used to assess comparative performance between nations, and, to a much less extent, between agencies. They therefore serve to provide some accountability for aid received, and for domestic commitment to shared goals. Their present weakness, however, is that the 'northern' side of the implicit contract is not being kept. Far from countries not being thwarted in their EFA aims by a lack of resources, sufficient aid has not yet been forthcoming, in many cases, even where such a demonstrated commitment has been made. The politics of the process are dependent upon this implicit contract being honoured. The challenge of 'scaling up' aid activities to a new, much higher level, is probably at the heart of whether the MDGs eventually make a major difference to the provision of education and to gender equality within it, over the coming decades.

Notes

* This paper develops and extends an earlier paper: 'High Hopes for Global Educational Progress by 2015 – How Adequate are the Contributions of International Agencies?', presented at the Development Bank of Southern Africa Conference on Investment Choices for Education in South Africa, September 2006.
1 The author was the founding director of the UNESCO EFA *Global Monitoring Report*, Paris, 2002–2004.
2 In addition to three earlier human rights treaties, these include the Convention on the Elimination of all Forms of Discrimination against Women, and the Convention on the Rights of the Child, which came into force in 1981 and 1990, respectively. Both of these include specific requirements to guarantee non-discriminatory rights of access to, and provision of, education.
3 For more discussion of these parallel legal and political processes, and of the specific undertakings made by signatories to the agreements, see Colclough 2005. A detailed description of the rights to education and to gender equality specified by international treaties and declarations is given in UNESCO 2003: Appendix 1.
4 OECD DAC, 1996.
5 A detailed account of the transition from IDTs to MDGs is given by White and Black 2004.
6 These estimates are in constant 2003 prices (UNESCO 2006: 89).
7 See UNESCO 2002: 133–163. This source estimates additional aid requirements of £5.6 billion in 2000 prices, which would amount to about $6 billion in 2003 prices.
8 In an earlier paper (Colclough 2004) I identified the main cost and national expenditure constraints to achieving UPE, concluding that the 2015 targets are achievable, subject to national governments introducing new efficiency measures, increasing educational expenditures and promoting a range of quality and demand-side reforms. The aid requirements were also specified. Here, the discussion of feasibility is based upon a concern with more conceptual matters, and with the types of theoretical understanding presupposed by UN discourse.
9 See Colclough with Lewin 1993: Table 1.3 and p. 214.
10 See Colclough *et al.* 2003: Table 2.2.
11 This elision was evident even in the selection of Task Forces set up under the Millennium Project, and which reported on progress towards the goals during 2005. There were ten of these, but Task Force 3 was asked to report on both the education and the gender goals (Goals 2 and 3). Task Force members soon found it necessary to have two reports – one on education and one on gender equality – with education being recognised as fundamental for the latter, yet comprising only one of the gender report's seven strategic priorities for policy change (UN Millennium Project 2005: 28–29).
12 The evidence is given in Colclough *et al.* 2003: 29–30.
13 For discussion of these issues see UNESCO 2003, chapters 3 and 4.
14 See, for example, Boserup 1970, Caplan 1981, Dey 1981.
15 Young *et al.* 1981 provides an influential early example of this new tradition.
16 The data are shown in UNESCO 2005: 72.
17 See UNESCO 2003: 284–292, UNESCO 2004: 236–247 and subsequent volumes in the series.
18 The indicators for each of the goals are: the net enrolment ratio in primary education as an indicator of progress towards UPE; the literacy rate of those aged 15 years and over, as an indicator of adult literacy; the survival rate to grade five as an indicator of

the quality of education; the simple average of gender parity indices for primary and secondary education and for adult literates, as an indicator of the gender goal. The other two 'Dakar' goals – for the enhancement of early childhood education and of life-skills programmes – do not yet have indicators which are conducive to quantitative measurement on an international basis.

19 See, for example, UNDP 2004: 258–264, where the methods, and associated technical problems of constructing the Human Development Index, and the other indices used by the Human Development Report, are outlined.

20 This is not necessarily to imply disingenuousness on the part of either government or agency representatives. Often, policies had indeed changed, and the data did reveal some improvement the following year. This was, however, rarely by so much as to change national or agency rankings in very significant ways.

References

Black, R. and White, H. (eds) (2004) *Targeting Development – Critical Perspectives on the Millennium Development Goals*, London: Routledge.

Boserup, E. (1970) *Women's Role in Economic Development*, New York: St Martin's Press.

Caplan, P. (1981) 'Development policies for Tanzania: some implications for women', in N. Nelson (ed.) 'African Women in the Development Process,' Special Issue, *Journal of Development Studies*, 17, 3: 98–108.

Colclough, C. (2004) 'Towards universal primary education' in R. Black and H. White, (eds) *Targeting Development – Critical Perspectives on the Millennium Development Goals*, London: Routledge, pp. 166–183.

Colclough, C. (2005) 'Rights, goals and targets: how do those for education add up?', *Journal of International Development*, 17: 101–111.

Colclough, C, with Lewin, K. (1993) *Educating All the Children: Strategies for Primary Schooling in the South*, Oxford: Clarendon Press.

Colclough, C., Al-Samarrai, S., Rose, P. and Tembon, M. (2003) *Achieving Schooling for All in Africa: Costs, Commitment and Gender*, Aldershot: Ashgate.

Connell, R.W. (1987) *Gender and Power*, Cambridge: Polity Press.

Dey, J. (1981) 'Gambian women: unequal partners in rice development projects?' in N. Nelson (ed.) 'African Women in the Development Process,' Special Issue, *Journal of Development Studies*, 17, 3: 109–122.

DFID/HM Treasury (2005) 'From Commitment to Action: Education', (available online at: www.fasid.or.jp/chosa/forum/bbl/pdf/135–3.pdf).

Kabeer, N. (1994) *Reversed Realities: Gender Hierarchies in Development Thought*, London: Verso.

Nelson, N. (ed.) (1981) 'African Women in the Development Process,' Special Issue, *Journal of Development Studies*, 17, 3.

OECD DAC (1996) *Shaping the 21st Century: The Contribution of Development Cooperation*, Paris: OECD.

Stromquist, N. (1989) 'Determinants of Educational Participation and Achievement of Women in the Third World: A Review of the Evidence and a Theoretical Critique', *Review of Educational Research*, 59, 2: 143–183.

Tomasevski, K. (2003) 'School fees as hindrance to universalizing primary education', Background paper for *EFA Global Monitoring Report 2003/4* (mimeo).

UN Millennium Project (2005) *Taking Action: Achieving Gender Equality and Empowering Women*, London: Earthscan.

UNDP (2004) *Human Development Report 2004: Cultural Liberty in Today's Diverse World*, New York: Oxford University Press.

UNESCO (2000a) *The Dakar Framework for Action: Education for All – Meeting our Collective Commitments*, World Education Forum, Dakar, Senegal 26–28 April, UNESCO, Paris.

UNESCO (2000b) *World Education Forum – Final Report*, UNESCO, Paris.

UNESCO (2002) *Education for All: Is the World on Track? EFA Global Monitoring Report 2002*, UNESCO, Paris.

UNESCO (2003) *Gender and Education for All – The Leap to Equality EFA Global Monitoring Report 2003/4*, UNESCO, Paris.

UNESCO (2004) *Education for All: The Quality Imperative EFA Global Monitoring Report 2005*, UNESCO, Paris.

UNESCO (2005) *Literacy for Life, EFA Global Monitoring Report 2006*, UNESCO, Paris.

UNESCO (2006) *Strong Foundations: Early Childhood Care and Education, EFA Global Monitoring Report 2007*, UNESCO, Paris.

United Nations (UN) (2000) *United Nations Millennium Declaration*, Document A/RES/55/2, United Nations, New York.

United Nations (UN) (2001) 'Resolution A/56/326', 6 September 2001, United Nations General Assembly, New York.

UNIVERSALIA (2006) *Formative Review of the Education for All Global Monitoring Report*, Volume II, Narrative Report, UNESCO, Paris, March.

Unterhalter, E. (2005) 'Fragmented frameworks? Researching women, gender, education and development' in S. Aikman and E. Unterhalter (eds) *Beyond Access: Transforming Policy and Practice for Gender Equality in Education*, Oxford: Oxfam, pp. 15–35.

White, H. and Black, R. (2004) 'Millennium development goals: a drop in the ocean?' in R. Black and H. White (eds) *Targeting Development – Critical Perspectives on the Millennium Development Goals*, London: Routledge, pp. 1–24.

Whitehead, A. (1979) 'Some Preliminary Notes on the Subordination of Women', *IDS Bulletin*, 10, 3: 10–13, Brighton.

Young, K., Wolkowitz, C. and McCullagh, C. (eds) (1981) *Of Marriage and the Market, Women's Subordination in International Perspective*, London: CSE Books.

5 Social capital, civil society and education for all

A gendered lens

Malini Sivasubramaniam

Civil society must be granted new and expanded political and social scope at all levels of society in order to engage governments in dialogue, decision-making and innovation around the goals for basic education. Civil society has much experience and a crucial role to play in identifying barriers to Education for All goals, and developing policies and strategies to remove them.

(Dakar Framework for Action Item no. 53)

Social capital is not a panacea, and more of it is not necessarily better.

(Woolcock 2001: 80)

Can social capital serve as a helpful conceptual framework for analysing the role of civil society organizations (CSOs) in the achievement of Education for All (EFA), and in particular girls' education? This chapter undertakes a critical examination of the contribution of the concept of social capital to the attainment of the gender goals of EFA, by examining the role of civil society organizations as one of the key actors in the equality agenda.[1]

The World Education Forum in Dakar, Senegal, in 2000, positioned civil society organizations at the forefront as important actors in global efforts to achieve the EFA goals.[2] This affirmation, in the post-Dakar period, has resulted in an unprecedented growth in the number of civil society coalitions and networks engaged in EFA policy processes at the national, regional and international levels (Mundy and Murphy 2001; Mundy 2006). Enthusiastically embraced by multilateral and bilateral agencies, CSOs continue to be valorized as crucial policy partners and advocates in achieving the EFA agenda.

Yet, the insights offered by the growing literature on civil society and education do not entirely address the role of CSOs in promoting gender equality. One way to scrutinize the participation of CSOs, particularly with a gendered lens, is by reference to the concept of social capital. Social capital is generated through successful collective action of civil society as development agents. While international agencies provide legitimacy to the role of civil society and encourage the formation of social capital, a gendered perspective and analysis is noticeably missing from both the civil society (Howell 2005) and social capital literature (Gidengil and O'Neill 2006). Arguably, then, the ubiquity of CSOs within the current discourse of partnership in EFA and girls' education raises some important questions, such as, do CSO coalitions and networks generate social capital that, in turn, is leveraged to promote gender equality in education?

This chapter proceeds as follows. I first explore the conceptual and methodological issues surrounding the usefulness of social capital in analysing EFA, and in particular girls' education globally. I consider the ways in which social capital has been represented and used by those offering a neo-liberal, political economy and/or feminist perspective. Comparing across these differing frameworks serves as an important starting point to understand how social capital can contribute to analysing the EFA agenda. The second section outlines the manner in which international and transnational initiatives compare with national and subnational initiatives in the area of girls' education. The intention here is to consider the limitations and advantages of social capital frameworks in relating to these national and transnational initiatives. The third and final section describes briefly specific examples of national and international initiatives in education. To better understand the role of civil society in promoting gender equality in education, I apply the different notions of social capital (*bonding, bridging* and *linking*) to two particular national and transnational initiatives to show why there is a differential impact. Finally, I conclude with some implications and caveats for gendered conceptualization of civil society and social capital.

Social capital: a conceptual and methodological framework

Social capital research has advanced to the forefront of contemporary thinking in policy and social sciences. In the literature, the origins of the concept are often attributed to sociologists James Coleman (1988) and Pierre Bourdieu (1986). More recently political scientist, Robert Putnam (1995) has done much to popularize the concept. As an analytical and conceptual tool, social capital is useful in understanding how dense interlocking networks of relationships can serve as a resource, and why these networks matter. Interestingly, social capital serves both as an outcome and a resource. Communities with a rich endowment of social capital are thought to be better able to deal with poverty (Woolcock and Narayan 2000), and combat community violence (Colletta and Cullen 2000). On the other hand, a lack of social capital has been linked to reduced access to education (Coleman 1988), and social fragmentation and isolation (Flora and Flora 1993). Table 5.1 summarizes some contrasting definitions of social capital.

Nevertheless, social capital remains a contested concept. Its ambiguity as Fine (2001: 190) contends is that 'social capital has a gargantuan appetite' and so invites a plethora of definitions and perspectives. This lack of consensus about its definition, operationalization and conceptualization, however, contributes to its malleability and to its conceptual weakness (Fine 2001; Harris 2001; Quibria 2003; Halpern 2005). Some critics even claim that the putative, positive outcomes of social capital have been overplayed and, conversely, its

Table 5.1 Contrasting conceptual and operational definitions of social capital

Theorist	Conceptual definition	Operational definition	Unit of analysis	View of social capital and education
James Coleman	'Social capital is ... not a single entity, but a variety of entities having characteristics in common; they all consist of some aspect of social structure, and they facilitate certain actions of individuals who are within the structure' (Coleman 1990: 302).	Social capital is a form of capital that exists in the relationship between people. Similarly, families can accumulate social capital to advance their children's education.	Individual/families	Instrumental – used for positive outcomes. Education viewed as a democratizing instrument.
Pierre Bourdieu	'... the aggregate of actual and potential resources which are linked to the possession of a durable network of more or less institutionalized relationships of mutual acquaintance or recognition or in other words, to membership in a group' (Bourdieu 1986: 248).	Social capital plays a role in the reproduction of unequal power relationships because it is used to maintain dominant political and social ideologies.	Social structures/networks	Inhibitive – used to reproduce power differentials. Education viewed as a legitimizing instrument.
Robert Putnam	'Social capital refers to features of social organization such as networks, norms and social trust that facilitate coordination and cooperation for mutual benefit' (Putnam 1995: 67).	Societies with more aggregate social capital demonstrate higher levels of civic engagement.	Community organizations	Instrumental – used for positive outcomes. Education viewed as a leveraging and democratizing instrument.

exclusionary, negative effects underplayed (Fine 2001; Harris 2001; Rankin 2002). Portes (1998) similarly points to the 'downside of social capital' where social networks can reinforce hierarchical positions of power. This contention parallels Bourdieu's (1986) caution about the role played by social capital in the reproduction of unequal power relations. In other words, social capital can be deployed for both positive and negative ends.

Clearly, social capital has its share of sceptics and proponents. However, recent scholarly work on social capital has stimulated new thinking about its usefulness as an analytical construct in advancing public policy issues (Saegert *et al.* 2001; Prakash and Selle 2004). Below I briefly distinguish between three alternative perspectives of social capital: *neo-liberal, political economy* and *feminist.*

There appears to be considerable consensus within the *neo-liberal* discourse that social capital is important for development (Coleman 1988; Putnam 1993, 1995, 2000; Woolcock 1998, 2001). Endorsed by mainstream development agencies, and the World Bank, the neo-liberal development discourse has adopted Robert Putnam's (1995: 67) conceptualization of social capital (see Table 5.1). Implicit in these discussions is the normative view that involvement in civil society generates social capital, which in turn contributes to the development of political democracy, economic growth and an array of desirable policy outcomes (Edwards *et al.* 2001; Kruse 2002; Putnam 1995).

Within the World Bank discourse on development, in particular social capital, has been elevated to the 'missing link' or 'social glue' in development. In fact, the bank's social capital website offers an expansive definition of social capital (as cited in Rankin 2002: 4)

> Social capital refers to the institutions, relationships, and norms that shape the quality and quantity of a society's social interactions. Increasing evidence show that social cohesion is critical for societies to prosper economically and for development to be sustainable. Social capital is not just the sum of the institutions [that] underpin a society – it is the glue that holds them together.

Several researchers (Fine 2001; Harris 2001; Mayer and Rankin 2002; Rankin 2002), however, are critical of this apolitical position adopted by the World Bank because of the unquestioning, seemingly deterministic relationship proposed between social capital, sustainable development and economic growth. Such a neo-liberal construction of social capital, as Rankin (2002: 2), argues 'conflates development with economic growth and embraces the rational, utility-maximizing individual as the locus of progressive change'. In doing so, this appropriation of social capital not only depoliticizes development but merely shifts the burden of responsibility from the state to the people themselves, without addressing structural impediments to development.

In education, this social capital rationale underpins structural adjustment programmes that shift the burden of the cost of education to poor parents.

Research demonstrates, however, that deploying community and parental social capital through cost-sharing and decentralization policies has negative consequences for girls' education in poor areas and promotes unfavourable equity effects in girls' education (Rose 2002).

While a neo-liberal perspective contends that social capital fosters trust and cooperation, which in turn encourages economic prosperity and effective governance, a *political economy* perspective argues instead that 'Social capital, and the character of civil society itself, are more likely to be shaped by broader economic and political trends' (Edwards *et al.* 2001: 100). From a political economy perspective, economic and political structures play a key role in fostering social capital (Harris 2001; Szreter and Woolcock, 2004). Whilst neo-liberal development discourses focus on the benign qualities of social capital, a political economy perspective in contrast, drawing heavily on Bourdieu (1986), views social capital as reinforcing power and structural inequalities. Consistent with Woolcock's (2001) contention that the efficacy of social capital must be understood in its institutional context, a political economy perspective necessitates a reconfiguration of state–society relations itself. In considering the broader macroeconomic and socio-structural context then, linkages between state and civil society become important.

State–civil society relationships, however, can be contentious as they represent a power differential. Particularly, when framed as a zero-sum relationship, the construction of social capital within these relationships can be difficult. Socio-political contexts can also constrain or facilitate the building of state–society relations. Nonetheless, relationships across the public-private divide are important, as Evans (1996: 21) points out, 'Social capital inheres, not just in civil society, but in an enduring set of relationships that spans the public private divide'. However, to accrue social capital necessary for creating gender responsive policy frameworks, CSOs need to build norms of trust and reciprocity with the state.

Unlike the anti-statist thinking of neo-liberal conceptualizations of social capital, a state–society perspective requires state involvement. Several researchers (e.g. Evans 1996; Woolcock and Narayan 2000), however, argue for a synergistic relationship between state and civil society. Synergy implies that 'civic engagement strengthens state institutions, and effective state institutions create an environment in which civic engagement is more likely to thrive' Evans (1996: 3). State–society synergy[3] can be instrumental for development, bringing the state back into the discourse. Synergy depends on two mutually supportive concepts: *complementarity*, which is the 'mutually supportive relations between public and private actors' (Evans 1996: 179), and *embeddedness*, which is the 'ties that connect citizens and public officials across the public–private divide'. (Evans 1996: 180). Woolcock and Narayan (2000) extend this concept of synergy further by arguing that different combinations of complementarity and embeddedness result in different outcomes in state–society relations. However, it is also important to acknowledge the role of the State in stimulating the creation of social capital. A synergistic partnership requires new political conjunctures and the political will to address gender concerns.

Finally, a *feminist* perspective of social capital shares many similarities with a political economy perspective. In considering the broader institutional environment of development, feminist scholars however have criticized social capital for its reticence about gender inequalities and gender hierarchies (Molyneux 2002; Van Straven 2002; Rankin 2002; Mayer and Rankin 2002). Likewise, Gidengil and O'Neill (2006: 4) argue that it is only 'A gendered analysis of social capital [that] brings to the fore larger questions about the distribution of social capital, differences in the nature of social capital, and differences in the way social capital is used.' This gendered analysis necessitates an examination of nuanced power relations. Such an analysis parallels Bourdieu's (1986) line of thinking, in which social capital is used as a means to maintaining social hierarchies. More precisely, this gendered critique is directed at neo-liberal conceptualizations of social capital that not only obscure structural inequalities, but also render women invisible in development partnerships. Molyneux (2002) argues that this hidden burden of development, often unloaded on women through development projects and policies, perpetuates the unchallenged gendered assumptions about women's roles. Where development policies are narrowly fashioned, social capital accumulation becomes a burden disproportionately borne by women. Likewise, even education for girls merely serves as a vehicle for other development goals, and is not promoted as a right in itself.

A gendered analysis of social capital can help to explain power asymmetries within networks by asking who is excluded. Cleaver's research in Tanzania (2003), for example, illustrates how some social relationships, collective action and local institutions may exclude some of the poorest by reproducing relations of inequality and marginalization. Similarly, Rankin (2002) in her work in Nepal points out that micro-lending groups are divided along lines of gender and caste, leading to higher bonding social capital within such groups but also to the exclusion of women from lower castes.

Extending the analyses of gender and social capital from micro-finance to education, it is possible to conclude that neither CSOs nor the social capital they generate is not neutral. In fact, as Van Straven aptly notes 'Civil society is not gender neutral and does not automatically contribute to women's wellbeing or empowerment' (2002: 22). Likewise, it is only when gender is brought into the frame of analysis, partnerships with CSOs in girls' education can be problematized (Rao and Smyth, 2004). This gendered analysis in state-civil society relationships is particularly crucial where there is the danger of gender advocates in civil society actors being co-opted through clientalism and state patronage.

Civil society itself is not an entirely homogenous entity and on many fronts is still 'a site of conflict and ideological struggle' (Howell 2005: 249). Therefore, norms of trust may be difficult to negotiate. Depending on how social capital is construed, coalitions and networks advocating for girls' education have the potential to strengthen exclusion patterns and unequal distributions of power. In such instances, CSO involvement only serves to exacerbate existing gender inequalities.

Theorizing social capital and gender outcomes in girls' education

It is important to recognize that not all social capital is alike. Different societies are characterized by the relative prevalence of different kinds of social capital in them, resulting in different outcomes. Szreter and Woolcock (2004: 654–6) distinguish for example, between three types of social capital:

a *bonding social capital,* which refers to trusting and cooperative relations between members of a network who see themselves as being similar, in terms of their shared social identity;

b *bridging social capital,* by contrast, comprises relations of respect and mutuality between people who know that they are not alike in some socio-demographic (or social identity) sense (differing by age, ethnic group, class, etc.); and

c *linking social capital,* as norms of respect and networks of trusting relationships between people who are interacting across explicit, formal or institutionalized power or authority gradients in society.

This typology points to the relative importance of horizontal (bonding and bridging) and vertical (linking) linkages in the field of social capital. From a feminist perspective of social capital, it is instructive in locating our discussion on CSOs and gender equality in education within a broader, contextual/social structural framework. Such a discussion helps us to pay attention to the 'regressive and progressive forms of associational life' (Rankin 2002: 18) and cautions us that not all civil society endowments of social capital are equal.

While there is widespread agreement that eliminating gender inequalities in education is imperative to achieving the gender goals of EFA, feminist scholarship has shown that providing access in itself is insufficient to ensure gender equality (Heward 1999; Stromquist 2003; Subrahmanian 2005). This implies it is important to distinguish between parity, equality and equity goals. Gender parity primarily attends to issues of access and enrolment, whereas gender equality demands are more 'gender-redistributive' (Kabeer and Subrahmanian as cited in Kirk 2005: 644). Subrahmanian has further suggested the need for the conceptual framework on gender to include the concept gender equity as a measure of the effectiveness of the measures used to monitor gender parity and gender equality. This is because gender equity 'places emphasis on redistribution of resources between men and women in a way that addresses gender-based asymmetries in investment and capacities of women and men' (Subrahmanian 2005: 406). To address inequitable gender policies, CSOs must challenge gender assumptions, asymmetries and exclusions in girls' education and move beyond advocating primarily for access.

Gender parity, equality and equity are not mutually exclusive. Similarly, there are no distinct boundaries between bonding, bridging and linking networks because groups can exhibit more than one function. Thus, CSOs may exhibit all

Table 5.2 Relative density of bonding, bridging and linking networks of social capital required for particular gender outcomes in girls' education

Gender outcomes	Bonding networks	Bridging networks	Linking networks
Gender parity	High	Low	Low
Gender equality	High	High/Low	High/Low
Gender equity	High	High	High

three networks, but vary in their relative endowment of a particular type of social capital. Drawing therefore on this taxonomic distinction, it can be postulated that progress in all three dimensions of gender outcomes (parity, equality and equity) requires a 'balanced distribution of a relatively rich endowment of all three of these forms of social capital' (Szreter and Woolcock 2004: 661) (see Table 5.2).

CSO coalitions which advocate for girls' education without challenging prevailing gender ideologies are only working towards improving gender parity, not equality or equity. In doing so, they are merely promoting a neo-liberal conceptualization of girls' education that is primarily conceived in a narrow, instrumental sense (Kirk 2005). A gendered social capital framework, on the other hand, problematizes social capital and provides a more incisive understanding of how the different forms of social capital contribute to different gendered outcomes. Thus, the potential exists to transform CSOs in positive directions and to generate more progressive forms of social capital.

Civil society coalitions, social capital formation and gendered education

In the post-Dakar period, there has been a significant growth in the number and reach of national and regional coalitions addressing issues of EFA and girls' education. For example, during Dakar, there were only two national education campaign coalitions in the Asia-Pacific region, presently there are at least 12. Similarly in Africa, 27 national EFA campaigns have been set up in the last five years (*Education Today* 2006).

There is ample evidence of this heightened level of engagement on the part of national CSOs. *Elimu Yetu* in Kenya is a national umbrella educational coalition of over 110 diverse partners, and similarly *E-Net* in the Philippines, boasts over 400 CSO actors working on joint advocacy strategies, including research, monitoring, campaigning and lobbying. The primary focus of these coalitions is to hold national governments accountable to meeting their commitments to their EFA goals. Post-Dakar, UNESCO revitalized its Collective Consultation of NGOs on EFA (CCNGO/EFA) as the primary mechanism to collaborate with CSOs and presently connects about 700 CSOs, two-thirds of whom are from the South (UNESCO 2004). In a similar manner, United Nation's Girls' Educational Initiative (UNGEI), launched at Dakar in 2000, provides a platform for CSOs, governments, INGOs and the private sector to work together to narrow the gender gap at the country level, particularly through interventions aimed at national education policies and plans.

Schnuttgen and Khan (2004: 2) term this emergence of a global polity in education as 'historically new in the field of education'. For the first time a broad range of CSO actors ranging from teachers' unions, grassroots organizations, trade unions, women's groups, faith-based organizations and human rights groups, among others have come together to form broad based coalitions advocating for EFA and gender goals. What is noteworthy about these global coalitions is that through their coalition building, they are able to influence national government decisions in an organized and informed way. In their role as advocates and policy partners, these coalitions have engaged with national governments by advocating policy change through budget tracking and expenditure monitoring, research, and evaluation of national EFA policy processes.

This unprecedented association of CSO actors, even in countries where there has been traditionally little state–civil society engagement, is supported technically and financially by regional networks and international NGOs (INGOs) (UNESCO 2004). INGOs have come to play a more prominent role in international discourse around EFA in what is seen as a 'new and unanticipated leadership in international EFA efforts by International NGOs' (Mundy and Murphy 2001). For example, a majority of the national EFA country coalitions are members of the Global Campaign for Education (GCE), a transnational network which works at the global stage to lobby governments on issues relating to the attainment of EFA goals.[4] Likewise, the Commonwealth Education Fund (CEF), a UK government initiative supports capacity building of national EFA coalitions in 16 Commonwealth countries. Regionally, ANCEFA (the African National Network for EFA) and ASPBAE (Asia South Pacific Bureau for Adult Education), both primarily funded by INGOs, provide a collective voice for EFA coalitions through their lobbying, networking, alliance building and information sharing activities.

Social capital in national and international initiatives on girls' education

In order to see how a social capital and gender typology (Table 5.2) can provide a useful framework for understanding CSO engagement and gender outcomes, I apply it to the analysis of two particular initiatives: the 'Girl Child Network' (GCN), a national group in Kenya and the 'Global Campaign for Education' (GCE), a transnational network comprised of national groups. My intent in analysing these two initiatives is not to contrast between them. These initiatives are clearly two different kinds of entities. Rather the purpose is to show why there is differential impact and to question if social capital (*bonding, bridging and linking*) can be relevant in the respective contexts.

In Kenya, the 'Girl Child Network' (GCN) is a national coalition of more than 280 local CSOs and community groups with its members spread over four regions: Mount. Kenya, Western Kenya, Coast and Nairobi (CIDA, 2006). Formed in 1995, the network's main goal is to help orphaned and vulnerable girls. Initially set up by CARE Canada as part of its 'Girl Child Program', it was funded by the Canadian International Development Agency (CIDA). The purpose of the network was to bring greater coordination between the hundreds of NGOs working in this sector in Kenya, and to serve as key national forum for advocacy and promoting the rights of the girl child (Girl Child Network 2004). GCN is a member of the national EFA coalition in Kenya and is one of the 13 partner organizations of the Commonwealth Education Fund (CEF). The network also receives funding from other bilateral donors and INGOs.

GCN operates within a rights based framework in its policies and approaches to issues of gender. With education as its core mobilizing strategy, GCN strongly advocates for the girl child's rights to education. As a network, GCN seeks to mainstream girl child activities through advocacy, information sharing and strengthening girl child programming in Kenya (Girl Child Network 2004).

Internationally, the 'Global Campaign for Education' (GCE) has given a highly credible voice and leadership to civil society in education. As a transnational advocacy network of over 400 CSOs active in over 100 countries, GCE has done much to catapult EFA issues onto the global stage. Initially set up in 1999 by four major INGOs (Oxfam International, ActionAid, Education International and the Global March Against Child Labor) to prepare for the World Education Forum in Dakar, GCE has been able to generate political support for education at major international meetings such as IMF–World Bank Annual Meetings and the G8 summits (Watt 2004).

As a unique coalition of Northern and Southern partners, representing a broad based coalition of international, regional and national CSO members, GCE has been able to leverage international support and resources to support the work of national and regional networks in advocating for EFA. As a global policy watchdog, GCE sits on the consultative board of many international initiatives, such as the World Bank's Fast Track Initiative (FTI), UNICEF's United National Girls' Education Initiative (UNGEI) and UNESCO's EFA working group and High Level Group.[5]

Global Campaign for Education (2003, 2005) contends that educating girls is the first step toward ending poverty and achieving human rights. Therefore, GCE promotes education as a basic human right and mobilizes public pressure on governments and the international community to achieve the EFA and gender goals. GCE also strongly advocates for state provision of free, compulsory public education for all children, especially girls.

Understanding gendered social capital

To better understand these national and transnational coalitions in education, I draw upon the analysis of Minkoff (2001) and Smith (2001) who examine social capital formation in national and transnational social movement organizations, respectively. Three claims can be made about how the engagement of national and transnational CSO networks and coalitions creates social capital which impacts policy advocacy around EFA.

First, national and transnational networks provide an infrastructure for communication and activism. Minkoff (2001) in her analysis of national social movement organizations shows how these organizations provide a means for accumulating social capital that can be used for collective activism. A parallel can be drawn with national and transnational CSOs in the post-Dakar period. For example, the GCN and the GCE have created respectively, a national and an international infrastructure for collective activism.

GCE has successfully established a new space for civil society advocacy in education (Watt 2004), while at the same time 'introducing more accountability for recipient governments and donor commitments to EFA commitments' (Mundy 2006: 39). On a cautionary note, Watt (2004) states that consensus building is a challenge within the coalition as its members have 'diverse expertise, capacities, and policy priorities'. These differences are clearly further exacerbated by the stark political and economic differences between its northern and southern partners. Therefore, policy and advocacy initiatives at times, have the potential to become contentious issues.

Likewise, GCN has successfully set up an infrastructure that connects the hundreds of previously uncoordinated CSOs working on gender issues in Kenya. This infrastructure enables bonding and bridging networks to be established to exploit the pooled potential of the different efforts being made for the benefit of the girl child.

The infrastructure created by these broad-based networks and coalitions has not only enhanced their credibility, but has also enabled a sustained and coordinated dialogue to take place. The expansion of technology has enabled easier networking nationally and internationally. Furthermore, these efforts have catalyzed increased coalition building efforts, which in turn have resulted in improved infrastructure for sustained and credible advocacy work. Both GCE and GCN represent CSO advocacy efforts which have successfully cultivated social trust and social capital.

Next, national and transnational networks facilitate the development of collective identities. As coalition building and capacity building initiatives develop, there is increased opportunity for CSO coalitions from the South particularly to influence EFA policy processes at the national and international level. Smith (2001: 201) contends that transnational social movements act as 'mediators between local interest and identities and global institutions'. This mediation generates social capital relevant to marginalized groups through the creation of a collective identity. Internationally, a similar claim can be made about the GCE which serves as a mediator for the local and global in EFA, and in the process generates social capital for CSOs, particularly those in the South. Without the collective identity provided by GCE, Southern coalitions would have limited access to and influence at international policy platforms. GCE's mediation provides a legitimizing effect for local coalitions and networks lobbying their governments on EFA reforms. GCE enables national and sub-national coalitions in the South to bring external pressure upon their governments by leveraging international laws and norms, thus creating what Keck and Sikkink (1998: 13) refer to as the 'boomerang effect'.

At the national level, GCN similarly creates a collective identity for CSOs working on gender issues in the country. In the process, GCN serves as an intermediary between local grassroots CSOs and the government. As part of this effort, the network is working to develop a nationwide policy which will make the protection of girls and women a priority (CIDA 2006). GCN has set up a countrywide database to keep track of girls who have sought help or have been helped by members of the network in any of its shelters. The database allows for follow-up, so that once the girl has left the shelter, counsellors or government officials can go to the girl's family to speak to them about her rights to schooling. Without the database, it would be difficult to trace these girls. GCN is also training district government officials on how to use and maintain the database. The database necessitates the formation of bonding and bridging networks between GCN's members in seeking to act collectively to achieve gender parity and equality.

A collective identity provides networks with social relations that can be mobilized to pursue shared goals for the common good. Both GCE and GCN represent examples of broad – based coalitions working towards the collective issue of quality, public education for girls. There is clear demonstration of the formation of 'bridging social capital' or 'linkages' between the various networks GCE and GCN are a part of. Woolcock (2001) points out that social opportunity requires high levels of both integration and linkage. In other words, because GCE and GCN engage and interact with a larger number of diverse actors, they would have more opportunities to form more linkages. These linkages would then help them to form higher bridging and linking social capital and to better contribute to more equitable gendered development outcomes.

Finally, national and transnational networks have helped generate and guide the public discourse around EFA. Both Minkoff (2001) and Smith (2001) concede that social movement organizations shape and expand the public sphere by promoting debate on issues of collective concern. This broadening debate helps excluded groups participate in formal institutions. One illustration of this is the spaces made available for traditionally marginalized CSOs through platforms such as the UNESCO EFA working groups and the World Bank Fast Track Initiative (FTI). For example, GCE sits on the steering committee of the FTI and so represents its members in the international discourse around gender and education. In this representation, GCE is building bonding, bridging and linking networks between its North and South members, and also between national governments and multilateral organizations.

Conversely, in 2001, the GCN was instrumental in the enactment of the Government of Kenya's Children Act, a bill designed to protect the rights of children, particularly girls (CIDA 2006). Lobbying parliamentarians and government officials, GCN accrued a density of bridging and linking social capital through coalition building between its members as well as negotiating power-differentiated network roles between CSOs and the government. GCN was able to leverage the social capital generated to promote the desired gender outcomes.

As coalition building and capacity building initiatives develop, there is increased opportunity for CSO coalitions, particularly from the South to influence EFA and gender policy processes at the national and international level. This is evident in the case of GCN. In fact, GCN, through its membership in the national education coalition in Kenya, is a member of GCE (Elimu Yetu Coalition 2005). Therefore, GCN is able to contribute to the global public discourse around gender goals through its linking networks with GCE.

In the context of social capital formation, GCE is a macro-representation of GCN because they both bring together diverse members within a network requiring the formation of horizontal linkages and they both work on advocacy issues requiring the formation of vertical linkages. Further, *GCN and GCE* represent initiatives which seek to build the capacity of CSOs to influence government policy decisions around gender and education. These initiatives have strong commitments to a rights-based framework to girls' education. GCE and GCN clearly deploy social capital for collective action in their respective local contexts. While there is evidence of all three endowments of social capital in both cases, they differ in their relative intensity depending on the issue pursued.

As national and transnational networks, GCN and GCE differ in how they frame structural issues that affect gender equality. GCE's emphasis on girls' schooling as a global good frames the issue of rights to education as more broadly linked to other concomitant barriers such as poverty reduction and debt relief. In the case of GCN, the framing of structural issues impeding girls' education is less global and more focussed on promoting and safeguarding the rights of the girl child. However, GCE and GCN demonstrate sufficiently high bridging and linking networks to ensure gender equality and equity outcomes. The examination of both GCN and GCE provides further evidence that the gendering of social capital requires the presence of all three networks of social capital to achieve the gender goals in girls' education.

Conclusion

In this chapter, I have examined the role of CSOs as policy actors engaged in EFA and girls' education, and I have asked if social capital is a useful framework to examine this engagement. My purpose has been to determine if and how CSO networks and coalitions stimulate the creation of social capital, and, more importantly, how effectively CSOs have promoted the gender goals of the EFA agenda through the generation of social capital.

While the involvement of CSOs in EFA is not without its limitations, tensions and constraints, national, regional and transnational coalitions and networks do generate social capital by providing an infrastructure for communication, facilitating the development of collective identities, and shaping the public discourse and debate around EFA. CSOs have an important role in furthering the gender goals of EFA. However, the mere accumulation of coalitions and networks is insufficient to ensure gender equality in education. From a feminist perspective, however, it is also important consider if, CSOs promote 'gender-redistributive' education policies through leveraging the social capital generated.

Social capital can serve as a useful conceptual framework for analysing the role of CSOs, particularly in girls education when gender is brought into the frame of analysis. Ultimately, there is a need for persistent attention not only to the quantity of social capital generated, but also to the quality. Social capital by no means guarantees gendered education. Viewing social capital through a gendered lens, we must *ask what kind of social capital is generated, how this social capital is used,* and, most importantly *who benefits.* The answers to these questions are not yet clear. Nevertheless, more research into gendered social capital can do much to augment its usefulness as an innovative conceptual apparatus for examining CSO engagement in EFA and girls' education.

Notes

1 I would like to thank the editors of this collection for their comments on earlier drafts of this chapter. I would also like to thank Karen Mundy for her insightful comments on an earlier draft. I define civil society as 'the broad range of formal and informal organizations that operate in the space between family and the state' (Kruse 2002: 5).
2 Gender equality is one of the six goals of the EFA agenda as well Goal 3 of the Millennium Development Goals. Information on the Dakar Framework for Action and EFA goals can be found at www.unesco.org/education/efa/index.shtml.
3 Evans does acknowledge though, that in some circumstances, a zero-sum relationship may be unavoidable.
4 A transnational advocacy network is defined as '... relevant actors working internationally on an issue, who are bound together by shared values, a common discourse, and dense exchanges of information and services' (Keck and Sikkink 1998: 2).
5 The Fast Track Initiative (FTI), is a World Bank proposal conceived in 2002 to accelerate progress in the education sector. As a global compact, it provides aid and technical assistance to countries which implement prescribed policy and institutional reforms. There are presently 31 countries which have been accorded FTI status. However, with growing funding gaps, donor commitments to the initiative have been criticized for falling short of international promise. See Rose (2003) for a more detailed critique of the FTI.

Bibliography

Bourdieu, P. (1986) 'The forms of capital' in J. Richardson (ed.) *Handbook of Theory and Research for the Sociology of Education*, Westport, CT: Greenwood Press.
Canadian International Development Agency (2006) 'Weaving a safety net for girls in Kenya', CIDA Canada. Available online at: www.acdi-cida.gc.ca/CIDAWEB/ acdi-cida.nsf/En/NAT-8282435-GKE (accessed 18 September 2006).
Cleaver, F. (2003) 'The inequality of social capital: agency, association and the reproduction of chronic poverty', Paper presented at 'Staying Poor: Chronic Poverty and Development Policy conference, University of Manchester, April.

Coleman, J. (1988) 'Social Capital and the Creation of Human Capital', *American Journal of Sociology*, 94: 95–120.

Coleman, J. (1990) *Foundations of Social Theory*, Cambridge: Harvard University Press.

Colletta, N. and Cullen, M. (2000) *Violent Conflict and the Transformation of Social Capital: Lessons from Cambodia, Rwanda, Guatemala, and Somalia*, Washington, DC: World Bank.

Education Today (2006) 'Civil Society Pushes the Boundaries', no. 17. UNESCO. Available online at: portal.unesco.org/education/en/ev.phpURL_ID=48879&URL_DO=DO_TOPIC&URL_SECTION=201.html (accessed 10 October 2006).

Edwards, B., Foley, M. and Diani, M. (2001) 'Civil society and social capital: A primer' in B. Edwards, M. Foley and M. Diani (eds) *Beyond Tocqueville: Civil Society and the Social Capital Debate in Comparative Perspective*, Hanover: Tufts University.

Elimu Yetu Coalition (2005) 'The challenge of educating girls in Kenya' in S. Aikman and E. Unterhalter (eds) *Beyond Access: Transforming Policy and Practice for Gender Equality in Education*, Oxfam GB. Available online at: www.oxfam.org.uk/what_we_do/resources/downloads/BA_7.pdf (accessed 4 June 2007).

Evans, P. (1996) *State–society Synergy: Government and Social Capital in Development*, International and Area Studies: University of California at Berkeley.

Field, J. (2003) *Social Capital*, London: Routledge.

Fine, B. (2001) *Social Capital versus Social Theory: Political Economy and Social Sciences at the Turn of the Millennium*, London and New York: Routledge.

Flora, C. and Flora, J. (1993) 'Entrepreneurial Social Infrastructure: A Necessary Ingredient', *Annals of the American Academy of Political and Social Sciences*, 529: 48–58.

Gidengil, E. and O'Neill, B. (2006) 'Removing rose coloured glasses: Examining theories of social capital through a gendered lens' in B. O'Neill and E. Gidengil (eds) *Gender and Social Capital*, New York: Routledge.

Girl Child Network (2004). *The Status of gender equity and equality in primary education in Kenya*. A report prepared for the Commonwealth Education Fund.

Global Campaign for Education (2003) *A Fair Chance: attaining gender equality in basic education by 2005*, Global Campaign for Education. Available online at: www.campaignforeducation.org/resources/Mar2005/b10_brief_final.doc (accessed 4 June 2007).

—— (2005). *Girls can't wait. Why girls' education matters, and how to make it happen now*. Briefing paper for the UN Beijing + 10 Review and Appraisal.

Halpern, D. (2005) *Social Capital*, Cambridge: Polity Press.

Harriss, J. (2001) *Depoliticising Development: The World Bank and Social Capital*, London: Anthem Press.

Heward, C. (1999) 'Introduction: the new discourses of gender, education and development' in C. Heward and S. Bunwaree (eds) *Gender, Education and Development: Beyond Access and Empowerment*, London: Zed Books, pp. 1–14.

Howell, J. (2005) 'Introduction' in J. Howell and D. Mulligan (eds) *Gender and Civil Society: Transcending Boundaries*, London: Routledge.

Keck, M. and Sikkinik, K. (1998) *Activists Beyond Borders*, New York: Cornell University Press.

Kirk, J. (2005) 'Gender, Education And Development: Are Women Teachers Women in Development?' *Canadian Journal of Development Studies*, 26: 633–49.

Kruse, S. (2002) 'SWAPs and Civil Society: The Roles of Civil Society Organizations in Sector Programmes', a report prepared for the Norwegian Development cooperation

(NORAD). Centre for Health and Social Development. Available online at: www.sti.ch/pdfs/swap279.pdf (accessed 23 September 2006).

Mayer, M. and Rankin, K. (2002) *Social Capital and (Community) Development: A North/South Perspective*, Antipode: Blackwell Publishing.

Minkoff, D. (2001) 'Producing social capital: national social movements and civil society' in B. Edwards, M. Foley and M. Diani (eds) *Beyond Tocqueville: Civil Society and the Social Capital Debate in Comparative Perspective*, Hanover: Tufts University.

Molyneux, M. (2002) 'Gender and the silences of social capital: Lessons from Latin America', *Development and Change*, 33, 2: 167–88.

Mundy, K. (2006) 'Education for all and the new development compact', *Review of Education*, 52: 23–48.

Mundy, K. and Murphy, L. (2001) 'Transnational advocacy, Global civil society? Emerging evidence in the field of education', *Comparative Education Review*, 45, 1: 85–126.

Portes, A. (1998) 'Social Capital: Its Origins and Applications in Modern Sociology', *Annual Review of Sociology*, 24: 1–24.

Prakash, S. and Selle, P. (2004) 'Why investigate social capital?' in S. Prakash and P. Selle (eds) *Investigating Social Capital: Comparative Perspectives on Civil Society, Participation and Governance*, New Delhi: Sage Publications.

Putnam, R. (1993) *Making Democracy Work: Civic Traditions in Modern Italy*, Princeton, NJ: Princeton University Press.

—— (1995) 'Bowling Alone: America's Declining Social Capital', *Journal of Democracy*, 3: 65–78.

—— (2000) *Bowling Alone: The Collapse and Revival of American Community*, New York: Simon and Schuster.

Quibria, M. (2003) 'The Puzzle of Social Capital: A Critical Review', *Asian Development Review*, 20, 2: 19–39.

Rao, N. and Smyth, I. (eds) (2004) *Partnerships in Girls' Education*, London: Oxfam Publishing.

Rankin, K. (2002) 'Social Capital, Microfinance, and the Politics of Development', *Feminist Economics*, 8, 1: 1–24.

Rose, P. (2002) 'Is the non-state sector serving the needs of the poor: evidence from East and Southern Africa', November 2002, DFID, for the World Bank's World Development Report 2004. Available online at: www.ids.ac.uk/ids/govern/pdfs/roseWDR.pdf (accessed 20 July 2006).

—— (2003) *The Education Fast Track Initiative*. Report prepared for Action Aid on behalf of the Global Campaign for Education. London: ActionAid.

Saegert, S., Thompson, J. and Warren, M. (2001) 'The role of social capital in combating poverty' in S. Saegert, J. Thompson and M. Warren (eds) *Social capital and Poor Communities*, New York: Russell Sage Foundation.

Schnuttgen, S. and Khan, M. (2004) 'Civil Society Engagement in EFA in the Post-Dakar Period'. Working Document for the Fifth EFA Working Group Meeting. Consultative Consultation of NGOs on EFA regional focal points and UNESCO. Available online at: portal.unesco.org/education/en/file_download.php/0c0af8d6.htm (accessed 20 July 2006).

Smith, J. (2001) 'Global civil society? Transnational social movement organizations and social capital' in B. Edwards, M. Foley and M. Diani (eds) *Beyond Tocqueville: Civil Society and the Social Capital Debate in Comparative Perspective*, Hanover: Tufts University.

Stromquist, N. (2003) 'Contributions and challenges of feminist theory to comparative education research and methodology' in J. Schriewer (ed.) *Discourse Formation in Comparative Education*, Frankfurt: Peter Lang.

Subrahmanian, R. (2005) 'Gender Equality in Education: Definitions and Measurements', *International Journal of Educational Development*, 25: 395–407.

Szreter, S. and Woolcock, M. (2004) 'Health by Association? Social Capital, Social Theory, and the Political Economy of Public Health', *International Epidemiological Association*, 33: 650–67.

UNESCO (2002) 'The Dakar Framework for Action, Education for All: Meeting our Collective Commitments'. World Education Forum, Dakar, Senegal, 26–28 April 2000. Paris: UNESCO. Available online at: www.unesco.org/education/efa/index.shtml (accessed 10 August 2006).

—— (2004) *EFA Global Monitoring Report: Gender and Education for All: The Leap to Equality*, Paris: UNESCO.

Van Straven, I. (2002) 'Social capital: What's in it for feminist economics?', Working paper no. 368. Institute for Social Studies.

Watt, P. (2004) 'Keeping education on the international agenda: the Global Campaign for Education' in I. Smyth and N. Rao (eds) *Partnerships for Girls' Education*, London: Oxfam Publishing.

Woolcock, M. (1998) 'Social Capital and Economic Development: Toward a Theoretical Synthesis and Policy Framework', *Theory and Society*, 27, 2: 151–208.

—— (2001) 'The Place of Social Capital in Understanding Social and Economic Outcomes' in *Canadian Journal of Policy Research*. Available online at: 142.236.154.1/sp-ps/arb-dgra/publications/books/oecd/en/5-woolcock.pdf (accessed 12 September 2006).

Woolcock, M. and Narayan, D. (2000) 'Social Capital: Implications for Development Theory, Research, and Policy', *World Bank Research Observer*, 15, 2: 1–49.

Part II

Researching agency, engagements and empowerment

6 Researching transitions

Gendered education, marketisation and Islam in Tajikistan

Anise Waljee

This chapter seeks to explore the complex web of forces and factors that shape gender relations and education in 'countries in transition' – particularly countries that have moved through major economic, political and cultural transitions. These transitions may be the result of economic modernisation and progress might be relatively smooth. In other cases, these transitions are the result of occupation by another country, civil war, aggressive dictatorship and social upheaval. On the whole, gender studies of education in the context of development have tended to assume relatively stable social formations and smooth economic and political transitions (particularly in relation to the goals of Education for All). This stance is deeply problematic, not least since it can involve misunderstandings of the reasons for existing patterns of gender relations and their connections to educational systems, and also ignore or fail to notice the structures and processes of opposition represented by women's actions within such societies. Transitions within a nation state will impact differently on men and women and gender power relations will be disturbed by such transitional stages, sometimes metamorphosing into new temporary shapes. Transitional gender relations are not normally the focus of international gender studies in education, concerned as they often are with access and outcome patterns, or with conventions, traditions and cultural patterns that pertain to Western capitalist societies whence they originate. In the event, these studies can represent either restricted models of analysis that demonstrate a superficial causal relationship such as access, outcomes and performance or else they fail to address, or find wanting, the cultural and religious specificity and economic realities of nations in transition, or the cultural norms that frame gender relations.

This chapter challenges such gender approaches and suggests that they are not only in danger of misrepresenting a nation but impose their own strictures/judgements on a nation's progress in relation to 'outsider' criteria. I suggest that the relationship between gender and education cannot be analysed in isolation of the impact of transition on the changing gender relationships being negotiated in other spheres of community life besides education. We need to take account of how communities respond to imposed changes in their lifeworlds (Keshavjee 1998)[1] and how such communities respond to current social transformations (whether religious, political or economic). I hope to demonstrate, therefore, the power of an historical and socio-political approach to the study of gender and education in development, an approach that recognises the political complexities behind the official statistics of educational access and achievement.

My strategy is to use a national case study – that of gender and education in Tajikistan, one of the Central Asian countries that formed a part of the former Soviet Union. Tajikistan borders Kyrgystan and Uzbekistan in the north, China, Pakistan and Afghanistan in the south and east. The majority of Tajiks are Sunni Muslims and have been since about the eighth century onwards when Islam was first brought to the region and slowly gained ground (Johnson 2004). An exception is Gorno Badakhshan which is Shi'a Isma'ili Muslim. There is a small and dwindling minority of Christians, Jews and people of other faiths in the country. About 64 per cent of the population is ethnic Tajik, with Russians, Uzbeks and Tartars comprising the rest (Harris 2004).

In its recent history, Tajikistan has sustained three transitions: the Russian conquest (1860s–1917), Soviet colonisation (1917–91) and the current transition from communism and a planned economy to some form of democracy and a market economy since independence in 1991. With a population of about six million, 40 per cent of whom were under the age of 16, Tajikistan was the poorest of the Central Asian countries. During the Soviet period it had a real GDP of purchasing power parity in $s (ppp$) 2,180 in 1991 which, by 1996, had dropped in real value to less than 40 per cent of its 1989 value. However in 1991 the Human Development Index for Tajikistan was 0.629, comparable with the medium income countries' average of 0.649 (UNDP 1991 cited in Falkingham 2000). At that point, two-thirds of the population was rural, life expectancy averaged at 70 years and women formed 40 per cent of the labour force. Literacy rates were very high, at 96 per cent, and, significantly, women represented one-third of the higher education student population (Falkingham 2000).

The discourse that frames existing or emergent gender analyses in Tajikistan read this history in somewhat stereotypical ways. Since independence from the Soviet bloc, the education sector in Tajikistan has demonstrated reduced enrolment rates for girls and their early withdrawal from the school system at secondary level (UNICEF 2004). In 1990, there were 104 girls per 100 boys in general secondary school; in 1998, there were only 63 girls per 100 boys. The gender gap in higher education has also widened, from 58 girls per 100 boys in 1990 to just 34 in 1998 (Falkingham 2000).[2] This increasing gender disparity has been seen as evidence of the regressive tendencies associated with the reversion of Tajik communities to cultural and religious (Muslim) identities that traditionally have assigned – and relegated – women to the roles of caregivers and homemakers (Harris 2004; Asian Development Bank Report 2000; UNESCO/UNICEF 2000).

But the reality as I hope to show is far more complex. In contemporary Tajikistan, gender relations are contextualised in the political, ideological, economic and social upheavals that attended the collapse of the Soviet Union and the subsequent civil war over a decade ago. They are affected by the structural and systemic (economic) reforms that form a part of the transition from communism to capitalism and from a planned economy to a market one as this is directed by the international community in the form of the IMF, the World Bank and other NGOs. Against this backdrop, gender roles and relationships are played out, perhaps most significantly, in the realities of the struggle for survival in a society in transition, in the changing cultural values, beliefs and practices that this entails and in the urgency to understand and manage radically changed circumstances. Access, affordability, safety (for both boys and girls) and relevance, all recent, transition-related issues, contribute to parental decisions about who goes to school in these changed times and circumstances. These decisions are a *response* to the radical changes that transition has imposed on them in the economic, ideological and political spheres of life rather than purely an *expression* of traditional gender preferences in relation to education. That response to radical change is also shaped by the communities' experience of previous pervasive impositions on their way of life (i.e. communism) and guided by the various traditions of Islam that the communities adhere to.

I begin the case study by briefly discussing the last two decades of economic reforms on the educational system in Tajikistan before demonstrating how the processes of marketisation and commodification also affected community life. Within these transitional and transformed social contexts, gender differentiation associated with Islamic practices came to symbolise communal identity and resistance. In conclusion, I suggest that as gender scholars we need to be far more cognisant of such transitional histories when studying gender relationships and education in societies other than our own.

Education and gender in contemporary Tajikistan

As in other parts of the Soviet Union, the educational system in what is now Tajikistan was universal, hierarchical and vertically structured. The curriculum was information centred and vocationally oriented to meet the job market in a state planned economy (Cummings and Dall 1995; Sayer 2002). Under Soviet rule, 'truths' emanated from Marxist Leninist ideology and nothing else was felt to be necessary with respect to philosophical thought or debate. The system worked towards the creation of the (ideal) 'new Soviet man' whose values and identity would cut across ethnic, geographical and cultural differences in the name of egalitarianism. Free education was considered a fundamental right of both sexes and every child was assured of a fully subsidised, sound, basic education leading either to higher or vocational education and then to guaranteed employment. Education in pre-independent Tajikistan, therefore, comprised a comprehensive network of kindergartens and compulsory education from ages 7–15 years. Post-compulsory education was available at technical and vocational schools and a number of higher education institutions including the Tajik State University and the Pedagogical Institute among others. Aspiring teachers took courses in pedagogy and practising teachers received professional development every five years from in-service training institutions. They were provided with centrally created curricula, textbooks, teaching aids and syllabus. Each district had subject specialists who could support then in the classrooms.

However, since independence in 1991 there have been severe cuts to Tajik government expenditure in the education sector. The government's share of GDP dropped from 58 per cent in 1992 to 17 per cent in 1998 and education expenditure as a percentage of GDP dropped from 11.1 to 2.3 in the same period. The total state expenditure on education dropped from 19.2 per cent to 13.5 per cent. Hence, educational provision in Tajikistan has become uneven in quality and relevance and inequitable in access. Education is no longer free: parents pay for books, uniforms, school supplies, contribute to school repairs and subsidise the salaries of teachers. State schools and tertiary establishments now attach user fees to popular courses such as English, economics and IT. Dropping enrolment rates at all levels in the system reflect this erosion of universal education. Since 1990, enrolment rates have fallen for three to six year olds from 15 per cent to just 6 per cent; enrolment in compulsory education (ages 7–15) has fallen from 94 per cent in 1990 to 89 per cent in 1998 and enrolment in post-compulsory education (15–19 year olds) has fallen from 51 per cent in 1990 to 36 per cent in 1998. As a result, literacy rates, estimated at about 95 per cent in 1990 are now below 65 per cent and dropping. These dropping enrolment rates indicate an increasing gender divide in access to schooling and achievement. There is an increasing loss of women within the educational system.

Such cuts have resulted in deteriorating infrastructures, collapsing school buildings, the lack of teaching/learning materials, low and delayed remuneration, and there has been a steady drain of qualified personnel from the sector as teachers leave in search of better employment or to trade in the markets. Many also emigrated because of the civil war. Between 1991 and 1997, for example, the number of teachers in general education schools fell from 99,122 to 91,285. The quality of education continues to decline as high school graduates replace the professionals and teacher development institutions barely function (Falkingham 2000). Teaching as a profession has also suffered a loss in status different from that in other occupations. Teachers used to be considered the custodians of wisdom and moral values – they were the transmitters of the received ideology in communist times (Niyozov 2004). But the current transition, requiring a shift from one ideological position to a diametrically opposite one has called their knowledge into question and shaken their own beliefs (Vende 1991; Birzea 1994; Niyozov 2002). They are now held responsible for misleading the community and, as a result, they are reported to be deeply suspicious of the new order that might prove to be equally false. There has been a massive loss of confidence in – and amongst – teachers and a loss of confidence amongst teachers – attracting new recruits to the profession is a challenge (Niyozov 2001).

This crisis in education and the increasing gender differentiation however has also intensified because of external factors. Particularly significant has been the advent of a market economy system that challenges the moral values of egalitarianism, responsibility for the collective community, generosity and care of the weak that both communism and the community's Muslim heritage promoted. The education sector itself reflects the changing values and practices that the current transition is generating. Under the IMF and the World Bank management, structural reforms to education include rationalisation of provision, the introduction of user fees and the introduction of private provision alongside state schools.

Therefore, to assume that the erosion of gender equity in education can be explained as a simple dichotomy comprising a return to a conservative interpretation of Islam, on the one hand, and a resistance to yielding up freedoms already gained, on the other, would be superficial. The contrasting/differing outlooks of the communities on the place and role of women is better explained as their responses to their Soviet past and their particular reconnection with global Islam. But before we turn our attention to these other cultural–religious considerations, we need first to understand the impact of the transition to a market economy on gender relations in Tajikistan in the last 15 years.

The transition and gender relations: economic considerations

Under communism, the Tajik state and its citizens operated on the basis of a well-defined, well-understood social contract. The state ensured social and material security through a system of sophisticated and well-resourced social services provision including free education, health care and childcare, generous pensions and maternity allowances as well as guaranteed employment. In return, the citizen was required to be loyal and to accept the paternal oversight of the state in all his/her affairs as well as to forgo certain personal, including ideological, freedoms (Birzea 1994). Human and social capital were prioritised at the expense of economic efficiency and viability. The transition years (1991 to date) saw a rapid decline in all state obligations. Employment is no longer guaranteed; education, health care and social services now attract user fees – the physical infrastructure such as roads, electricity and communication networks, the basic amenities – are barely maintained, serviced or repaired and corruption is rising (UNDP 2006).

The collapse of the Soviet Union (1990) was rapid and total. Almost overnight, an entire political, ideological and economic system crumbled, leaving in its wake both initial euphoria, as nations either regained their former independence or came into being for the first time, and chaos, as they struggled with the complexities of the political, economic and social transformations in which they found themselves.[3] With budgetary support from Moscow suddenly withdrawn, the new nation states had to reinvent their political identities, rescue their collapsing economies and redefine/rediscover their moral frameworks (Birzea 1994). In Tajikistan, resurfacing ethnic identities and affiliations which were more clearly stratified along political lines than in other Central Asian republics found violent expression in a civil war (1992–3)[4] that also brought Islam into the political arena, Roy (2000).

This was transformation at its more radical. The ensuing deep sense of betrayal and abandonment led to a paralysis that precluded both a coherent response to the situation, as well as any analysis of what caused the collapse, that might have informed that response. As a result, the international community in the shape of the IMF, the World Bank, bilateral donor agencies and other NGOs, stepped in to direct the economic and social transition of the countries of Central Asia to a market economy and 'democratisation'. Their approach to the task, as we have seen in the education sector, is strikingly close to that of the communists 70 years ago in its total disregard for the value of what already existed and its firm conviction that what was being offered was self-evidently better.[5] The parallels go further. Then, as now, this was an external phenomenon that totally transformed the communities' whole way of life, over which they had little control, and that demanded of them that they adjust to an ideology (communist) that was diametrically opposed to the ideology they had been living by until that time. But while communism focused on modernising the communities through 'freeing' them from their religious fetters, the current transition seeks to globalise them through admitting them into the free market economy.

Embedded in this scenario are the demands of the international community for structural and systemic economic reforms that have their genesis in long established capitalist systems and are dictated in part by neo-liberal agendas (Stromquist and Monksman 2000). At the communal level, the transition to a market economy has led to widespread poverty in Tajikistan.[6] Disparities of income had always existed in Soviet times but the phenomenon is new in its universality. The human development index had dropped from 0.629 in 1991 to 0.540 in 1998 (UNDP 1991 cited in Falkingham 2000). What is evident in speaking to communities is how these macroeconomic policies of 'community self-reliance', 'privatisation of assets' and 'user fees' translate into the lives of ordinary people in Tajikistan.

Women appear to be the most affected by this economic transition. When market economics and the World Bank and IMF policies dictate that user fees should apply to social services, women as primary caregivers and as needing reproductive health themselves, are disproportionately affected by the resulting decline in quality and affordability of such services. Cuts in childcare provision, pre-natal and ante-natal care divert and reduce women's productive capacity. As old diseases (malaria, tuberculosis, malnutrition, chronic anaemia) resurface and new dangers (HIV/AIDS, narcotic dependence) appear, they put a greater strain on the scarce family resources and on women's time, as well as posing risks to their own health. Families increasingly turn to local traditional healers or simply wait longer before seeking conventional medical care (Falkingham 2000). The application of user fees to basic amenities such as electricity (where this is available) and telephones has resulted in families voluntarily cutting consumption resulting in increased cold-related illnesses such as pneumonia and bronchitis and in isolation. In winter in the rural mountain provinces the temperature can drop to as much as $-18°C$ with no heating for up to six hours at a time. Avalanches and snow falls can isolate villages for months and wipe out entire families and villages at a stroke and without warning.

The decline in infrastructure has had an impact on women in other ways as well. Lack of adequate and regular water and heating supplies have forced them to spend more time on household chores since this now includes fetching water and firewood from a distance for cooking and cleaning.[7] Women's workload has also increased since independence as they join the men on the farms as labourers. Given that the state can no longer provide adequately remunerated employment, there is more reliance on land for subsistence and more pressure on it. The corruption that attends land distribution in privatisation reforms has served to increase the gap between the well-off and the poor. Female headed households are particularly discriminated against since one of the criteria applied to land allocation is the ability to till the land (Falkingham 2000). Women are considered not capable of undertaking this activity (ibid). Yet they are solely responsible for all work in their kitchen garden that feeds the family as well as for bringing in water and firewood.

The demands on women's time has been cited as the main reason for their lack of participation in public life and leadership positions (Kanji and Gladwin 2000). The transition has disadvantaged women in the job market as well. During Soviet times, women were employed in the social sectors such as health and education. These were the areas where remuneration was traditionally lower and the government was slower to make the necessary adjustments after independence (Falkingham 2000).[8] Increased unemployment is leading to the migration of men to places such as Moscow leaving the women to take the total responsibility for the family. According to the IMF reports, a surge in remittances is one factor that has led to the impressive economic performance of the country over the last couple of years. Yet in effect the practice reduces social cohesion. The incidence of female headed households, already on the increase as a result of the civil war, is exacerbated. They receive intermittent and often intercepted and diminished monies from the absent men who sometimes marry a second wife.

While a full study of the emotional and psychological impact of transition is beyond the scope of this chapter, it is important to make a few remarks in passing. Transition has brought with it enormous stresses to communities not just through the drop in income, but also because of the strategies resorted to for coping with the poverty that threatens survival. In the initial stages of economic decline, the belief that this was a temporary setback caused households to borrow from others to maintain their families. Later, as the situation deteriorated, assets were sold off for essentials such as food, clothes, school fees, medicines. And finally, as the communities realised that the poverty they were experiencing was now chronic, families cut consumption to the very basics with women eating smaller portions of food to ensure the family had enough to eat (Falkingham 2000). Women were more concerned about how to provide food and more willing to borrow or trade to do so (Kanji and Gladwin 2000). Men, overwhelmed by the shame of not being able to provide for their families, often resorted to alcoholism, drug addiction and even suicide to obliterate the pain (Unicef 1999 cited in Falkingham 2000). Anecdotal evidence suggests that, at the height of the civil war crisis in the province of Badakhshan, the rate of male suicide increased, and throughout the country there is evidence that domestic violence is on the increase (Falkingham 2000; Harris 2004).

Poverty is a phenomenon that is both new and invested with such a deep sense of shame and failure that families still find it hard to use the term with reference to themselves (personal communication). Communism guaranteed the right to work and poverty under these circumstances could only be the result of individual negligence or indolence or weakness: all of which were anathema to the very ideology of communism. One corollary of this was that buying and selling was shameful, greedy and selfish (personal communication). Entrepreneurship was a bourgeois activity exploitative and demeaning. And it went against the cultural hospitality tradition to sell rather than to give to others what they were in need of.[9] But in Tajikistan as elsewhere, these cultural practices yielded to economic pragmatism. Gender roles, it seems, are being redefined by the need to respond to the pressures and exigencies of a market economy and the need to survive the transition and not simply by demands on the women to revert to their former roles in the pre-communist era. But if women have been the first to pay the price of transition they have also been courageous and enterprising, ready to take and hold new initiatives and create the space for their families' survival and their own development against enormous odds. The collapse of the Soviet Union saw women taking the lead in trading in the bazaars: an activity both foreign to their (ideological) experience and considered (culturally) demeaning but critical to their families' survival. As the transition to a market economy legitimised engagement in small enterprise activity, this has now come to be dominated by men.

Women are acknowledged to have a better business sense of what is likely to be in demand and what is not. And they are considered less likely to give away goods although they will be flexible about prices where they see genuine need (Kanji and Gladwin 2000). It is women who travel, for example, to Kyrgystan, Turkey and Dubai to buy the goods: their gender ensures that they are less likely to be intercepted to pay 'taxes' at unofficial 'checkpoints' along the way (Falkingham 2000). However this increases the already heavy burden on them even though it affords them mobility, freedom and the options to develop networks beyond family and clan constraints. This entrepreneurial partnership creates the space for a more equal relationship between the genders and contrasts sharply with the stereotypical view of women within Muslim societies being assigned to a more domestic and secondary role. A parallel space in education is evident both in the up-take of employment by young women graduates from rural provinces in urban towns and cities and even in neighbouring Afghanistan, living alone and away from their families, as well as in the small but increasing numbers of female graduate students abroad. It is telling that most conventional gender analyses in education look only at the student–parent population and do not seek to engage young, recently qualified, economically independent women to see how they have used the spaces opened up to them. It is this fragmented view of distinct 'sectors' that limits such analyses particu-

larly in communities where their lifeworld does not work in such compartmen-
talised ways.

Economic pragmatism has also seen women in rural provinces (such as
Badakhshan) becoming the main breadwinners even leaving their villages and
families to work with NGOs in the small provincial capital town or the
country's capital. Nor is this a trend for the young only. Older women, especially those with English skills, are in demand with the NGOs for their
experience as well as their translation abilities. The disruption to cultural patterns are felt both in the reversal of the norm of parents providing for children
(university graduates can now command up to 20 times the salary of a senior
government official if they can speak English and have some IT skills) as well as
in men staying in the villages to work whatever land there may be while their
wives live away during the week and return over the weekend, or even longer
intervals if their work takes them out of the province.

In the next section, in contrast with this modernising of gender relations, we
find spiralling differences between men and women in response to war, poverty
and the revival of community values and customs. Here we begin to see the role
that religion, in this case Islam, comes to play in this transitional society, creating new gender conditions that pull between the past and the present, the traditional and the modern, the local and the global. Any understanding of the
increasingly differentiated gendered patterns in education needs to take these
cultural scenarios into account.

Islam and gender: the cultural scenario

The Central Asian interpretation of Islam has always been distinguished by its
eclecticism, characteristic of Islam's ability to absorb foreign influences and
accommodate the prevalent, traditional customs and beliefs amongst the
peoples it encountered and converted. Under Soviet rule, overt religious practices were illegal but covert Muslim traditions and customs prevailed in all
communities, finding expression in marriage and funeral rites and in private acts
of worship in the safety of the family home. The way communities dealt with
the assault through education, first under the Russians and then under
communism, on their Muslim way of life is salient to understanding their
response to the current transition.

The introduction or rather imposition of an education system was almost
always a matter of furthering a tacit political agenda: visible 'benefits' had their
raison d'etre in invisible webs of control. Education while being presented as a
vehicle for modernising (the inferior 'other') was designed to undermine the
communities' culture and prevent potentially liberalising alliances with other
broader Muslim movements (Johnson 2004). Enforced school attendance compelled the nomadic Kazakhs and Kyrgyz into a sedentary life, curbing their
freedom of movement and association between communities; the introduction
of the allegedly easier Cyrillic script effectively disconnected the young from
their Muslim (Iranian or Turkish) past (Shorish 1984) and the closure of

Qur'anic schools (the *makhtabs* and the *madrassahs*) deepened the disjuncture between the communities and their religious and literary heritage as well as their access to prevailing Muslim political thought. Likewise, the emancipation of women, premised on the principles of universal suffrage through gender equity education policies had its basis in the breaking of traditional patterns of socialisation and in creating a new 'surrogate proletariat' (Johnson 2004).

The initial response of progressive elements within the community was to seek a compromise between the traditional and the modern but which would leave their lifeworld intact. The response took the form of the *Jadid* or 'new' movement in Muslim education concerned with developing a system of well-organised, standardised education through schools offering both secular and religious knowledge (*usul-i-jaded*). The movement was characterised by the emphasis it placed on the power of knowledge and the role of the human intel-lect, its belief that schools should be the focus of both religious and secular studies and its insistence on an organised, standardised, disciplined and system-atic approach to this more broad based education. It sought to expand the cur-riculum to include subjects such as history and geography and to change pedagogies to be more child centred, while retaining the core Islamic values and practices (Johnson 2004; Shorish 1984). The Jadidists also tried to establish indigenous literary language teaching and to create a more modern historiogra-phy, and to introduce contemporary literary and dramatic genres into the curriculum.

The Jadidists gained influence rapidly, offering both an intellectual and a political strategy that addressed the new realities with a revitalised, Muslim approach to knowledge, freeing it from the corruption and the 'obscurantism' that was rendering it obsolete under the traditional leadership in the region. (Johnson 2004). In the process, they antagonised traditional Islamic interests, since they challenged their status as the custodians of culture as well as know-ledge.[10] They also challenged the Russians who saw the development of indigenous languages as representing the first signs of nationalistic tendencies in the development of indigenous languages. As a result, the movement was bru-tally crushed but, as with the cultures and faith of the communities, the move-ment has lived on in the minds of progressive Muslims in the region. Its history has parallels, I suggest, with what is happening in the negotiation of gender roles in contemporary Tajikistan. Women there deal with the impositions of the current transition to a market economy that has radically changed the circum-stances of their lives and community networks of support as well as with the conservative Muslim elements within the communities that would seek to hold women back in the name of Islam – a process that began with the civil war.

There are other fallouts from the civil war: safety overrides all other consider-ations. Communities had to look inwards to their own codes of conduct for security and survival. It was the veil that offered protection to women in these circumstances. The powerful symbol of the status of Tajik women, ironically, resided not in the Soviet policies of equity and equality (Soviet doctrine had lost its credibility by then) but in the deep-rooted respect for what the veil symbolises in gender relations in Islam going back in time to an era prior to Soviet rule. This is not to suggest that all veiled women were automatically safe, but it does signify an important aspect of gender relations regulated by Islam that is often overlooked. However, what was a strategy for protection has subsequently become the determining discourse in some regions of Tajikistan such as Garm and is legitimised in the name of religion. In these circumstances, women are relegated to the home, their opportunity for participation in public affairs or even in determining their own affairs is severely circumscribed and controlled. As noted earlier, girls in these communities withdraw from school at an early age and are often married off prematurely.

However, within Tajikistan, there is considerable diversity in the ways in which communities interpret Islam and gender roles in relation to it. In the province of Badakhshan, for example, gender relations are dictated by the long established cultural and religious practices of the majority who are Shi'a Isma'ili Muslims and followers of the Aga Khan. Their interpretation of Islam is characterised by an emphasis on the role of the intellect, the importance of an individual search for meaning that is close to the Sufi tradition, and an emphasis on the development of women. These principles are unequivocally interpreted as a fundamental/neces- sary part of faith. Isma'ili Badakhshani women neither veil themselves as a matter of course,[11] nor are their lives controlled and confined by the male members of the community to the extent that is common in some parts of Tajikistan. Nor is this a purely Ismai'li phenomenon. In urban Dushanbe, young (Sunni) women increas- ingly strike out on their own from unsatisfactory relationships with men, demon- strating their resourcefulness and independence economically and emotionally.

Another factor affecting gender and education is the role *external* Muslim influences have played in shaping communities' outlook on Islam and women within Islam. Soviet gender egalitarianism represented the secular approach to gender and social relations. With the reconnection to world Islam, this seculari- sation of relations is rejected, as are atheism and other ideological principles of the Soviet regime. In some parts of Tajikistan, therefore, there is a nostalgic if unrealistic desire to return to pre-capitalist gender relations. Moreover, the liberal form of interpretation of Islam in Central Asia is now being called into question by the more conservative custodians of the faith in the diaspora who conveniently but mistakenly hold that the years of atheistic teaching and isola- tion from the *Ummah* (Muslim community) have diluted the communities' understanding of their faith. Conservative elements have therefore sought to re- orient the Tajiks to their own form of Islam with some success in places like Garm. In contrast, in Badakhshan the globalising influences have been one of a reconnection with the larger Isma'ili *Ummah* that has encouraged the promo- tion of women and the education of girls.

It is in the cultural arena perhaps that the greatest care needs to be taken in seeking to understand gender issues and gender relationships and their impact on education. As I have already indicated, cultural norms and values are in a state of transition. In a society in transition towards capitalism, family and extended family relationships are particularly impacted upon. Where economic stability is no longer guaranteed, traditional communal norms of hospitality, of mutual support and care are under strain. Families can become isolated and women are less able to combat ill-health, shoulder the burdens of extra work-loads without extended family help and can experience increased marital viol-ence. Men, forced to migrate for work or reluctant to return home because of their role in the civil war, create new families by resorting to second marriages. They are sanctioned within Islam but not subject to the attendant protective laws for women under Islam because Tajikistan is not (nor do its leaders wish it to be) an Islamic state. Conversely, women, especially younger women, are negotiating their space both within their marriages[12] as well as exerting the right to opt out of unsatisfactory marriages and become economically independent.[13] Divorce is not always seen as a stigma from which there is no reprieve: mar-riages between divorced women and single men are not uncommon even when the women have children from earlier unions. Gender relations in Tajikistan comprise a complex web of influences that scholars would do well to acknow-ledge if they are not to present a partial or even distorted picture of the reality.

Analysing gender in other societies: final reflections

The study by Western scholars of gender relations in Central Asia raises issues of voice and interpretation that need to be asked. In the light of the discussion in this chapter, we need to be wary of Western notions of feminism. We need to look at the way that feminism itself has been redefined by women outside Western norms and how the lives of men and women have been reshaped by such norms, especially when imposed upon different cultures.

One perspective worth considering is whether the Tajik communities' response to the assault on their way of life by communism gives us more insight in under-standing how women work with and around some of the constraints placed on them than a study of contemporary gender differences. Far from enacting roles, donning, changing and removing masks, women do what the community has traditionally done: they live a paradox in which they are able to allow multiple realities to co-exist side by side without themselves being pulled asunder through the diametric opposition of those realities. Educators taught atheism in school in the full knowledge that practices at home remained religious. Communist party officials, once they were retired, took on religious roles and were well able to move between party politics and personal belief. While there was no doubt an element of contradiction in what they did, pragmatism prevailed and they lived the paradox between their public and private lives. Women likewise manage to live the paradoxes that they are confronted with: discriminated against in employ-ment and then left to head households alone; experiencing domestic violence but also able to assert economic independence; going abroad to study but getting married first so they can take their spouses with them.

When Tajik women have the time and capacity to engage in an analysis of their own strength they are unlikely to define their feminism by drawing exclus-ively on either their Soviet and previous Islamic history, or on the current external interpretations of Islam visited on them. Also, might they in keeping with the rejection of these transmissions not reject the Western values imposed on them through economic and political transition and globalisation? They may even engage with other Muslim women to whom their access is as yet limited and one day challenge an Islam that is interpreted for them by men. What kind of feminism might emerge from these considerations and perspectives is something that remains in the realm of supposition until Tajik women choose to engage Western academics in a debate about their perspectives on gender issues, on equal terms rather than as subjects of other academics' studies. In the meantime, those of us who seek to research gender relations in education in such contexts as Tajikistan need to ensure that our research is not another (this time an academic) imposition or colonisation of their situation with all that the term implies. It might be wise to engage in an approach where we look to ourselves even as we look out at other cultures. It is important to remember that economic necessities, domestic violence, the repression/exploitation sexually and otherwise of women is as common a feature in our so-called liberated Western societies as it is in Tajikistan. What we write as researchers needs to remain interim, tentative, offering questions rather than providing answers. It should push the debate towards the uncertainty and the richness of diverse perspectives rather than steering it towards the conviction that we can understand and resolve what is and will remain a complex web of gender relations, framed in various transmissions and transitions and not yet spun to completion.

Ultimately, as this chapter has sought to demonstrate, Western (even feminist) conceptualisations of gender relations will always remain at best incomplete and at worst misguided. To gain a better understanding of what is played out in such relations it is crucial to pay more attention to political, economic and cultural context so as to understand how communities have historically dealt with imposed ideologies that are diametrically opposed to their values. Above all, it is important to recognise that Tajik women are already engaged in redefining their own gender roles and their voices and their actions already lead the way. If we cannot follow, it is because we have not learnt the language of their struggles and their successes.

Notes

1 The term is used by S. Keshavjee (1998) to denote the particular characteristic of Islam that it is not just a faith but a whole way of life. It accurately describes the inter-relatedness of what in Western terms has been dichotomised into the 'secular' and the 'sacred'.

2 These national figures, however, do hide the differential regional responses to gender. For example, in Badakshani, parents were found not to differentiate between educating girls and boys even when poor. Considerations included need: 29 per cent felt girls needed education more than boys, 27 per cent would educate the boy as the potential future breadwinner. The rest felt the ability of the child would be the deciding factor (Kanji and Gladwin 2000).

3 In the case of Central Asia, the artificially constructed 'republics' under Soviet rule

had been carefully designed to placate nationalist aspirations but prevent the development of any genuine economic viability as independent nations (Roy 2000).

4 Although the war supposedly ended in 1993, hostilities went on much longer and the peace treaty was not finally signed in 1997. Sporadic civil unrest continued until 2000.

5 While the interventions and policies of the INGOs are critiqued by African writers who attest to their hegemony, their capacity to render governments economically dependent and take decision making out of their hands in the name of transparency and 'the market' (Hoppers 2000), INGO roles in the former Soviet Union are not subject to the same scrutiny.

6 Women are reported to define an impoverished life as their inability to keep up networks through sharing hospitality, the lack of education, the inability to participate in public affairs (Kanji and Gladwin 2000).

7 Children as young as four years old are trained to carry even small amounts of water from the standpipes while the adults may have to go further afield.

8 Also personal communication from the Deputy Minister of Education.

9 During the civil war, families that had some goods to sell from better-off members outside the country found it hard to 'sell' anything and ended up sharing them. Speaking to communities in 2004 about what has changed for them, the assertion that 'if you take a cup of sugar even from your sister she'll ask for it back' attests to the loss felt in community networks that could have eased economic hardship in the past.

10 For a full treatment of the Jadids, see Adeeb Khalid (1998).

11 A headscarf is worn in the event of a death and when travelling to the more conservative regions such as Garm.

12 Women in career employment negotiate the right to work late and on weekends, and to travel extensively for weeks if necessary before entering into marriage (interview notes with two young women as part of my forthcoming Ph.D).

13 A young mother of two who discovered her husband was unfaithful stayed in the marriage on condition that she could set up her own independent business.

References

Asian Development Bank Report (2000) 'Tajikistan: 2001–2003', Country Assistance Plans, Dushanbe: Asian Development Bank.

Birzea, C. (1994) *Education Policies of the Countries in Transition*, Publishing and Documentation Service, Strasbourg: Council of Europe.

Birzea, C. (1996) 'Education in a World in Transition: Between Post-communism and Post-modernism', *Prospects*, 26: 673–682.

Brown, B. (1998) 'The Civil War in Tajikistan 1992–1993' in D. Mohammad-Reza, G. Fredric and A. Shirin (eds) *In Tajikistan: the Trials of Independence*, Richmond, Surrey: Curzon.

Cummings, W.K. and Dall, F.P. (1995) *Implementing Quality Primary Education for Countries in Transition*, New York: UNICEF.

Djalili, M.-R., Grare, F. and Akiner, S. (eds) (1998) *Tajikistan: The Trials of Independence*, Richmond, Surrey: Curzon.

Falkingham, J. (2000) 'Women and Gender Relations in Tajikistan', Country Briefing Paper, Dushanbe: The Asian Development Bank.

Harris, C. (2004) *Control and Subversion Gender Relations in Tajikistan*, London: Pluto Press.

Heyneman, S.P. and DeYoung, A.J. (eds) (2004) *The Challenges of Education in Central Asia*, Charlotte, NC: Information Age Publishing.

Hoppers, O. (2000) 'Globalisation and the social construction of reality: affirming or unmasking the "Inevitable"' in N. Stromquist and K. Monksman (eds) *Globalization and Integration and Contestation across Cultures*, Lanham, MD: Rowman and Littlefield Inc.

International Monetary Fund, (2005) 'Republic of Tajikistan: 2004', Article IV Consultation and Fourth Review Under the Poverty Reduction and Growth Facility-Staff Report, Washington: International Monetary Fund.

Johnson, M.S. (2004) 'The legacy of Russian and Soviet education and the shaping of ethnic, religious, and national identities in Central Asia' in S.P. Heyneman and A.J. De Young (eds) *The Challenges of Education in Central Asia*, Charlotte, NC: Information Age Publishing.

Kanji, N. and Gladwin, C. (2000) *Gender and Livelihoods in Gorno-Badakhshan*, Dushanbe: The Mountain Societies Development and Support Programme.

Keshavjee, S. (1998) *Medicines and Transitions: The Political Economy of Health and Social Change in Post-Soviet Badakshan – Tajikistan*, Ph.D thesis, Cambridge: Harvard University Press.

Khalid, A. (1998) *The Politics of Muslim Cultural Reform: The Jadids of Central Asia*, Berkeley: University of California Press.

Niyozov, S. (2002) 'Understanding teaching in post-Soviet, rural, mountainous Tajikistan: case studies of teachers' life and work', unpublished Dissertation, Ph.D, Toronto: University of Toronto.

Niyozov, S. (2004) 'The effects of the collapse of the USSR on teachers' lives and work in Tajikistna' in S.P. Heyneman and A.J. De Young (eds) *The Challenge of Education in Central Asia*, Charlotte, NC: Information Age Publishing.

Roy, O. (2000) *The New Central Asia the Creation of Nations*, London: I B Taurus.

Sayer, E.J. (ed.) (2002) 'Opening Windows to Change: A Case Study of Sustained International Development, Vol. 1': *Oxford Studies in Comparative Education, 1*.

Shorish, M. (1984) 'Planning by Decree: The Soviet Language Policy in Central Asia', *Language Problems and Language Planning*, 8, 1: 35–49.

Stromquist, N.P. and Monksman, K. (ed.) (2000) *Globalisation and Education: Integration and Contestation across Cultures*, Lanham, MD Rowman and Littlefield Inc.

UNDP (2006) 'Survey on corruption', available online at: www.Principal.tjk.undp.org (accessed 12 June 2006).

UNESCO/UNICEF (2000) 'Where have all the girls gone?' Available online at: www.unicef.org.

UNICEF (2004) 'Where have all the School Girls in Tajikistan Gone'. Available online at: www.unicef.org/girlseducation/index_school_girls.html (accessed 30 April 2004).

Vende, V. (1991) 'Transformation Dynamics in Complex Systems', *Journal of the Washington Academy of Sciences*, 81, 4: 163–184.

7 Researching gender

Explorations into sexuality and HIV/AIDS in African contexts

Fatuma Chege

Ranking among regions of the world that can ill-afford modern medicine for managing HIV and AIDS conditions, many of the countries in the Eastern and Southern Africa Region (ESAR) have embraced education as the potent 'social vaccine' against HIV infection that is accessible to their communities. However, cultural beliefs around matters of sexuality and reproductive health issues have continued to thrive in an apparent culture of silence that hampers effective HIV/AIDS education and the participation of children and young people in the related life skills. Many duty bearers, including parents and teachers, lack accurate sexual health knowledge and the life skills that are key to effective sexuality and HIV/AIDS education (Pathfinder 1999). Sexuality issues pose problems even among educators who are expected to offer guidance in terms of knowledge and attitudes as noted in the studies cited herein.

HIV/AIDS in the ESAR continues to affect not only the quality of education at all levels but also the demand for education in terms of quantity, performance and transition, thus retarding the achievement of Education for All (EFA) goals and by extension, the Millennium Development Goals (MDGs), particularly those that target education, health and poverty. Evidence abounds on how the rates of HIV infection and AIDS-related attrition among teachers and school administrators has continued to erode the progress made towards achieving universal primary education (UPE) targets (Kickbusch and Payne 2004; UNAIDS 2003). In some of the countries of Eastern and Southern Africa, the situation raises great concern for the future of education as noted in Zambia, where an estimated 815 primary school teachers died of AIDS in 2003, thus corresponding to 45 per cent of teachers trained that year (UNESCO 2004). This means that nearly half of the newly trained teachers replaced the teachers who had died instead of boosting the existing teaching workforce. According to UNESCO (2004), the impact of HIV/AIDS in the education sector will be greater than is currently projected, mainly because of future orphans whose parents are currently living with HIV/AIDS. There is also a view, that although some countries of Eastern Africa (such as Uganda, Ethiopia and Kenya) have shown a decline in HIV infections, most of the success stories tend to be more a consequence of public educational practices outside the formal school system where the majority of children spend their waking time.

Most studies recommend a comprehensive approach to the HIV/AIDS epidemic that embraces not just the adults (teachers and parents/guardians) but also the children in their active capacities as members of families and communities as well as their capacities as pupils/students of particular schools and other educational institutions. Based on his work with children on sexuality and HIV/AIDS life skills, Mabala (2003), however, points out that many children appear fatigued of being targeted as the problem and threatened with death should they indulge in sexual relations. He contends that, if treated positively as sexual beings with capacity to feel and think for themselves, children can respond appropriately and make the HIV/AIDS scourge an opportunity through which to revitalise response to the pandemic in new and innovative ways that are young-person friendly. According to Mabala (2003):

> If given the chance, if given the knowledge, life skills and opportunities they require, young people, as rights holders, as the group most threatened by AIDS, and as the most energetic members of society, can lead an effective response and help to shape policies and programmes that are effective in preventing the spread of HIV/AIDS.

This chapter argues that education systems, particularly in sub-Saharan Africa where sexual intercourse is the leading medium for HIV transmission, ought to invest in curricula that embrace issues of sexuality. The development of this strategy depends, I want to argue, first from a life-cycle approach that is gender sensitive and, second, by focusing on the potential of young people and children in the fight against HIV and AIDS. Those who are affected most need to be empowered in the best way possible with skills that would enable them to deal with the challenges in their lives. Such empowerment should be built on knowledge and information about gender and sexuality, about HIV and AIDS and also on the teaching of relevant and complementary skills and positive attitudes.

Arguably, collaborating with children who constitute the future generation of any nation is bound to yield social and health dividends that have long-term positive implications. Instead of looking at young people as part of the problem of the HIV/AIDS pandemic, we need to look for strategies and solutions for the malady from among them. One way of doing this is to engage young people in the process of HIV/AIDS education, not just as consumers of information but also as generators of relevant knowledge that is responsive to their needs, aspirations, anxieties, fears, hopes and dreams. This should be enhanced by teacher capacities designed to respond to the relatively complex combination of teaching, caring and protecting, not only the children in their care but also the self. It is in this context that this chapter highlights the role of children and young people in the ESAR in generating knowledge and providing insights on gender, sexuality, sexuality education and HIV/AIDS and how such different types of knowledge can be used to enhance positive gender relations.

Researching gender and sexuality with African children

The project on which this chapter is based was funded by UNICEF, Eastern and Southern Africa Regional Office (ESARO). It involved field research in a range of countries comprising Botswana, Kenya, South Africa, Rwanda, Tanzania, Zambia and Zimbabwe. The aim of the project was to explore the potential of young people and children to generate information on issues of sexuality and HIV/AIDS education, which could be used as a curricular resource in schools. Our observations revealed that teachers tended to shy away from engaging their students with interactive learning activities, particularly in the area of sexuality. Conversely, many of the children and young people in our project exhibited eagerness to address issues of gender and sexual relations with friendly adult researchers. Evidently, the kinds of relationships that the researchers established with the young people were exactly the type that teachers ought to establish when addressing sensitive issues of sexuality and HIV/AIDS. However, many of the teachers who taught sexuality and HIV/AIDS education faced serious difficulties when responding to sensitive questions about sex and sexuality (Pattman and Chege 2003). They expressed feelings of embarrassment and vulnerability during the lessons, resulting in most of them adopting a moralistic, didactic and authoritarian approach in order to assert their positions and protect themselves from ridicule. To enhance their authority and protect themselves from ridicule and possible embarrassment, the teachers avoided learner-centred methods such as group discussions, brainstorming, debates and visual activities such as drawing. Instructively, these pedagogic approaches are exactly what the researchers used with considerable success in engaging young people in addressing issues of sexuality and HIV/AIDS.

In order to enable young people to participate as key actors in the process of generating data, the researchers were trained, specifically in young person-centred approaches that enabled them to work consciously with young persons and children as subjects who were experts on issues regarding their gendered and sexual lives (see Chege 2001). This strategy complemented the logic of qualitative research methods that acknowledge the position of researchers and their research subjects as actors who engaged intersubjectively, influencing each other through the research process. The researchers were encouraged to pay particular attention to what the young people said in the interviews with regard to their relationships with others of the same or opposite sex. They were also trained on how to capture *unspoken* language including the silences and other non-verbalised communication for purposes of analysis (see Brown and Gilligan 1992, and Taylor and Gilligan 1997). Hence, emotional tones, facial expressions, physical disposition, how much or how little children spoke, as well as the interruptions by others and so on, became part of the data. Also underscored was the value of gender sensitivity, examining the similarities and differences of boys' and girls' 'performance' during interviews – whether in mixed or single sex groups, or individually. The researchers were also encouraged to form mixed teams of female and male, young and older people, with varied experience and fluency in the local language – in order to respond appropriately to different research situations, considering the local cultures that did not foreground the voices of children and young people.

The researchers were also trained on how to ensure that the group and individual interviews were conducted in a *gender sensitive* and friendly manner that was responsive to the particular research settings in which the young people were constructing their identities. Such settings included sites in schools, homes and community, as well as the different interview settings of different gender compositions and sizes. The need to let the subjects 'set the agenda' and dictate both the pace and direction of the interviews was stressed. The researchers were also encouraged to identify and pursue any pertinent points raised by the interviewees themselves.

Our project employed a number of methods for generating data from group and individual interviews, non-participant as well as participant observation, drawing, diary keeping and essay writing. Simulating group interviews was a major component of the research training. This involved engaging the researchers in criticising each other's performances and making suggestions for improving effectiveness of interviews, transcribing interviews and comparing notes on each other's transcripts. This activity proved to be core in raising awareness regarding the tendency by researchers to paraphrase what interviewees said, and thus distorting the interviewees' 'voices' to reflect the researchers' own interpretations or opinions. Simulations helped the researchers to recognise how their efforts to keep up with the interview schedules could sometimes preclude them from listening to, or even following up on, issues raised by the interviewees.

These interviews emerged as important sites where interviewees not only addressed the research themes but also the forum in which they expressed appreciation for the opportunity to talk about themselves and about issues that they perceived to be of importance to them, freely and without fear of intimidation. This could not be taken for granted as Davies (1999) rightly observed that the experience of participating in loosely structured interviews designed to enhance inter-subjective and dialogical relationships among research subjects as well as between them and researchers was a relatively new phenomenon for many African children. An important outcome of the interviews, in methodological terms, was the ability to solicit different types of data on sexuality among very young children, thus disproving popular arguments regarding the asexuality of the very young. By so doing, the different interviews that were facilitated by different categories of researchers, yielded good practices that could be adapted to inform pedagogical practices on matters of gender relations as well as sexuality and HIV/AIDS.

In addition, in some countries such as Tanzania, adolescent girls and boys were trained to work alongside experienced adult researchers in generating data on sexuality and HIV/AIDS. The young researchers doubled as community thespians who articulated drama and role plays developed around the research themes of sexuality and HIV/AIDS. In the community theatre an audience of adults and children of both sexes were engaged in observation and open discussions on themes presented. The discussions were facilitated by the young people with the help of adult facilitators and the process recorded on video for analysis.

In this chapter, I focus on interviews to demonstrate their potential in addressing gender relations, childhood sexuality and HIV/AIDS within educational settings. In the section below, I discuss the role of group interviews in eliciting sensitive data *and* developing empathy between the sexes. The key focus is not on the findings per se but also on the methodological value of the types of interviews that can serve as prototypes of pedagogical practices. The examples show how *single-sex* interviews were used to provide safe spaces for girls and boys to discuss sensitive issues of sexuality. They also demonstrate how *mixed-sex forums* were created in safe environments to expose and challenge oppressive gender relations. As a result, the group interviews became important venues whereby young people were able to talk freely and in uninhibited ways about sex, sexual relations, HIV/AIDS and other pertinent concerns, without feeling threatened by possibilities of humiliation, violence or stigmatisation.

Interviews and the fallacy of sex for the under sixteens

One of the major issues facing HIV/AIDS and sexuality education in the ESAR is the question regarding the appropriate age for introducing sexuality and HIV/AIDS education to children. This question hinges on the politics surrounding children's sexual innocence, which is founded on the assumption that children are born asexual and that they only become sexual at some stage in the process of their maturing. In this study, this assumption posed a major hindrance. National governments, through their ministries of education problematised HIV/AIDS and sexuality education in ways that made it impossible to conduct interviews on sexuality with children below sixteen years old. They argued that children who were below this age did not have ideas of sex and hence, this kind of study was bound to corrupt the presumably innocent minds of children, making them sexually active before adulthood. For instance, like many of the teachers and parents who were interviewed, personnel in the Ministry of Education in Zimbabwe were of the view that children under the age of sixteen either did not have sex or did not even think of having sex. By implication, this kind of assumption meant that young children would be denied the right to sexuality education, thus condemning them to a life of ignorance and uncertainties with regard to risks associated with sexual health, including HIV infection. Arguably, for both the girls and boys to learn how to become women and men, they need relevant knowledge, skills and the right attitudes that would deliver them into the future with confidence about their sexual and gendered identities.

Researchers in Zimbabwe were only allowed to interview school children that were over the age of sixteen. Importantly, however, researchers found that, contrary to the official claims regarding children's sexuality, older boys were engaging in sexual relations with younger girls aged ten and eleven. Apparently, while older girls had sexual relations with boys who were older than them, or with men, their male peers tended to seek sexual relations with relatively younger girls in what the boys described as the exploitative nature of boys and men. The excerpt below presents a mixed-sex group discussion where boys boast about what they described as their 'oppressive nature' towards the younger girls whom they bragged of 'sleeping with' and eventually 'ditching' them. In addition to these findings discrediting official claims regarding children's sexual innocence, the importance of the group discussion as shown below lies in concretising group dynamics of how interviews can serve to challenge oppressive gender relations as is observed in the interaction between the girls and the boys in the group. The gendered dimensions are explicit in the ways that the girls tended to romanticise love, while the boys talked about sex and violence.

CANAAN (B): These days, kids have big bodies. By the time she gets to Form 1, she will be having affairs.

INTERVIEWER: Even those in Grades 4 and 5 [aged 10–11 years]?

KOKAYI (B): Er, yes ... those in Grade 4, yes. Those are the ones we are jumping for these days. (Laughter)

INTERVIEWER: Why do you go for such young girls?

KOKAYI: You know what, yes, us boys have an oppressive nature. Once I sleep with a girl I lose interest in her, so usually I want to go for those who still have 'intact closed presents'. (Laughter and grumbles)

INTERVIEWER: What presents?

KOKAYI: Official opening – when you sleep with a virgin!

INTERVIEWER: So how do you feel about it?

KOKAYI: I feel good – it's nice. After the official opening, you can just ditch her ...

INTERVIEWER (TO THE GIRLS): So if a boy dumps you, what do you do?

DAYA (G): It depends on how much you loved him. If you really loved him, you will be pained.

KAMBO (G): I ... I won't feel that way. I will actually look around for a replacement boyfriend, and I will show off to the boy who dumped me.

MOYO (B): That's when I will beat you.

CHIPIWA (G): Why should you beat me? Isn't it you would have dumped me?

CANAAN: Yes, I will beat her because what she will be doing to me is painful, showing off to me ...

CHIPIWA: But it is you who would have ditched me.

In Zambia, study findings confirmed that thinking and acting sexually was not something that happened at the arbitrary selected age of sixteen. For example, young children aged six were observed constructing sexuality and presenting themselves as sexual beings who spoke openly and animatedly about sex. Interviews with these children further dispelled official make-believe that young children do not think or act sexually. The findings from Zambia are unique in that by the time of the study, no research in the ESAR had captured this kind of data with such young children speaking candidly about sex. This is perhaps because dominant public opinions regarding presumed child innocence may have influenced researchers in the relevant areas.

From the video recording of the interview with the Zambian six-year-old girls and boys, no signs of embarrassment or shyness were noted among the children who appeared so keen to contribute to the conversation about sex and 'having sex' that they leaned forward, put their hands up animatedly and even stood up to try and attract the interviewer's attention. Importantly also was the observation that the interviewer, a young woman in her twenties, sat between the boys and girls on an equal level that created a sense of belonging. She made effort to maintain eye contact with all the pupils around her and did not appear shocked or embarrassed by what the children said with regard to their engagement in sexual activities. They talked of having 'husbands' and 'wives' and named the human genitals explicitly or using representative terminologies. The interviewer kept smiling encouragingly and reassuringly and asked questions in a matter-of-fact way about what the children meant or did when they claimed to have had sex. The excerpt below demonstrates the freedom with which the children constructed themselves as sexual and gendered beings.

INTERVIEWER: How do you know whether you are male or female?
STEVE: By the small penis.
BWALYA, MUSONDA, BEATRICE AND ELIZA: [All smiling] Penis ...
STELLA: [Smiling] Vagina ...
INTERVIEWER: What do you do with the penis and the vagina?
BEVE (B): [have] sex.
INTERVIEWER: Who do you have sex with?
GELI (G): With my husband.
INTERVIEWER: Where do you have sex?
BEVE: [Holding chin and smiling] In the bush or bathroom ...
MUSODA (B): [Holding his head and smiling] Under the bed ...
GELI: [Playing with a bottle and looking shy] In a small house.
INTERVIEWER: Where is the small house?
GELI: In the bush.

Arguably, it is precisely because of the kind of relaxed, friendly, non-judgemental relationship that the interviewer established with the young children that the interview yielded the kind of data cited above. Contrary to popular belief that 'sex talk' was gendered in terms of who should or should not speak about pertinent matters, the interviews with the young Zambian children demonstrate clearly that both the girls and the boys were keen to speak about sex in uninhibited ways. It is noteworthy too that at a relatively young age, the Zambian children talked about their identities in heterosexual relationships in a manner similar to that of much older, post-pubescent children. Even as some developmental psychologists, influenced by Freud, have argued that the experience of sexuality for young children is qualitatively different from sexuality as experienced by adults, Gregory (1987), for example, confirms the research findings with regard to children's tendency to seek sexual pleasure with themselves or heterosexually. Gregory observes that:

> By and large the [sexual] explorations of the child are sensually diffuse rather than erotically specific, though well before the onset of puberty both boys and girls may masturbate to some kind of orgasmic experience without there being, in the boy, any ejaculatory consequences.
>
> (ibid.: 705)

Very specifically, the interviews with young people (including those in pre-pubescent stage) show that when working with children, the social context is a key factor that determines the level of confidence among the interviewees and the nature of content in what they could possibly share with adult educators or researchers without fearing punishment. Hence, the place and the people present – female and male – often played a vital role in determining how children constructed themselves, and what they said about themselves in relation to others, in terms of gender and sexual relations. This underscores other findings on multiplicity and fluidity of identities (Hall 1992) and the way these are enacted differently in different contexts and with different people. This has important implications for educators – particularly sexuality and HIV/AIDS teachers – who need to reflect (and encourage their pupils to reflect) upon the ways in which they constructed their identities and positioned themselves in relation to others of the same and opposite sex.

Becoming the 'other'

Based on discourse theory, which requires that what the different sexes say about themselves and others be treated as constructions rather than descriptions of their identities, this study captured the process in which femininities and masculinities were constructed as polar opposites and lacking similarity. In an attempt to elicit gendered perceptions of one gender by the other, girls and boys in the study were asked to imagine that they had changed sex for one day. The outcome of this research activity was that girls and boys in the different countries expressed aversion at the idea in almost similar ways and, consequently, portrayed the polarity with which they constructed gender identities. The common revulsion expressed suggests that many of the girls and boys were strongly invested in constructing themselves in opposition to their views of the opposite sex. Notably, even adults expressed similar revulsion when asked to imagine that they had changed their sex for one day. For example in Zimbabwe, one Ministry of Education official described the question about changing sex as attempts in expecting the 'unnatural'. Further, in a dissemination workshop for this research, more men than women seemed be relatively more opposed to this idea with some of them claiming that only men with 'hormonal abnormalities' could imagine being women. It is noteworthy that schoolboys in South Africa and Tanzania constructed boys who expressed a willingness to become girls for a day, as 'homosexual'. In South Africa, homophobia seemed to play a signific-ant part in the ways that boys tried to assert themselves as masculine by warding off possible accusations of femininity. Declaring an interest in becoming girls clearly posed an imagined threat to male identities – implying just how fragile those identities were. Studies on boys and masculinity in Britain and other Western countries have also shown how preoccupied boys are with distancing themselves from girls and activities and characteristics that they define as femin-ine (e.g. Epstein 1997; Nayak and Kehily 1996, Frosh *et al.* 2002).

Findings from other countries in Eastern and Southern Africa are similar, thus strengthening the view that boys, more than girls have greater investment in the power-based masculine construct while girls, more than boys, invested more on the relational and character attributes that are identified with feminin-ity. The interview excerpts below demonstrate these assertions by highlighting boys' and girls' sense of gender boundaries.

Zimbabwean girls would not like to be boys

INTERVIEWER: You will be sad if you were a boy – why?
CHIPO: Yes, because I will be having attitudes of a boy when I am a girl.
INTERVIEWER: What are the attitudes of a boy?
CHIPO: Drinking beer.
NYASHA: Taking alcohol.
JAPERA: Being attracted to simple things.

Kenyan boys would not like to be girls

WAKESA: Girls respect you and I will inherit property from my father.
CHEGE: Boys are brave and girls keep on laughing – I hate that.
GICHINGA: They are not easily raped.
KAGAI: They don't get pregnant.
MBUI: They will be head of the house.
MUKIRI: Girls wash dirty things in the house.

Some girls wish to be boys sometimes (Kenyan boys and girls)

ABSCO (G): Sometimes I'd like to be a boy. For example, if you want to go [out] with your friends, if you are a boy you just go. If you are a girl, you have to get permission first ... of course, they are concerned about you ... but at times you will just be wanting to go with your friends and just talk ... sometimes you will just be wanting to visit your friend, a girl-friend ... sometimes it is boring, because if I was a boy I would just come back anytime!
INTERVIEWER: Boys, do you ever want to be a girl?

BOYS: Ah, no.

OWINO (BOY): We only thought of it as kids when we were playing home ... as kids ... and were cooking. [Laughter from the group]

WARUI (BOY): It's unimaginable ...

The boys and girls associate masculinity with certain privileges and freedoms as evident in other gender and sexuality studies (see Commeyras and Montsi 2000; Chege 2001). Nevertheless, many of the girls in the study, like the Zimbabwean girls, expressed revulsion at the idea of imagining what it would be like to change their sex. They spoke about boys as being 'simple', 'immature' and 'troublesome'. In addition, many of the girls were keen to present themselves as 'good' by distinguishing themselves from other girls who were seen as behaving too much like boys by being too sexual, going out, drinking and attracting people of the opposite sex. This may explain why the Zimbabwean girls characterised boys in the way they did, distancing themselves as 'good' girls from these popular characteristics of boys. But the strong desire of most girls to remain girls, despite the apparent attractions of being male may stem from a sense that girls enjoy more support from each other than the boys receive from amongst themselves.

Using the two-stage interview sessions, researchers encouraged the Zambian girls and boys to address problems of the other gender. In the first stage, same-sex groups were asked to identify the sorts of gender-related issues that they thought people of the opposite sex had to deal with. In a follow-up stage, the boys and girls came together to present and discuss their findings. Even with the evidence of polarisation and the expressed aversion of being the other gender, it was interesting to note how empowering single-sex group discussions were for the girls. Furthermore, the experience of working in single-sex groups clearly encouraged girls, in particular, to be more outspoken when they joined the ensuing mixed-sex group discussions. Researchers found that, in some of the mixed-sex plenary sessions, the girls were as outspoken and critical as the boys – a fact they attributed to the confidence and support they had gained in the single-sex group. It was also in such groups that girls and boys developed the kind of gender empathy expressed when they were asked to reflect consciously on the problems that the other genders encountered in society and their role in addressing the same. This experience reflects the pedagogical tenets of societal conscientisation (see Freire 1972).

Analysis of data showed that this two-stage strategy of group discussions addressing gender issues and relations could be effectively incorporated in the kind of learner-centred and gender-sensitive pedagogy for addressing HIV/AIDS and sexuality education. This would help embrace the learners' views as key resource materials in informing gender issues in education.

Gender expectations

One major problem that emerged consistently about boys revolved around the economic responsibilities boys were expected to fulfil, the better exam marks they were expected to achieve, their presumed susceptibility to peer pressure, their presumed physical toughness and sexual proclivity, and their relative detachment from their mothers and fathers. In a girls' group discussion in Zambia, participants empathised with the problems of boys, observing that:

> Boys faced problems at home mainly because they were considered stronger than girls. They were always given hard jobs to do [and] even when they can't do it, they will just continue because their parent commanded [them] to do so.

In addition,

> When men got married, they faced problems of looking after the family. [Also] unemployment and school dropout resulted in men being unable to meet expectations of supporting families. [Hence, boys are pressured to outperform girls in school.]

It was further observed that:

> Boys were teased by other boys and girls for being physically small and for having a small penis.

In Zimbabwe, rather surprisingly, given the ways in which the boys prided themselves in being 'free' and saw girls as subordinated people who were tied to the home, some teenage boys confirmed the girls' view that boys' advantage over girls was exaggerated on some issues. The boys complained about their parents favouring their sisters over them as captured in a boys' group discussion below:

CHARLES: If you have a sister, when she asks for money from your parents, they just give [it to] her without asking any questions. All she does is state how much she wants and she gets it. But for me, a boy, I have to explain and usually they don't give me the cash. They would rather buy me what I want than give me the money.

OWEN: My parents expect [a lot] from me. When I get what I call my best results, they still expect me to have done better, so we have problems. If I try to explain, they won't listen. They simply accuse me of being playful in school. I think they expect too much from me.

JONAH: In my family, I talk to my sisters and [we go] around together. But the way we are treated is different. The girls are regarded highly and us boys are simply brushed aside as being a mischievous lot. Even though my sisters are as mischievous as the boys, it's never discovered.

For educators and other duty-bearers, understanding the dilemmas facing boys and girls from their own perspective is primary to understanding how stereotyping works in the politics of gendering the sexes. Teachers can build on these understandings to improve on their interaction with students and even engage young people in their care to challenge gender differentiation with the aim of developing healthy gender relations based on empathy.

Allowing boys to address the problems facing girls was an equally important process of developing empathy as found in some of the research countries. When asked to identify the problems that girls commonly experienced, Zambian boys focused on sexuality claiming that girls were sexually disadvantaged because they were identified with unwanted pregnancies, rape, prostitution, early marriages and sexual abuse. According to the boys, girls' problems emanated from the fact that they were constructed as the 'weaker' sex; their physical movements were restricted, they faced low academic expectations and were considered to be less powerful than boys. The girls concurred with these views and observed that:

> Teachers [both male and female] have a negative attitude against the girls. They say boys are brighter or cleverer than girls and treat them as such. For this reason, women were given lower jobs than men, like teaching and nursing. Where there are men, they will always be appointed for higher posts. Very few women are in high positions.

Notably, almost all the girls' groups identified sexual harassment and abuse as the most pressing problem faced by girls. Some of girls observed that sexual harassment was experienced from grandfathers to school peers. The following are some captions from girls' group discussions in Kenya:

> After [male] grandparents or stepfathers pay for school fees, they want sex from you in return.

> A teacher starts giving you more marks, invites you to his home and asks for [a] sexual favour. If you refuse ... you get to be a victim in class.

> Bus conductors or call boys touch you and make you [feel] uncomfortable. They use offensive language. They also favour you by not making you pay the fare.

Research findings from the interviews indicated that few girls and boys were aware of their rights as children. There were suggestions that the schools lacked functional mechanisms through which girls – or even boys – could channel their grievances with regard to sexual harassment or other gender constraining issues. Considering the link between power relations involved in sexual harassment and abuse and HIV/AIDS, sexuality matters needed to be addressed by schools, not just generally but also specifically and formally as key to healthy relations between the genders (see Posada 1999).

The value of bringing girls and boys together in an attempt to develop positive gender relations and empathy was captured in an interview with a Zambian parish counsellor, Mary, whose view was that nurturing healthy gender relations was dependent on teachers' attitudes and abilities to facilitate boys and girls to get together as friends. This, she argued, would help minimise the tendency to focus on sex as the only reason why the two sexes should relate. She explained that engaging girls and boys in various activities helped to demonstrate the many commonalities between the genders and consequently divert attention away from sex per se. She said:

> It is the same when you mix these boys and girls, you know that feeling [sexual] goes away. (...) We want to make them feel they are brothers and sisters, which should be the case. I remember when I was growing up ... sorry to take you back some 50, 60 years [laughter] ... we used to bathe with boys in a stream with no costumes and we didn't see each other's nakedness, because [of the way we] were brought up like. That is the culture we want to bring to these children ... that there is really nothing peculiar or strange about each other.

Mary's explanation implies that, separating boys and girls so that they do not engage in sex, may only serve to construct the relationship between them as essentially, and only, a sexual one. Hence segregating boys and girls, in her view, made them ultimately more likely to engage in sex when they did get the chance to mix.

Conclusion

Our findings from the countries cited in this chapter show that young people were eager to discuss sexuality and by extension sexual and reproductive health issues including HIV/AIDS with friendly and non-judgemental researchers. It is therefore important that gender relations that influence the nature and form of sexual activity be addressed with young people taking up their positions as sexual beings who are actors and experts of their experiential encounters. Development of empathy should be encouraged through group discussions where young people are provided the space to explore the merits and demerits of healthy gendered relations. Discussions of this nature should be done in a manner that is participatory, subject centred, gender sensitive and non-threatening.

In order to implement sexuality and HIV/AIDS education effectively among children and young people, the study suggests that teachers focus more on identities of girls and boys and the link between constructions of 'self' and 'other' and how this could put them at risk of contracting HIV. They also need to develop safe environments through single-sex discussions as well as mixed-sex settings in which both genders feel safe to express themselves, their expectations and fears. Teachers and other educators should encourage the development of empathy between the genders focusing more on commonalities between them.

It is important that educators present safe spaces through which to challenge the assumption that sexual desire is mainly male and that heterosexual relations invariably involve males harassing females. In order to minimise sexual vulnerability of girls and to establish more equal sexual relations between girls and boys, HIV/AIDS and sexuality education should be designed in ways that encourage girls to express themselves more openly regarding their sexual desires and expectations in relationships. While sexual harassment must not be tolerated in schools, it is important that schools respond not just by simply punishing boys, and potentially making them more hostile to girls, but rather through reflective discussions that promote mutual understanding and empathy and equal relationships between the genders.

Educators should be trained to tap the sexual experiences and practices of children and young people in order to tailor education for the very young children who have an equal right to access sexuality and HIV/AIDS education that is gender and age appropriate. Given the common taboos that surround talking about sexuality in many African communities – particularly between adults and children – it is clearly not easy to be an effective HIV/AIDS and sexuality education teacher. Teachers need to be enabled, through training, to take an active role in challenging misconceptions on gender relations and encourage girls and boys to respect each other, listen to one another and participate equally in all learning activities, including sexuality education. While research has shown that young people find it easier to talk about sexuality issues in single-sex groups, it is vital that such topics do not become characterised as exclusively male or female. We have seen that with assurance of protection from humiliation and harassment, boys and girls are willing and even eager to talk about these issues in the presence of each other, and even in the presence of caring and trusted adults.

Acknowledgements

I would like to thank Rob Pattman, who was a co-researcher in the UNICEF-sponsored project, for allowing me to report the findings of the project.

References

Brown, L.M. and Gilligan, C. (1992) *Meeting at the Crossroads: Women's Psychology and Girls' Development*, Cambridge, MA: Harvard University Press.

Chege, F. (2001) *Gender Values, Schooling and Transition to Adulthood: A Study of Female and Male Pupils in Two Urban Primary Schools in Kenya*, University of Cambridge, unpublished PhD thesis.

Commeyras, M. and Montsi, M. (2000) 'What if I Woke Up the Other Sex?', Botswana Youth Perspectives on Gender in *Gender and Education*, 12, 3: 327–46.

Davies, L. (1999) 'Researching Democratic Understandings in Primary School', *Journal of Education*, 61, May: 39–48.

Epstein, D. (1997) 'Boyz own stories: masculinities and sexualities in schools' in C. Griffin and S. Lees (eds) 'Masculinities in Education', *Gender and Education*, Special Issue 9: 105–14.

Freire, P. (1973) *Education for Critical Consciousness*, New York: Seabury Press.

Frosh, S., Phoenix, A. and Pattman, R. (2002) *Young Masculinities: Understanding Boys in Contemporary Society*, London: Palgrave.

Gregory, R.L. (ed.) (1987) *The Oxford Companion to Mind*, Oxford: Oxford University Press.

Hall, S. (1992) 'The Question of Cultural Identity' in S. Hall, D. Held and T. MacGrew (eds) *Modernity and its Future*, Cambridge: Cambridge Polity Press.

Humm, M. (ed.) (1995) *The Dictionary of Feminist Theory*, London: Prentice Hall/Harvester Wheatsheaf.

Kickbusch Ilona and Payne Lea (2004) 'Ensuring health security in an interdependent world' in Angela Drakulich (ed.) *Issues before the 59th General Assembly of the United Nations*, New York: UN.

Mabala, R. (2003) 'A Multi-Country Initiative to Promote HIV/AIDS Life Skills Education among Young People in Southern Africa'. UNICEF ESARO, unpublished report.

Nayak, A. and Kehily, M. (1996) 'Playing it Straight: Masculinities, Homophobias and Schooling', *Journal of Gender Studies*, 5, 2: 211–30.

Pathfinder International, Africa Regional Office (1999) *Adolescent Reproductive Health in Africa: Paths into the Next Century*, Nairobi, Kenya: The Africa Regional Office.

Pattman, R. and Chege, F. (2003) *Finding Our Voices: Gendered and Sexual Identities and HIV/AIDS in Education*, Nairobi: UNICEF ESARO.

Posada, C. (1999) 'Gender and rights analysis of life skills: HIV/AIDS prevention teaching and learning materials', Paper for UNICEF, Latin America and the Caribbean (TARCO) Region.

Taylor, J.M., Gilligan, C. and Sullivan, A.M. (1997) *Between Voice and Silence: Women and Girls', Race and Relationship*, Massachusetts: First Harvard University Press.

UNAIDS (2003) 'Progress report on the global response to HIV/AIDS epidemic'.

UNAIDS (2003) 'HIV/AIDS in sub-Saharan Africa'. UNIAIDS Fact Sheet, September. Available online at: www.unaids.org/html/pub/Publications/Fact-Sheets03/FS_AIDS_in Africa_2003.

UNESCO (2004) *Education For All. The Quality Imperative. EFA Global Monitoring Report*, Paris: UNESCO Publishing.

United Nations (2005) 'Beijing At Ten. Achieving Gender Equality, Development and Peace', *Anniversary Newsletter*.

USAID (2003) 'Increasing learning opportunities for orphans and vulnerable children in Africa'. Africa Bureau Brief. Available online at: pdf.usaid.gov/pdf~docs/PNACT987.pdf.

WorldWide HIV&AIDS Epidemic Statistics (2002). Available online at: www.avert.org/worldstatinfo.htm.

8 Schooling girls

An inter-generational study of women's burdens in rural Bangladesh

Janet Raynor

Bangladesh has recently been widely showcased as having made good progress in development generally, in education, and in girls' education in particular (UNDP 2005; World Bank 2005; Herz 2006). While it is true that girls' enrolment at both primary and secondary levels has increased significantly in the last few decades, with girls now being enrolled in roughly equal numbers to boys at primary and lower secondary levels (Ahmed *et al.* 2006), it is not yet clear how this affects the quality of the lives of women and girls: their capabilities, their ability to do and be what they have reason to value. Without intending to denigrate the quantitative progress that has been made, a superficial examination of indicators such as enrolment figures might give an impression that the burdens related to being born a girl in Bangladesh are being lifted along with enrolment – as evidenced by claims that the country has already achieved the third Millennium Development Goal of promoting gender equality and empowering women (e.g. Bangladesh Sangbad Sangstna 2005; Zia 2005). Such claims arise from a restricted understanding of gender, education and development, with attention further restricted to accessible indicators of gender disparity in education, reduced even further to basic education enrolment figures. Little attention has been paid to higher levels of education where gender gaps widen, nor to other possible gender disparities in education such as exclusion in the classroom, subject choice or achievement in schools, nor to what impact education might have beyond the classroom.

This chapter attempts to situate developments in education in Bangladesh within the context of the perception of women and girls as *burdens*, and the burdens they have to bear because of being born female. They are perceived as burdens because – for example – they are generally seen as 'non-productive', because of the need for large dowry payments to 'marry girls off', the perceived wasted investment in daughters who will be 'lost' after marriage, the need to preserve a girl's 'purity' and the related risk to family reputation should the girls be perceived to be breaking the moral codes. The burdens they have to bear because of being born female include generally having to work harder and longer for lower returns, discrimination against them in terms of education and employment, the low status they have in the family they are born into and marry into, the increased risk of physical and mental abuse, the restricted mobility imposed by a lingering purdah system, and even to having to eat 'least and last' within the family (Abdullah 1985). Linked to all this is the pervasive son preference, with an estimated 1.6 million 'missing' women (Seager 2005).[1] In this setting, I examine to what extent education (formal, non-formal or informal) is helping to ease women's burdens and increase their capabilities.

In this chapter, I first describe the ways in which a capability approach can be developed in a study of women's empowerment through education. I then describe some of the preliminary findings from an inter-generational study of women in a rural community in Bangladesh and how the capability approach can be utilised and developed.

A gender empowerment and capability approach

Bangladesh has made progress in overall enrolment of children in schools, and in having roughly equal numbers of girls and boys for the first eight years of school, but as yet there is no strong evidence that it has brought about significant societal transformation in terms of empowerment of women. According to the UNDP's annual human development reports (based on Amartya Sen's vision of a capabilities approach), Bangladesh's performance in 2003 in the overall Human Development Index put it just within the UNDP's 'medium development' category of countries. However, it remains among the lowest-ranking countries in terms of the Gender Empowerment Measure (UNDP 2003–2006). While it can be argued that this measure's focus captures only limited aspects of empowerment/disempowerment, such measures do highlight imbalances, even if they are only proxy indicators of an even wider set of inequalities.

Bangladesh's focus on access to schools as one proxy for empowerment is understandable. It is easy to quantify, and easier to achieve than the more challenging and less tangible qualitative aspects of education – including an education that helps develop empowerment, or the development of capabilities. But for education to help bring about empowerment, it is necessary to think about models of education that are 'inclusive, participatory and democratic', and to 'think critically and differently about pedagogy, about teaching, learning, in relation to young people's identities' (Arnot 2004: 3–4). Similar points have been made in relation to gender and education in Bangladesh (Raschen and Shah 2006). The focus should not be on how many girls we can get into schools – with schools sometimes of questionable quality, and with children sometimes learning questionable values. Rather, from economic, human development or feminist perspectives, the question should be: how can education lead to the empowerment of girls and women? I believe that a capabilities approach provides an appropriate conceptual framework and policy perspective for education, and can help identify ways in which education can contribute to empowerment.

Elaine Unterhalter (Chapter 2, this volume) examines ways in which basic needs, rights and capabilities are used as justifications for gender equality in education, analyses the assumptions about equality and difference associated with each, and argues that a capabilities approach allows for a fuller picture of the extent to which education or schooling helps people lead lives they have reasons to value. Nussbaum (2000a, 2002), in her feminist modification of the more general capabilities approach developed by Amartya Sen (Sen 1980, 1999), argues that an understanding of 'the special problems that women face because of sex in more or less every nation in the world' is essential to an understanding of the more general issues of poverty and development, and that '(a)n approach to international development should be assessed for its ability to recognise these problems and make recommendations for their solution' (Nussbaum 2002: 48).

Intending the concept of capabilities to be as relevant in Chennai as in Chicago, Nussbaum's thinking was to develop and refine Sen's theory partly through considering the lives and thoughts of women in India. While there have been justified critiques of Nussbaum's representation of Indian women (as cited for example, in Robeyns 2005: 11), and while there are many differences between India and neighbouring Bangladesh (such as the dominant religion and size of country) there are more similarities than differences (such as the prevailing cultural practices and the shared colonial history) between these two countries. These similarities can be seen, for example, in Chanana's analysis of women and education in pre-independence India, which included what is now Bangladesh (1994). Also, the lives of the women in Nussbaum's studies (2002, 2003) appear quite similar to the lives of women I have met in Bangladesh. The issues Nussbaum addresses, of global application, could be considered, certainly in the first instance, as relevant to Bangladesh. To Nussbaum, the central question of the capabilities approach is 'What is she actually able to do and to be?' (2002: 58), and this is essentially the question I am asking in relation to girls' education in Bangladesh.

Nussbaum's list of ten central human functional capabilities allows for 'a thicker account of the goals of development in terms of a set of fundamental entitlements' (ibid.: 56). The capabilities she lists give a much wider vision than simply the future wifehood or motherhood that many studies focus on (e.g. Cleland *et al.* 1996; Amin and Lloyd 2002). Nussbaum has always stressed that her list is of general capabilities, open to revision to fit specific situations. My study of developments in women's education in rural Bangladesh uses this list as a framework to deepen the understanding of those 'special problems' (the burdens) that girls and women in poor families in Bangladesh face because of their sex, and through the recognition of the problems explore possible solutions that are or can be targeted through education. My starting point, therefore, has been to adapt Nussbaum's capabilities to the particular context of gender and education in Bangladesh.

'Empowerment' means many different things to many different people, but for the purpose of this study I take it to be synonymous with the capabilities that Nussbaum spells out. Education in Bangladesh is linked – among other things – to marriage options, the chances of being subjected to violence, dowry

Table 8.1 Nussbaum's capabilities modified

Nussbaum's capabilities ...	Girls and boys, women and men learning about:
1 Life	Essential aspects of areas such as laws and rights in relation to inheritance, marriage/child marriage, dowry, nutrition, immunisation or pre- and post-natal care.
2 Bodily health	Essential aspects of bodily health such as adequate nutrition and reproductive health, access to resources to enable continued good health, non-humiliating access to adequate sanitation facilities (including in schools, and including acceptable provision for menstrual hygiene management).
3 Bodily integrity	Laws, obligations and rights in relation to mobility, harassment, assault and sexual violence (including 'domestic violence'), and choice in matters of reproduction.
4 Senses, imagination and thought	Imagination, thought and reasoning – in a 'truly human' way, a way informed and cultivated by an adequate education, including, but by no means limited to, literacy and basic mathematical and scientific training.
5 Emotions	Being able to have attachments to things and people outside ourselves. Not having one's emotional development blighted by fear and anxiety.
6 Practical reason	Forming conceptions of the good and engaging in critical reflection about the planning of one's life.
7 Affiliation	(a) Being able to recognise and show concern for other human beings, to engage in various forms of social interaction; having empathy; having the capability for both justice and friendship and (b) having the social bases of self-respect and non-humiliation; being able to be treated as a dignified being whose worth is equal to others.
8 Other species	Being able to live with concern for and in relation to animals, plants and the world of nature.
9 Play	Being able to laugh, to play, to enjoy recreational activities.
10 Control over one's environment	(a) Being able to participate effectively in choices that govern one's life and (b) being able to access resources; having the right to seek education or employment on an equal basis with others, entering into meaningful relationships of mutual recognition with others.

Source: Adapted from Nussbaum 2002: 60–62.

demands, purdah and mobility, and financial empowerment – if not financial independence. Although such themes are included in the general Bangladeshi development literature, they are rarely considered in direct relation to education. Also much of the research relating to gender and education in Bangladesh has focused on easily quantifiable aspects such as school enrolment or age of first marriage, and gives little insight into how education impacts on the socially constructed reality of those who have traditionally been marginalised and unheard.

The study

My work in Bangladesh connected me to BRAC, the largest NGO in the country, and I was able to draw on its support in contacting families for this study. BRAC was set up in 1972 to work on relief and rehabilitation in newly independent Bangladesh, and has since focused on poverty alleviation and empowerment of the poor, especially women, in rural Bangladesh. The societal vision is 'a just, enlightened, healthy and democratic Bangladesh free from hunger, poverty, environmental degradation and all forms of exploitation based on age, sex, religion and ethnicity' (BRAC 2005). Its work attracts praise and significant funding from a wide range of development partners, reaching people and areas that the government has not been able to reach. It is particularly well known for its non-formal education programme.

The study I conducted is a form of inter-generational research involving girls and women in rural Bangladesh. The focus is on a small number of families, interviewing school-age adolescent girls, their mothers and paternal grandmothers (these grandmothers were chosen because of the influence within the patrilocal marriage system that the mother-in-law may have over household decisions). Defining women by reproductive roles – as mothers or grandmothers – can be restricting. However, because of the research design and the fact that interviews spanned three generations in each family, the participants were inevitably linked through reproduction. Therefore, it would be artificial and unhelpful to avoid using family relationship terms. But where I use terms such as mother or grandmother, it is not because she is *a* mother, but because she is *the* mother or grandmother of someone in the study, and this is directly relevant. Similarly, such terms are used to locate each person within the generational structure of the study (older, middle or younger generation). The inter-generational study is of particular interest in terms of the history of Bangladesh as a relatively newly independent country. The older generation was of school age – but unlikely to have been allowed an extended education – when what is now Bangladesh was known as East Pakistan, and a few were of school age under British rule up to 1947. The middle generation was of school age at or around the time of the 'war of liberation' from Pakistan in 1971, a time of major disruption to most aspects of life, including education. But the younger generation was born around the time (1990) of a marked increase in the likelihood of girls being allowed to go to school and stay in school. Thus, it is reasonable to expect to see marked changes and different viewpoints.

In the context of such an inter-generational study, the distinction between formal, non-formal and informal education was also important. By *formal education* I mean that undertaken in schools, following the national curriculum or that of the Islamic education system (*madrasahs*). All the girls I spoke to had formal education at least up to Class 6, and some were in the tenth, eleventh or twelfth year of school. Few of the mothers or grandmothers had had much formal education; although some had a few years of basic schooling, none had gone beyond primary level. *Non-formal education* – in the context of this study

– is that provided by BRAC, such as in BRAC primary schools, or the Adolescent Development Programme (ADP) that supplements the education provided by formal secondary schools. Some of the girls had attended BRAC primary schools and most had been part of the ADP. None of the women had been part of any BRAC education initiative, but several had had some non-formal Islamic education in their homes or that of a neighbour. *Informal education* I use to describe learning that is acquired outside of any formal or non-formal structure, as with the learning that takes place within the home in relation to skills traditionally developed by girls and women – such as cooking, sewing or market gardening.

A capabilities focus on the views and experiences of these different generations helps give different perspectives on the meaning of education and empowerment over time. This can facilitate an analysis of patterns of empowerment, or shifting concepts of empowerment over time. An inter-generational history allows for thick, cumulative descriptions spanning long periods, obtainable in a much shorter time than in a longitudinal study, and can indicate changes that can take place in subsequent generations rather than in just one lifetime. Empowerment and education can be seen within a gender line (in this case, of women) in the context of family structures, as well as in the wider world.

As part of my study, I spoke to representatives of the three generations in seven families, each interview lasting about an hour, and each person interviewed on two occasions about six months apart. After the first round of interviews, transcripts were analysed, leading to a list of themes/questions to be followed up or initiated in the second round. The interviews took place in a rural district I shall call Naripur, and all names, place names and other indicators that might aid in identification of an informant have been changed. Naripur is one of the poorest districts in Bangladesh, with less than 15 per cent of households having electricity. Over 70 per cent of household heads have had no education, and under 45 per cent of households have one or more members who have completed five years of schooling (these members will often be the children, the first generation to attend school for a significant period of time). The district has one of the lowest rates of school enrolment for both girls and boys, but there is higher participation in NGO education ('Naripur' facts drawn from Amin *et al.* 2002; Huq-Hussain *et al.* 2006). Through my work with BRAC, I had some familiarity with Naripur, and this knowledge helped inform the interviews. These were loosely structured around Nussbaum's list of capabilities, but with conversations moving in directions determined at times by participants and at times by myself, allowing for revelation of information that might not have been forthcoming in a more structured interaction. As Nussbaum says, 'we need to rely on the ingenuity of those who suffer from deprivation: they will help us find ways to describe, and even to quantify, their predicament' (2002: 73). Keeping Nussbaum's list in mind enabled me to keep focused during the interviews, and to examine – for example – how girls' or women's lives may be affected by the presence or absence of a specific capability, or which capabilities can best be developed through some form of education.

Education easing women's burdens?

The accounts the women and girls gave of their lives ranged from fascinating to depressing to heart-breaking to inspirational, sometimes all of these in one person's story, and I was left with an immense admiration for these women taking what little control they could over what limited opportunities they had. A number of recurring topics or themes emerged, including – for example – agency, attendance, career plans, curriculum, decision making, dowry, family, inequalities, literacy, livelihoods, marriage, menstruation, mobility, numeracy, poverty, role-models, security, stereotyping, school stipends, subject choice, teachers and toilets. Only a very small number of these can be touched on in this chapter. Here I concentrate on using a capabilities lens to observe similarities and differences across the three generations.

With the older generations, *empowerment* – if acknowledged at all – was framed within the domestic setting and traditional family roles. Most had not been to school; their informal education was linked to a strengthening of traditional roles (which in turn could be linked to either empowerment or disempowerment), but was not perceived as education at all. To them, 'education' is about schooling. This perception led to a devaluing of their own knowledge and skills, and there was evidence of feelings of inferiority in relation to the daughters and granddaughters whose education they are now supporting. This reduced the capability of affiliation and self-respect in that the women do not see themselves as equal to others. The extract below shows Morsheda (grandmother) not attributing any formal educational value to her own skills, her conception of 'maths' being restricted to the arithmetical calculations she has seen her granddaughter doing.

JANET: Can you think of any other occasions when you use maths?
MORSHEDA: [silence] ...
JANET: For example, when you're cooking or sewing, and you need to measure things?
MORSHEDA: No ... when I cook, I just put in the ingredients according to my ideas. I don't measure anything, I don't use maths. Most of the women in our country don't use measures.
JANET: I know, but that's a mathematical ability – getting the proportions right.
MORSHEDA: I don't see that as maths.
JANET: What about sewing? Do you do sewing?
MORSHEDA: Yes. I make lots of things.
JANET: Do you use maths to do this?
MORSHEDA: There's no maths there.

Interestingly, Morsheda originally said she had no education, but later told me she had gone up to Class 5 in a *madrasah*. Her original denial of any schooling was partly because she did not see what she learned in that school as 'education' any more than she sees what she has learned informally as such. She asked her grandmother to withdraw her from school because she was being harassed by boys between there and home ('If you want me to keep my dignity, my reputation, don't send me to school any more.'). Her reputation – and thus chances of a 'good marriage' – was her strength and priority. However, this not only led to limited opportunity for affiliation outside the home, it also exemplifies the absence of the capability of bodily integrity, with the concern for that integrity eclipsing a concern for education, and the wider set of capabilities education could help develop.

Zubaida, the mother of one of the girls doing well at school, did not go to school herself, but on being questioned acknowledged that she had some sort of training in preparation for her life as a wife and mother. She was married at the age of 12, but stayed in her parents' home until she had started menstruating ('became a woman') – about six months later. During this period she underwent an apprenticeship.

JANET: OK. Now, who taught you about things like looking after babies?
ZUBAIDA: My mother, and grandmother – I learned from them.
JANET: What about things like cooking and household jobs?
ZUBAIDA: After I got married, when I stayed six months in my parents' home, my grandmother taught me everything. How to prepare rice for cooking, how many vegetables I need for that type of fish, and how much … everything. Cooking, and household work, how to sweep, how to manage, how to look after children and everything.
JANET: So that was your education, really.
ZUBAIDA: … Yes, and after the training, I was prepared to go to the new household.

This 'apprenticeship' led to her being received favourably into her new family, and being given preferential treatment by her mother-in-law. My questions allowed her to see herself as having been educated in some way (and visibly pleased at this new view of herself), but she bitterly regrets not being literate. Her son lives in another part of the country and he writes to her but she cannot read his letters, and nor can she write to him. This restricts her ability to maintain attachments to her son (i.e. a restriction of the capability of 'emotion' in Nussbaum's sense).

With her son living elsewhere, Zubaida has good reason to value being literate, but this view is not shared by all. A surprising number of those grandmothers or mothers who were literate or who had sent their children to school had negative views of the value of their education. Here is Morsheda again, once she had admitted to having attended school, and to being literate:

JANET: … You're literate, you have up to Class 5 education. Can you tell me what practical use your literacy has in your life?
MORSHEDA: No use. There's no use.

Another grandmother, who had sent her children to school:

JANET: Do you think your children got anything valuable from their education?

NASREEN: No. Nothing, no benefit.... Three children, two of them are just staying at home, and another one, the older one, he went to a madrasah, and now he's going from village to village talking about ... but he's illiterate.... He went up to Class 9, but ... he can only sign his name.

This exemplifies some of the disincentives to send children to poor quality rural schools, and the lack of paid employment for those who have been to school, and makes it easier to understand the devaluing of formal education. However, one mother, who did not see her own schooling as having been directly useful to her, now saw it as having some value:

JANET: OK. Did you learn anything in your five years of schooling that helped prepare you for your married life?

AFROZA: No.

JANET: So what do you see as the value of your education?

AFROZA: It has very limited use, our education; because all the time we're busy with the family and household work ... looking after my parents, cooking ... but when the children are studying sometimes I help them with their studies. Not with their maths, but I help them to learn Bengali. That's the use of my learning.

This is reminiscent of the mantra often heard in Bangladesh: 'if you educate a mother you educate a family' – that is, her education is instrumental, a means of transmission to her children, rather than a way of significantly expanding her own capabilities or an easing of her own burdens. Again we can see that formal schooling – as it is in Bangladesh – has very little relevance in the lives of many older women in rural Bangladesh. It is surprising, therefore, to learn of the hopes that the mothers and grandmothers have for the education of their daughters and granddaughters – hopes which bear little relation to their own experiences. These hopes are shared by the daughters, all of whom see their education as a way of building a life they have reason to value, and one which they hope will be very different to their mothers'. In one way or another, hopes were expressed for the development of all the capabilities on Nussbaum's list, from learning about inheritance rights (Nussbaum's 'control over one's environment') to 'being educated' negating the need for a dowry (self-respect/'affiliation') to being able to engage in critical reflection in the planning of one's own life ('practical reason'). Most were linked to an easing of burdens; all involved visions of increased empowerment and one that was different from that of the older generation.

Significantly, however, the aspects of education that were most valued by the girls were those gained through the non-formal education that most of them had received – that is, through BRAC. In particular, they valued what was offered through BRAC's adolescent centres.

JANET: OK, you've been to secondary school, and [the BRAC programmes]. Which did you like best? Which do you think was most useful to you?

ROUSHAN: I like [BRAC] best, we learned about important things, like periods and child marriage.

JANET: Did you learn about these at school at all?

ROUSHAN: There's one lesson about periods in Home Economics. It tells us that we need to keep clean ...

JANET: Right ... And you said that you thought the lesson on child marriage was important. Did you learn about that in school?

ROUSHAN: Umm ... I'm not sure. We had some discussions with a teacher about it.

JANET: Ok. And do you remember anything else that you covered in [BRAC] that you also covered at school?

ROUSHAN: ... Yes, there's a paragraph about HIV/AIDS in science, in biology.

Through BRAC, Roushan has been equipped with the knowledge she needs to manage her menstruation (which also helps prevent her being absent from school), and with knowledge of the laws and advocacy arguments useful in arguing against child marriage. Here, we can see a girl using her capability of 'senses, imagination and thought'. We can see Rehana thinking in 'a way informed and cultivated by an adequate education, including, but by no means limited to, literacy and basic mathematical and scientific training' (Nussbaum, 2000b). The education she has received has obviously helped develop her potential agency. However, this knowledge came not from her formal schooling, but from BRAC. Her 'schooling' only gave her cursory information on these important matters, or – as with child marriage – not as part of the formal curriculum. What is in the formal curriculum does not give her adequate information (for example, a paragraph on HIV/AIDS in school, compared to a whole unit in the BRAC course). Discussions with the girls showed that equally important to attending the *Kishori Kendro* was the opportunity for affiliation and friendship, and the chance to relax, to play games and to read magazines.

Although all three generations had great hopes for the opportunities that could be opened up by a formal education for the younger generation, there were numerous examples of the formal system limiting those opportunities. An example, from Roushan again, is given here. When I met her, she was in Class 10 – the year of the Secondary School Certificate exam – and getting good grades in all subjects. However, her options had already been restricted:

ROUSHAN: I wanted to do science, but there were no other girls who wanted to do science.

JANET: Not one?

ROUSHAN: No, not one. There was only me who wanted to do science, and the teacher asked me to do arts. Because there was no other female in the science group, only males doing science.

JANET: So how did you feel when the teacher said that?

ROUSHAN: I felt bad ... I wanted to be a doctor, that's why I wanted to do science.

This represents a severe limitation of a number of capabilities. Although Roushan displays the ability to plan her own future (to study science so that she could go on to study medicine), that plan has been destroyed by cultural practices that discourage girls from taking science, which led to her being the only girl wanting to study science, and the teacher's reluctance to let her enter the class. The teacher's decision was in no way based on her academic ability. There were many such examples of gendered restrictions. As in this example, some restrictions were imposed by the school, and several of the girls had similar stories. Other restrictions were imposed by families, often giving in to community pressure and expectations, or financial priorities. Quite a few of the girls (and the women of older generations who had been to school) told of having to attend lower quality schools than their brothers because of concerns for the girls' security in travelling to more distant schools, or of – unlike their brothers – not being able to have the necessary extra tuition to do well in their exams (private tuition is seen as a standard part of formal education in Bangladesh). All lead to and represent a reduction of empowerment possibilities.

Unlike the older generations, the girls valued what formal educational opportunities they had, even though they were aware of some of the limitations placed on them simply because they were girls. They saw their education as increasing their earning potential, negating the view of them as non-productive, and reducing the pressure on them to be 'married off'. Another positive theme that emerged, an aspect of the girls 'being educated', was already evident and benefiting the older generations, and that was the children in the role of advisers. There were several instances of parents deferring to their 'educated' daughters (for example, in selecting the best school for a younger sibling), or learning from their children. Most of these examples – such as laws relating to dowry or child marriage, or menstrual hygiene management or nutrition – were linked to the BRAC non-formal education. Such stories were told with pride by all generations – the mothers and grandmothers proud of their educated daughters and granddaughters, and the girls proud of the enhanced status their education gave them within the family. This sense of self-esteem and being able to command respect from others was seen to be one of the most important capabilities developed, and it develops regardless of the quality or content of the education received. This alone helps to ease some of the burdens.

Generational effects and capabilities

While it is clear that just the fact of being seen to be 'educated' is in itself an enhancement of capabilities and that being educated is seen as a path to wider empowerment possibilities, there is indication that some capabilities are not being developed well through education, while others are actively being inhibited. This seems to be particularly true of the formal education system. Girls repeatedly reported how they especially valued what they had learned through BRAC, and although the BRAC programmes do not have an explicit link with capability approaches, it is much closer than the formal system to helping develop central human functional capabilities. Moving away from a preoccupation with access and enrolment, a capabilities framework can help highlight to what extent and in which areas education can enhance or reduce chances of living a life one has reason to value. Such an approach provides a useful framework for an examination of the impact of education, and also for helping to shape the content. For example, if we can see that education is not enabling the capability of having control over one's environment, then the curriculum, content, processes and practices can be adjusted so that such a capability can be developed.

In a chapter of this length, it has not been possible to detail the evidence of generational shifts, nor to address all of the capabilities in Nussbaum's list, but there is enough information to indicate that an analysis shaped by a capabilities approach can illuminate the changing impact of the changing nature of education, and in what ways education can help increase agency and empowerment. Table 8.2 is a tentative summary of selected capabilities and their meanings to the three generations studied. The three capabilities chosen are ones that preliminary analysis indicates have particularly strong links with education.

As for the value of value of inter-generational research, a study of this type can show the shifting understandings of the meaning, value and purpose of education, and also of what it means to feel empowered. Although the older generations of women – if they had any formal education – placed little value on it in

Table 8.2 Generational effects on capabilities

	Bodily integrity	*Practical reason*	*Affiliation*
Mother-in-law (period of colonial rule)	'Purity'/reputation a powerful influence on life chances – more important than schooling	Planning of own life done mostly by others, but helping shape lives of younger generations	Very strong affiliations within the family, interactions with others determined by older males
Mother (period of independence war)	As above for self, but willing to push for daughter's increased mobility	Still little control over own destiny, but more likely to be willing to argue for sending daughters to school	Limited beyond the family, but the independence war widened potential interaction with others
Daughter (period of expanding educational opportunities)	Willing to brave the world outside the home, learning about laws and rights	Likely to plan a life involving regular paid employment, putting off marriage and controlling family size	Attending school automatically increases circle of contacts, but gendered biases may restrict further opportunities for girls

their own lives, both they and the younger generation had enormous hopes for what opportunities education might open up to the girls, and saw education as helping reduce the burdens of women. Their hopes may be over-optimistic, but the girls in this study can be seen as part of a new wave of educated young women who might just have the chance to take more control over their own lives. An expansion of girls' education is just one of the changes taking place in rural Bangladesh. There are also increased livelihood opportunities, less pressure for girls studying or earning to be married early and more possibility of girls achieving more of their potential, which are central concerns in a capability approach. The better-attuned their education is to their valued beings and doings (and a capabilities analysis helps highlight this), the better their chances of success.

Note

1 The concept of 'missing women' highlights the higher mortality impact on women related to unequal treatment in areas such as nutrition and medical care (particularly in Asia). See Amartya Sen's controversial article: 'More Than 100 Million Women Are Missing', New York Review of Books, 1990, copy available at: ucatlas.ucsc.edu/gender/Sen100M.html (last accessed 29 December 2006).

References

Abdullah, M. (1985) 'Seasonal Variations, and the Intra-household Distribution of Food in a Bangladeshi Village', *American Journal of Clinical Nutrition*, 41: 1305–1313.
Ahmed, M., Nath, S.R., Hossain, A. and Kalam, M.A. (2006) *Education Watch 2005 – The State of Secondary Education: Progress and Challenges*, Dhaka: Campaign for Popular Education. Available online at: www.campebd.org/download/EW2005Full-ReportEnglish.pdf (accessed 1 June 2006).
Amin, S. and Lloyd, C.B. (2002) 'Women's lives and rapid fertility decline: some lessons from Bangladesh and Egypt', *Population Research and Policy Review*, 21, 4: 275–317.
Amin, S., Mahmud, S. and Huq, L. (2002) *Baseline Survey Report on Rural Adolescents in Bangladesh*, Dhaka: Department of Women's Affairs, Ministry of Women and Children's Affairs, Government of Bangladesh.
Arnot, M. (2004) 'Gender equality and opportunities in the classroom: thinking about citizenship, pedagogy and the rights of children'. Paper presented at the Beyond Access seminar: 'Pedagogic Strategies for Gender Equality and Quality Basic Education in Schools', Nairobi, 2–3 February 2004.
Bangladesh Sangbad Sangstna (2005) Bangladesh finds World Summit fruitful: Reaz. News from Bangladesh. Available online at: www.bssnews.net/index.php?genID=BSS-06-2005-09-198id=7 (accessed 8 May 2007).
BRAC (2005) About BRAC: BRAC. Available online at: www.brac.net/about.htm (accessed 29 December 2006).
Chanana, K. (1994) 'Social change or social reform: women, education and family in pre-independence India' in C. Mukhopadhyay and S. Seymour (eds) *Women, Education and Family Structure in India*, Boulder, CO: Westview Press.
Cleland, J., Kamal, N. and Sloggett, A. (1996) 'Links between fertility regulation and the schooling and autonomy of women in Bangladesh' in R. Jeffery and A.M. Basu (eds)

Girls' Schooling, Women's Autonomy and Fertility Change in South Asia, New Delhi and Dewberry Park, CA: Sage Publications.

Herz, B. (2006) *Educating girls in South Asia: promising approaches*: UNICEF ROSA. UNGEI. Available online at: www.ungei.org/unicefrosa_educatinggirlsinSouthAsia.pdf (accessed 6 June 2006).

Huq-Hussain, S., Khan, A.U. and Momsen, J. (2006) *Gender Atlas of Bangladesh*, Dhaka: Geographical Solutions Research Centre/USAID.

Nussbaum, M.C. (2000a) *Women and Human Development: The Capabilities Approach*, Cambridge: Cambridge University Press.

Nussbaum, M.C. (2000b) Women and work – the capabilities approach: The Little Magazine. Available online at: www.littlemag.com/2000/martha.htm (accessed 28 November 2003).

Nussbaum, M.C. (2002) 'Women's capabilities and social justice' in E. Molyneux and S. Razavi (eds) *Gender, Justice, Developments and Rights*, Oxford: Oxford University Press.

Nussbaum, M.C. (2003) 'Women's education: a global challenge', *Signs: Journal of Women and Culture in Society*, 29, 2: 325–355. Available online at: www.journals.uchicago.edu/SIGNS/journal/issues/v29n2/290227/290227.web.pdf.

Raschen, M. and Shah, F. (2006) *Bangladesh Gender Profile*, Frankfurt am Main: KfW Development Bank. Available online at: www.kfw-entwicklungsbank.de/DE_Home/Service/OnlineBibl48/PDF-Dokumente/AMD_42_e.pdf.

Robeyns, I. (2005) 'Selecting capabilities for quality of life measurement', Social Indicators Research, 74, 1: 191–215.

Seager, J. (2005) *The Atlas of Women in the World* (3rd edn), London: Earthscan.

Sen, A. (1980) 'Equality of what?' in S. McMurrin (ed.) *The Tanner Lectures on Human Values*, Salt Lake City: University of Utah Press.

Sen, A. (1999) *Development as Freedom*, Oxford: Oxford University Press.

UNDP (2003–2006) *Human Development Reports*, New York: UNDP. Available online at: www.hdr.undp.org (accessed 11 July 2003 to 9 November 2006).

UNDP (2005) *Human Development Report 2005: International Cooperation at a Crossroads – Aid, Trade and Security in an Unequal World*, New York: UNDP. Available online at: www.hdr.undp.org/reports/global/2005/pdf/HDR05_complete.pdf (accessed 7 September 2005).

World Bank (2005) *Global Monitoring Report 2005: Millennium Development Goals – From Concensus to Momentum*, Washington, DC: World Bank/IMF. Available online at: www.web.worldbank.org/WBSITE/EXTERNAL/TOPICS/GLOBALMONI-TORINGEXT/0,,contentMDK:20445926~pagePK:64022011~piPK:292245~theSitePK:278515,00.html (accessed 4 June 2005).

Zia, B.K. (2005) 'High Level Plenary Meeting of the UN: Statement by her Excellency Begum Khaleda Zia, Prime Minister, People's Republic of Bangladesh'. Paper presented at the 2005 World Summit, New York, September. Available online at: www.un.org/webcast/summit2005/statements/ban050914eng2.pdf (accessed 21 January 2006).

9 Acts of citizenship

Women's civic engagements as community-based educators in Mumbai

Anju Saigal

This chapter examines the civic participation in education of low-income women in a slum community in Mumbai, India. The women work with a civil society organization (CSO), Pratham, which is engaged on a large scale with the country's efforts to universalize elementary education. The organization, and consequently the women's participation as community educators, had its genesis in the context of international and Indian policy emphasis on civic participation as an important and effective strategy for achieving the goals of Education for All (World Conference 1990; World Education Forum 2000). While such an emphasis on civic participation has undoubtedly created spaces for active citizenship in the educational arena (see for example, Collective Consultation of NGOs on Education for All 2001; Jagannathan 2001; Robinson 2000), the domain of civil society itself is generally left unproblematized. As Alvarez *et al.* (1998: 17) observe, civil society is rarely 'one homogeneous happy family ... [It] is also a terrain of struggle ... [intersected by] unequal power relations, and the enduring problems of racism, hetero/sexism ... and other forms of exclusion'.

In this chapter, I explore civil society as a terrain of struggle. The women in my study[1] belong to the same socially excluded communities they seek to work with; their own lives are not very different from those whom they seek to teach. Many of them have dropped out of school or further education; only a small minority continue in higher education. The story of their entry and action in the arena of community-based education work is embedded in a complex interplay of class and gender relations, as well as social relations they share with community members.

The prevailing discourse on participation raises questions for women's citizenship. The current emphasis on participation in education has emerged in the context of neo-liberalization and redefined roles of state and citizen. Since the 1990s, the liberalizing Indian state has recast its role as facilitator rather than provider, encouraging civil society participation in educational service provision (Wazir 2000). In this context, the role of citizens has been simultaneously reconceived in terms of their 'active exercise of responsibilities, including economic self-reliance and political participation' (Schild 1998: 94). This discourse of citizen responsibility creates a contested site for women's engagement as community educators. As such, the liberal state constructs women as linked both materially and ideologically to the private sphere, and men with the public sphere. This linkage of women's roles to the functions of the private sphere, namely, 'motherhood, caring, service ... [effectively] invokes the status of non-citizen, or non-worker' (Dillabough 2000: 164). There is a tendency then to see women's caretaking roles in their communities as extensions of their *natural* roles in the private sphere. As community-based educators, their acts would constitute those of cultivating citizens, rather than claiming citizenship themselves (ibid.).

Critiquing the false dichotomy of the separate spheres model and narrow definition of politics, feminist scholarship has shown that low-income/working class women's community-based action is political, since it is an 'attempt to change the social and political institutions that embody the basic power relations in ... society' (Morgen and Bookman 1988: 4), and constitutes acts of citizenship (Mirza and Reay 2000; Naples 1998). In this chapter, thus, I examine women's civic action in education as 'citizenship acts'. Centrally, I argue that the story of their civic participation is as much about their inclusion (and exclusion) as it is about their efforts for inclusion of their community members. This process though is a conflicted and negotiated one, through which the women create enabling spaces for themselves as well as for their community members. In the first analytic section, I examine the site of the domestic space in which the women use ideologies of 'good womanhood' to negotiate their entry into the domain of work and civic action. In the second section, I focus on women's efforts in the community site, and illustrate their actions as those of 'creating community'. Finally in the concluding section, I suggest that women's acts of citizenship can be understood in terms of their right to have a right to participate, and discuss the implication of the study for initiatives for educational change.

New contexts for women's civic engagements

Pratham emerged in the broader context of the Indian government's efforts toward universalization of education in the 1990s, where it sought partnerships to share in the provision of educational services with parents, communities, CSOs and the private sector (Wazir 2000). Primarily the brainchild of two professors, Madhav Chavan and Farida Lambay, Pratham was initiated in 1994 as a partnership with the Municipal Corporation of Greater Mumbai. The idea was to create a societal mission to help the government achieve universalization of pre-primary and primary education in Mumbai. Pratham's efforts were linked with the government education system, and geared toward improving children's access, attendance and achievement (Chavan 2000). Pratham has since expanded its operations beyond Mumbai and today has a presence in 14 states, where it works with local governments and low-income communities. While UNICEF provided the initial funding and supported the organization for the first three years, over time, leading corporate houses, the Indian disapora in

North America, Europe and the Middle East, and overseas funding agencies have financed the effort, which has reached over a million children across the country (Pratham website).

While its programmes and strategies are adapted to the given context, Pratham has four basic programmes targeted toward children in the age-group 3–12 years. These are: the Balwadi programme (pre-school programme), Learning to Read/Reading to Learn programme (accelerated learning programme for children who are enrolled in school but are non-literate), Outreach programme (programme for children not enrolled in schools and at-risk populations catering to their learning and health needs), and the Library programme (for all children in the community). The programmes are run in communities and/or in government schools.[2] Pratham's focus today is largely on educational achievement. It has developed highly structured accelerated learning programmes geared toward mastery of basic literacy skills.

Pratham recruits local women with a tenth or twelfth grade education to implement its programmes; however this qualification is flexible depending upon the availability of qualified women. The women educators are identified during yearly surveys in communities, which are conducted to assess educational need, as well as through social networks. Pratham provides the women with training, teaching–learning materials and regular supervision. Following Pratham's 'complete coverage' approach, teachers are allocated small local areas in which they have to ensure that the target group of children are receiving educational services, either through Pratham or other organizations. The teaching–learning takes place mostly in women's homes, and sometimes in other spaces in the community. Pratham gives the teachers a small honorarium. In an effort to make the programmes self-sustaining, teachers are expected to collect a small fee from children's parents. At the time of this study over 24,000 women worked with Pratham throughout India as community educators.

The participants in my study are drawn from a large, Muslim-dominated community, comprising over 150,000 residents. The area faces difficult issues like child labour, inadequate municipal school facilities, low literacy rates, high levels of poverty and a high crime rate. Pratham has been engaged in facilitating educational services here for the past ten years. At the time of data collection, Pratham had recruited 64 teachers (with the exception of the Outreach programme). Of these, I focused on 18 women for my study. A summary comparative profile of basic demographic information for 43 teachers in this community, collected through a survey questionnaire administered to teachers is presented in Table 9.1, as well as information on the sub-sample group of 18 teachers.

As indicated in Table 9.1, the typical teacher at this community is unmarried, Muslim and below 23 years old. There are a few older, married women, as well as divorced women who work as teachers. Most of the teachers have an educational completion level that is twelfth grade or below. Survey questionnaires administered to teachers in similar communities in Mumbai indicated that the teacher profile here was correspondingly similar. In the sample group, the characteristics of most teachers fit that of the majority in this area.

Table 9.1 Profile of teachers at Baiganwadi: entire teaching group and sample group teachers

	All teachers [n = 43]	*Sample group teachers [n = 18]*
Age:		
16–23 years	39	14
>24 years	4	4
Educational grade completed:[a]		
<10th	23	9
10th–12th	17	8
>12th	1	1
Marital status:[b]		
Unmarried	38	13
Married	3	3
Separated/divorced	1	2
Religion:		
Muslim	41	16
Hindu	2	2

Notes
a   Two respondents in the 'All teachers' group did not respond to the question.
b   One respondent in the 'All teachers' group did not respond to the question.

Data for this study was gathered between June 2004 and April 2005. I used ethnographic methods to gather data and grounded theory methods for analysis, since these methods lend themselves well to develop an inductive understanding of the women's viewpoints, assumptions and experiences. Data collection methods included a combination of participant observation, informal and narrative interviews, survey questionnaire, secondary data and reflexive photography. Eighteen teachers were invited to participate in the study. Their selection was based on purposeful sampling (Patton 1990). In selecting the participants, the criterion was to incorporate heterogeneity of the population under study in terms of their backgrounds and experiences. The objective was not to create a representative sample; instead, I sought a diversity of experiences in order to construct rich grounded theory.

Grounded theory methods (Charmaz 2000; Glaser and Strauss 1967; Strauss 1987; Strauss and Corbin 1998) were employed for data analysis. Developed by the sociologists, Barney Glaser and Anselm Strauss, these methods comprise 'systematic inductive guidelines ... to build middle-range theoretical frameworks' (Charmaz 2000: 509). Analysis is an ongoing part of the data collection phase, and informs the data gathering process. The methods involved an iterative process of open and focused coding, categorizing, memo writing and developing analytic themes for individual participants and across cases. Emergent patterns were identified through this process, which helped develop a theoretical understanding of low-income women's participation in community-based education work.

Becoming a teacher: good womanhood and the public space

For the women in this study, notions of 'good womanhood' (Luttrell 1997) define their primary identities and responsibilities in relation to the domestic space. The women's primary roles are defined by their social reproduction responsibilities within their families. When they do opt for paid work, which is usually in low-paid, home-based, small-scale industrial activity, they do so out of economic necessity to supplement household income. Further, women are segregated to the domestic space; the norms are particularly strict for the post-pubescent, unmarried women (a group that constitutes a majority of Pratham educators). These restrictions on women's mobility may be understood in terms of the patriarchal discourse in the South Asian context, where women's exclusion from the public space serves to protect their sexual purity and the associated family honour (Standing 1991). Engagement with teaching work contests notions of 'good womanhood'. While their work is structured as home-based work, teaching work carries with it the connotation of professional work and identity. Moreover, the women are required to be physically mobile for conducting community surveys, and attending meetings/training sessions. Both these aspects of women's work as educators conflict with their primary identities and roles as linked to the segregated domestic arena.

For a majority of the women educators, their engagement as educators marks their first entry into the public work–civic space. This entry means that family members need to allow for greater freedom for the women in the public space, as well as accept the women's roles as economic actors. Thus, the women's desire to work as educators initiates in the domestic domain, a process of negotiation over their access to the public space and meanings associated with their gender identity (Diaz-Barriga 1998; Krauss 1998). In what follows, I analyse these negotiations against the backdrop of their educational histories and gender and class relations. I illustrate that the women's negotiations are contradictory in that they involve applying the very logic of good womanhood in order to secure their participation in the public domain. In so doing, they simultaneously create an enabling space for themselves, and reinforce the norms that constrain the same.

'I like it – this is why I am doing it'

Meena is a tenth grade dropout, having failed her final board exams because she was simultaneously tending to her sick mother. While she does want to finish her tenth grade, she says that she does not have the economic means to appear for the exam again. Between her mother (who was also present at our interview session) and her, they recount instances of their abject poverty through the years. Meena's father had stopped contributing economically a long time ago, leaving Meena's mother and older brother to support the household. Her brother dropped out of school early on to support the family; her mother works as a cleaner at various small establishments. Meena's mother tells me that she feels bad that her daughters have to work, but they have no choice since they need the income. (Meena's sister currently works at a small-scale factory unit). Surprisingly, Meena provides a different rationale for her participation in teaching work. In response to my question of why she did not opt for the same work as her sister, Meena says:

> If both of us are away from morning to night who will look after the home? This is why one had to stay home. [After dropping out of school] I would stay at home the entire day. There was not much to occupy my time the entire day, so I joined the *balwadi* programme.

In this, Meena frames her primary responsibility as being that of keeping her home and speaks of her educational engagement as only an activity to pass spare time. A cousin introduced her to Pratham. While her mother agreed, her brother was opposed to her working. Meena recounts: 'He [said], "my sister will not go outside. Will I take my sister's salary? Don't we have food to eat?"' Meena goes on to agree with her brother's opinion on this, saying: 'His opinion is right. No one has done it at our home. Among our relatives, none of the girls [young, unmarried women] have gone [to work].'

Meena's brother's response to his sister working stemmed from his objection to her becoming a wage earner. This would be an affront to his role as the primary breadwinner, as well as the respectability of the family. Meena concurred with his perspective, and tried to convince him that she wanted to teach because she 'like[d] it'. As she relates:

> I told him that the work is that of a teacher. Very young children have to be taught at a *balwadi*.... There is no problem ... I am not opting [to work] for money. I like it [teaching] – therefore I am doing it. This is the main thing. The money is not the main thing.

She goes on to explicate her position to me:

> My brother will give me as much [money] I ask of him. If I ask my father he will give me, my younger brother also gives [me money]. My mother also gives sometimes. But the thing is that I like it [teaching].... I always had this desire since I was young.

Meena here explains her motivation for teaching work as stemming from her own interest in teaching. This interest is framed in non-economic terms and, therefore, as non-conflicting with her gender identity as an economic dependent on the male providers. In other words, in keeping with her primary domestic identity and notions of good womanhood, it is legitimate for her to pursue work in the public space out of personal interest, and not as an economic activity. Her brother accepts her argument and she is able to engage in teaching work.

Interestingly, there are competing meanings of work and economics at play in Meena's narrative. In another context, when I ask Meena if she can save her wages in order to reappear for her examinations, she responds:

> No. The household is running because everyone contributes. The two sisters contribute some, and we manage our expenses from that – like, if we have to buy clothes. My brother and mother contribute toward the electricity and groceries. [We manage] because everyone contributes.

I think these conflicting accounts stem from disconnections between what she believes to be her dominant identity and the practicalities of everyday life. Nonetheless, her framing of her role as primarily domestic and as an economic dependent allows her to negotiate domestically, her entry and continuation in teaching work.

Doing sahi kaam *(the right kind of work)*

Rubina and her three sisters work with Pratham. While her two single sisters are doing their undergraduate studies, Rubina's schooling was abruptly terminated after her ninth grade when she had to tend her eldest married sister, when the latter was ill. She lost an academic year and never returned to school. This, to date, remains her biggest regret. Rubina tells me that her sisters are supporting their educational expenses through their work at Pratham. In fact, as she explains, work with Pratham came at an opportune time, when they were facing difficult economic problems at home. At the time, their father decided that he would not have the wherewithal to educate his daughters after the tenth grade. Now, she says, 'with Pratham, we are able to take care of all our expenses, and our parents are not troubled [with the expense]. They take care of our food, [and the sisters] are able to take care of [their] expenses for their education.' Unlike Meena, who frames her role as non-economic, Rubina discusses her sisters' and her contribution toward economically sustaining her household.

Rubina's desire to teach stemmed from watching her older sister teach at home and helping her out with her class. As she tells me: 'Being exposed to teaching I also began to like it. At the time I thought, "I should also do something. Why should I waste my time sitting around?"' But her entry into teaching was eased by the fact that her older sister was already working as a teacher. It was the older sister who negotiated her mobility in the public domain. As Rubina explains: '[T]here was no permission to go outside. There was no permission to work outside the home.' One of Rubina's sisters had earlier acquainted me with the 'rules' of gender segregation their father enforced. For instance, the women have to wear their *burkha*, even when they step out to use the public toilet. Given this context, when her sister suggested that she had found work at Pratham with the help of a friend, it met with their father's resistance. She argued with him, as Rubina tells me that 'no men worked there … [She] had to teach children in the neighborhood. That too at home. And there was no male present at the … meetings held at the office.' Rubina's sister thus framed teaching children as a harmless activity. In her argument, she did not challenge the norm of gender segregation, but applied its logic to work in the public space. Her father relented, and soon her sisters followed suit. When I ask Rubina the reason for her father's consent for her teaching work, she says they are allowed because teaching work is *sahi kaam*, the right kind of work, in the sense of being respectable. It is not *faltu*, meaning useless, in the sense of disreputable work. She explains:

> Because it is *sahi kaam*…. Meaning, we are sitting at home and doing our work. We are teaching children, we don't go out anywhere. There is nothing *faltu* [about this work]…. And we can meet our expenses through this. With this, we can help improve our weak material conditions, [help] our parents.

Rubina's words here illustrate her justification for her participation in this work through the construct of good womanhood. Teaching is *sahi kaam*, and not *faltu*, because it does not conflict with norms of gender segregation and restricted mobility for women. Teaching becomes an appropriate occupation for women, and thus their participation in this work is legitimated.

Constructing community for change

Mirza and Reay (2000: 69), in their research about Black supplementary school women educators, speak of the educators' idea of community as a 'pragmatic, conscious construction of a "Black home"…. They [educators] were not simply a part of the community. They were also engaged in actively constructing it through their work as radical Black educators'. The work of teachers in this study resonates with this notion of being part of and actively constructing a community. In socially and educationally excluded communities, the women as teachers are the often the first non-school agents to initiate any attention to children's educational needs in their communities. Their action, on the one hand, is embedded in existing social relations with people in their localities. On the other hand, as teachers, they form networks with each other as also with Pratham, and they individually and collectively act as educational resources meeting the deficits of the government education system. Notions of community then are 'grounded in the women's own labour' (ibid.).

The following accounts illustrate that the women teachers in their roles as teachers and community members perceive themselves as community caretakers of children who lack educational resources (Naples 1998). Acting as such, constructing community involves a process in which the women make strategic use of their position and authority as teachers. This deployment is an adaptable one; the women's actions involve bargaining and accommodations with community members, and are contingent upon circumstances that call for their action.

The 'daughter' who is also teacher

Ameena, a young 19-year old has been living in the same neighbourhood since she was a child. Her role as a community-based educator is one that is mediated by pre-existing relations with community members. As she explains:

How will you describe your relationship with the [students'] parents?
They all live here and know me. And I have just become a teacher. From childhood, they [students' parents] have considered me a daughter.

Do you think there has been any change in the relationship?
No. The relationship has not changed. They consider me a daughter. And where applicable, they also give me the status of a teacher.

Here, Ameena highlights that her familial relations with her neighbours continue despite the fact that she has taken on a new role. However, her remark that 'they also give me the status of a teacher' implies that they do relate to her in new ways as well.

At times, it appears that her 'daughter' identity is foregrounded. For instance, she relates an incident of a parent sending her *idi* (a gift given to children in one's family during the festival of *Id*), through their child: 'The parent thought that this is like my daughter and they should give *idi* like they would to their own children.' At other times, the identity as daughter is conflated with that of her role as a teacher. Thus, her students' parents would often tell her to teach their children as she would her own siblings. As she says: '[T]hey tell me I should teach their children like my younger brothers and sisters. Mostly, they consider me a daughter.' In most instances, then, according to Ameena, the parents interpret her identity as teacher in a familial-relational sense.

Nonetheless, there is acknowledgement of her authority that comes with her role as teacher. She says she is called 'teacher' when she teaches the children, and parents seek her advice for problems with their children. However, her familiarity with the parents appears to be key to getting their participation. Ameena is one of the few teachers who does not face difficulty in securing parental cooperation for their child's regular attendance and completing homework. Relating the instance of four children who had irregular attendance, she says that those children lived outside her immediate neighbourhood. In contrast, referring to the children who are regular, she says, 'These children ... come from my own area. They know me. If they don't attend one day, the parents will tell me why – what the problem was.'

Ameena's own feelings toward her dual relationship with community members are revealed when she tells me that, despite pressures from the Pratham administration, she chooses not to insist that parents pay fees. This is because, '[T]his area ... is poor. People have three, four, five children. So they cannot give.... They do not pay because of poverty.' Despite pressures from Pratham to collect a fee from parents, she chooses not to do so. Also, she knows that if she does insist, then parents will stop sending the children. Moreover, she says, parents consider her as 'one of their own'. As she puts it: '[I] don't force them much. They consider me as one of their own. They tell me – "Teacher, if we have [the money] we will happily give it". What can we do if they don't have it?'

Ameena's decision not to insist on fees is embedded in her social relations with and empathy for parents who cannot afford to pay; instead she chooses to resist organizational pressures. Further, her decision is based in the practicalities of the circumstance: if she insisted, then parents would stop sending their children. Valerie Walkerdine (1990) speaks of the paradox embedded in the notion of the woman teacher: to be a woman means to lack knowledge and power; contradictorily, to be a teacher implies legitimacy to have knowledge and power (cited in Munro 1998: 1). Rather than reflect contradictions, Ameena's response suggests a reworking of this paradox through broadening her role as daughter–teacher in her community. She constructs her sense of responsibility toward her community, positioning herself as a daughter–teacher. Showing me a photograph of a second class she had recently taken on, she tells me: '[We] could not find [another] teacher. I thought, there are so many children in the area, roaming around. So I decided to teach the class.' I knew that Ameena had no spare time, handling as the eldest daughter in her household, all domestic responsibilities for her family of five. Illustrating family accommodations so that she could teach the children, she says: '*Ammi* [mother] said, "Teach the class. I will take care of the work that is left over."'

The cultural worker

While both Saira and Ameena live close by, the locality where Saira's children come from is much poorer than that of Ameena's. Children work on either home-based small-scale industrial activities here, or collect garbage on the dumping ground. Saira claims that children in her neighbourhood do attend school. However, given the nature of existing material conditions and the economic alternatives available, getting children to attend her class is very challenging. Nonetheless, Saira says of the area, which by her own claims is '99 per cent illiterate': 'At first children were not literate and didn't want to come to study. But now it is so good that children themselves wait thinking, "when will I go to school?"'

Saira is a 35-year-old mother of four children, who had joined Pratham eight years ago primarily for economic reasons. On earlier visits, I had witnessed her complaints about parental non-participation. Surprised with her response above, I probed more deeply. Saira told me about the work children did in her locality, how earlier children used to be engaged in collecting and selling garbage for an income. 'Now this has reduced', she says, going on to relate what she tells parents to persuade them to send their children to her class:

'You are making them do *ganda* [dirty] work. What will be the effect of this on your child? If you are not literate, do you feel that your child should also not study?' ... After explaining all this there has been a lot of change.

As her account reveals, Saira uses her authority as teacher to argue for a change in the way in which people view education. Through this she tries to bring about a cultural shift in support of literacy and education among people excluded from this domain.

Saira narrates the example of a mother who was unwilling to send her child to the *balwadi*. She recounts the mother's words:

Who has benefited from an education? My children will not study ... After being educated, [people] are still roaming around [jobless/doing meaning-less work].... They are doing the same tailoring work, the same work in hotels.

To this Saira responded:

Fine, he is working in a hotel or doing tailoring work, but at least he knows how to read and write! ... If he has to go somewhere by bus, he can find the address.... If he receives a letter, he will be able to read it. He will not be at the mercy of someone else.

The woman accepted the argument but still did not send her child. The next day, Saira went to her again and said:

Look don't spoil your child's life.... You can meet the tailor and ask how he benefits knowing how to read and write. Today he has become a tailor, he is able to take measurements, there are numbers written on the measuring tape – only if he is literate will he know how to read them.

She convinced the parent in this way; nonetheless it took several more visits and making the class attractive to the particular child to sustain this participation. When the parent began noticing changes in her child, she began sending him herself. Saira says that she later got the child enrolled in the local public school that he now attends.

Saira's narrative reveals that the nature of her work of creating enabling spaces for her community members is shaped by her context, and she uses her agency to bring change in that very context. She strategically employs her legitimacy as teacher to make a case for education. She follows up her arguments with persistent strategic action that is not only limited to the child's participation in her class, but is carried on into school. While this case demonstrates her contesting people's attitudes toward education as a strategy, sometimes, she is accommodative. For instance, she makes allowances for girls who have to do household chores, and has them attend class at least for a short while. She also fetches children from their homes for her class virtually everyday. When I ask her why she does it, she explains her actions through an empathetic understanding of the choices people have to make on account of poverty. As she says,

> One has to go to fetch the children at their homes because of the environment at their homes. There is a lot of poverty in this area. Fathers do not earn much. Mothers and children do the work of *lokhandkatta*[3] ... If they make two–three kilos, they earn five rupees. The parents make them do this work. And when I go to fetch them and ask why they haven't sent their child, they say, 's/he is just coming'. They take interest, but they make the children work because of their own compulsions.

Saira's accommodation here stems from her sense of empathy with 'compulsions', or material circumstances of people in her locality. Displaying class affiliation, she goes on to tell me that she herself engages in small-scale work in her spare time and has her daughter do the same, in order to earn a few extra rupees.

In sum, Saira uses her legitimacy as teacher to gain people's participation. In order to create change, she uses her authority strategically and contingent upon circumstance, contesting parental attitudes at times, and at others accommodating them. Through all this, she does not distance herself from her community; instead through giving the example of her own material need, she emphasizes that she too is part of the community in which she is trying to bring change.

Conclusion: the right to have a right to participate

Low-income women's acts of citizenship are characterized by their engagement in creating enabling spaces for themselves and their communities. This process, marked by their efforts to secure their own right to participate, span domestic, work and community sites. Further, it is political; albeit conflicted and negotiated, the process is embedded in domestic and community relations, mediated by gender relations and material conditions in their context. For the women themselves, participation in the public space is a question of threatening notions of good womanhood. As the analysis reveals, they deploy the same discourses of respectability to enter the public space as teachers. Positioned as teachers, they act as educational resources, and mobilize the same for children of their localities. In so doing, they create community grounded in their own labour.

Writing about the Brazilian context, Evelina Dagnino notes: '[T]o be poor means not only endure economic and material deprivation but also to be submitted to cultural rules that convey a complete lack of recognition of poor people as subjects, as bearers of rights' (1998: 48). This description speaks to circumstances of people living in poorer slums in Mumbai, who live in shanties under constant threat of eviction, have little access to services like potable water, sanitation, public health or educational facilities. The women in this study themselves have been excluded from the domain of education; however, today are engaged in educational change in their communities. For these women then, the acts of citizenship do not constitute simply a struggle for basic services, but also 'their very right to have rights' (Dagnino 1998: 48).

Often, it is in communities like these (including the site in which the present study is located) where the need for educational services is most, community women are mobilized for civic action. However, while referring to them as 'citizens' (Pratham website), the recognition of their citizenship is only insofar as their ability to garner resources for their community members. As a typical promotional literature titled *About Pratham* puts it:

> One of the biggest achievements of Pratham has been that it has managed to mobilize thousands of community women, across India, to take charge of the educational needs of their community. These young women exhibit an amazing and infectious 'can-do' attitude, which is truly what the Pratham Movement is all about. These young and empowered women, in turn, mobilize their entire community to take responsibility of their children's education and try to find ways and means of providing for that.
>
> (Pratham UK: 1–2)

Undoubtedly, the 'empowered woman' contradicts the dominant image of the Third World woman as powerless and victimized (Mohanty 1988). Nonetheless her agency, as represented here, is valorized and lies in creating citizens rather than in becoming a citizen herself. In contrast, as this research demonstrates, the women's effort to create citizens is one that is intertwined with their own claim to citizenship. As women living in poverty, they claim the right to have the right to participate in these terms.

Acknowledgement of women's citizenship would recognize the broader emancipatory potential embedded in large-scale civic movements for educational change. For the women teachers, the actual practice of education work is embedded in their social contexts, and involves conflicts and negotiations of power, both in their personal and their work lives. However, in the absence of collective consciousness building, their resistance is fragmented and isolated. Through understanding the dynamics of women's grassroots action, large-scale educational initiatives have the potential for much wider societal transformation. This will mean creating facilitative structures, and programmes for consciousness building in order to sustain and develop the women's participation, as well as their inclusion. It is through such praxis that democratic structures in society can truly be strengthened.

Notes

1 This chapter is drawn from my larger ethnographic study on the civic participation of these women community educators.
2 In Mumbai, after a long, tenuous relationship with the government school system, particularly with resistance from the teacher union, Pratham moved all its programmes to local communities. At the time of my field research, the only regular interaction

with school system officials was with respect to the Outreach programme to coordinate efforts to bring all children under the educational ambit.

3 This is small-scale informal work where people beat small bits of metal into shapes that go on to being used as clasps for straps around packaging boxes.

References

Alvarez, S.E., Dagnino, E. and Escobar, A. (1998) 'Introduction: the cultural and the political in Latin American social movements' in S.E. Alvarez, E. Dagnino and A. Escobar (eds) *Cultures of Politics/Politics of Cultures: Revisioning Latin American Social Movements*, Boulder, CO: Westview Press.

Charmaz, K. (2000) 'Grounded theory and constructivist methods' in N.K. Denzin and Y.S. Lincoln (eds) *Handbook of Qualitative Research*, Thousand Oaks, CA: Sage Publications.

Chavan, M. (2000) *Building Societal Missions for Universal Pre-school and Primary Education*, Paris: UNESCO.

Collective Consultation of NGOs on Education for All (2001) *Reason for Hope: The Support of NGOs to Education for All*, Paris: UNESCO.

Dagnino, E. (1998) 'Culture, citizenship and democracy: changing discourses and practices of the Latin American left' in S.E. Alvarez, E. Dagnino and A. Escobar (eds) *Cultures of Politics/Politics of Cultures: Re-visioning Latin American Social Movements*, Boulder, CO: Westview Press.

Diaz-Barriga, M. (1998) 'Beyond the domestic and the public: colonas participation in urban movements in Mexico City' in S.E. Alvarez, E. Dagnino and A. Escobar (eds) *Cultures of Politics/Politics of Cultures: Re-visioning Latin American Social Movements*, Boulder, CO: Westview Press.

Dillabough, J.-A. and Arnot, M. (2000) 'Women in teacher education: their struggle for inclusion as "citizen-workers" in late modernity' in M. Arnot and J.-A. Dillabough (eds) *Challenging Democracy: International Perspectives on Gender, Education and Citizenship*, London: RoutledgeFalmer.

Glaser, B. and Strauss, A. (1967) *Discovery of Grounded Theory*, Chicago: Aldine.

Jagannathan, S. (2001) *The Role of Nongovernmental Organizations in Primary Education. A Study of Six NGOs in India* (Policy Research Working Paper 2530), Washington, DC: World Bank.

Krauss, C. (1998) 'Challenging power: toxic waste protests and the politicization of white, working-class women' in N.A. Naples (ed.) *Community Activism and Feminist Politics: Organizing across Race, Class, and Gender*, New York: Routledge.

Luttrell, W. (1997) *Schoolsmart and Motherwise: Working-class Women's Identity and Schooling*, New York: Routledge.

Mirza, H.S. and Reay, D. (2000) 'Redefining citizenship: black women educators and "the third space"', in M. Arnot and J.-A. Dillabough (eds) *Challenging Democracy: International Perspectives on Gender, Education and Citizenship*, London: RoutledgeFalmer.

Mohanty, C. (1988) 'Under Western Eyes: Feminist Scholarship and Colonial Discourses', *Feminist Review*, 30: 61–88.

Morgen, S. and Bookman, A. (1988) 'Rethinking women and politics: an introductory essay' in A. Bookman and S. Morgen (eds) *Women and the Politics of Empowerment*, Philadelphia: Temple University Press.

Munro, P. (1998) *Subject to Fiction. Women Teachers' Life History Narratives and the Cultural Politics of Resistance*, Philadelphia, PA: Open University Press.

Naples, N.A. (1998) *Grassroots Warriors: Activist Mothering, Community Work, and the War on Poverty*, New York: Routledge.

Patton, M.Q. (1990) *Qualitative Evaluation and Research Methods*, Thousand Oaks, CA: Sage Publications.

Pratham. Available online at: www.pratham.org (accessed 29 December 2006).

Pratham UK. 'About Pratham', available online at: www.faculty.london.edu/vacharya/assets/documents/AboutPrathamInDetail.pdf (accessed 29 December 2006).

Robinson, C. (2000) 'Partnerships in Education for All: NGO and civil society experiences', available online at: www.unesco.org/education/partners/cco/English/Paternship2.htm (accessed 2 November 2005).

Schild, V. (1998) 'New subjects of rights? Women's movements and the construction of citizenship in the "new democracies"', in S.E. Alvarez, E. Dagnino and A. Escobar (eds) *Cultures of Politics/Politics of Cultures. Re-visioning Latin American Social Movements*, Boulder, CO: Westview Press.

Standing, H. (1991) *Dependence and Autonomy: Women's Employment and the Family in Calcutta*, New York: Routledge.

Strauss, A. (1987) *Qualitative Analysis for Social Scientists*, New York: Cambridge University Press.

Strauss, A. and Corbin, J. (1998) *Basics of Qualitative Research: Techniques and Procedures for Developing Grounded Theory*, Thousand Oaks, CA: Sage Publications.

Walkerdine, V. (1990) *Schoolgirl Fictions*, New York: Verso.

Wazir, R. (2000) 'Profiling the problem' in R. Wazir (ed.) *The Gender Gap in Basic Education. NGOs as Change Agents*, Thousand Oaks, CA: Sage Publications.

World Conference on Education for All (1990) 'World Declaration on Education For All. Meeting basic learning needs'. Available online at: www.unesco.org/education/efa/ed_for_all/background/jomtien_declaration.shtml (accessed 14 May 2007).

World Education Forum (2000) 'Education for All: Meeting our collective commitments', Dakar: World Education Forum.

10 Gendered experiences of teaching in poor rural areas of Ghana

Leslie Casely-Hayford

International agencies and governments agree that in order to achieve Millennium Development Goals and Education for All goals in sub-Saharan Africa over the next decade requires strategies that remove the barriers to educational attainment (UNESCO 2003). A number of strategies have been identified, particularly in relation to improving the enrolment, retention and attainment of girls. For example, the low presence of female teachers serving in disadvantaged rural communities has been identified as one of the main constraints militating against girls' access and completion of basic education (Sutherland-Addy 2002; Casely-Hayford 2000; Brock and Cammish 1997a). One of the most effective approaches for improving female educational attainment therefore is to use female teachers as role models for girls (Rugh 2000; King and Hill 1993). Studies also suggest that low self-esteem among girls is a key factor preventing them from attaining higher levels of education and that gender sensitive teaching methods can improve girls' retention rates in school (Casely-Hayford 2002b; WUSC 2000). Further, research by the Foundation for African Women Educationalists (FAWE 1999) suggests that girls are more likely to stay in school particularly if the school deals with reproductive health issues and if girls are able to talk to a woman in authority.

This chapter reports on the findings of the Ghana Female Teacher Study[1] (Casely-Hayford with Wilson 2001), which investigated the needs of female teachers in six remote rural areas in northern, southern and middle Ghana. Within each of these zones, the two districts were selected[2] that had the lowest percentages of female pupil enrolment rates in the country and the lowest proportion of female teachers working at basic education level.[3] Female teachers constituted 14.3 per cent of Juabeso Bia and 15.5 per cent in Wassa Amenfi in the southern belt; 13.1 per cent in Kintampo and 10.6 per cent in Sene (10.6 per cent) in the middle belt; and 7.8 per cent in Tolon Kumbongo and 14.3 per cent in East Gonja in the northern belt of the country. The project explored the experiences of female teachers, the reasons why very few female teachers accept postings to these areas and why girls are not entering the teaching profession.

The first section of the chapter briefly describes the qualitative research methodology that was used to capture the reasons why women came to be rural teachers in such poor communities, the difficulties they experienced in integrating into the community and in balancing personal and professional lives. The final section of the chapter considers the ways in which secondary school girls in the community perceive female teachers' status and their likelihood of entering the teaching profession.

Experiencing the lives of female teachers

The study was carried out by Sarah Wilson and myself in 2000 and was financed by Ghana's Ministry of Education in order to review key policies that could increase female enrolment into teacher training colleges and increase their deployment to rural areas. After extensive interviews at the national level with Ministry of Education officials and other key stakeholders we decided to employ an ethnographic approach by living with the female teachers in the rural areas we studied. We focused on the lives, aspirations and experiences of 22 female teachers serving in 20 poor rural communities in the six sampled districts across Ghana. Interviews were also held with male colleagues serving in the same schools and other female teachers in more prosperous areas that were nearer to the district capitals and education circuit centres. The data collected from these interviews allowed for triangulation, a comparison of the perceptions and attitudes of teachers in diverse contexts. Informal interviews were also conducted with girls in their final year at senior secondary school (SSS) concerning their career interests, choices and attitudes toward the teaching profession. This gave the research team important insights into the reasons why rural Ghanaian girls do not see female teachers as role models and become teachers themselves.

The research team lived in the communities in which the teachers worked, engaging in their daily lives at the school and within the community setting. The aim of taking a more ethnographic approach was to reach a deeper understanding of the challenges female teachers faced. However, this strategy demanded considerable endurance since we needed to adapt to the living conditions in remote rural areas, which often lacked clean water, access to food and clean accommodation. The research strategy brought us face to face with some of the same problems female teachers faced such as poor roads and inaccessibility, lack of clean accommodation, a lack of food and potable water, as well as personal insecurity, malaria and poor medical care.[4] Our experience of living for only a short time in these remote areas exposed us personally to some of the main reasons why long-term postings in remote rural schools are avoided by most women.

Another effective research technique was the use of in-depth interviews, which we conducted with each female teacher. Using a life history approach we were able to capture the main events leading up to their posting and changes to their lives after moving to a remote area. This approach also allowed the team to build rapport, trust and shared understanding of the steps leading up to the decision and the life changes that followed in accepting to live and serve in a deprived rural area. It meant that we could share experiences in our own lives with those of the teachers in the study and build a sense of commonality.

Table 10.1 Teacher participation by kindergarten, primary and junior secondary school levels across the six study districts

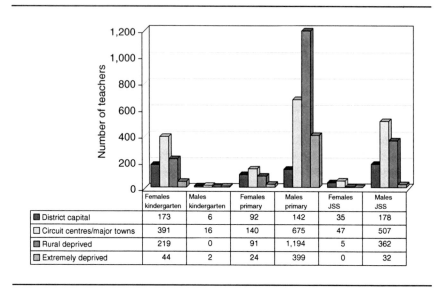

	Females kindergarten	Males kindergarten	Females primary	Males primary	Females JSS	Males JSS
■ District capital	173	6	92	142	35	178
□ Circuit centres/major towns	391	16	140	675	47	507
■ Rural deprived	219	0	91	1,194	5	362
▨ Extremely deprived	44	2	24	399	0	32

The Ghana Female Teacher Study indicated that the majority of teachers living in these rural areas were male with only a few female teachers who were often found teaching in circuit centres and at the kindergarten level.

In-depth interviews also suggested that there were two types of female teacher serving in the rural areas: the *long serving female teacher* who was often 'untrained' and had married into the community; and, second, the *newly trained young female teacher* who was serving a two-year term and did not want any close association with the rural area she was serving. The individual interviews and female teacher profiling activity revealed that there were often no professionally trained female teachers who were married and in the childbearing phase working in these areas. Some of the different experiences of these two groups of teachers are described below.

Becoming a rural teacher: the gender dimensions

The majority of female teachers we spoke to were encouraged by family members to become teachers. Some women had taken up teaching as untrained pupil teachers and discovered their interest in teaching before entering training college. Others had been assisted and encouraged by a religious leader to enter the teaching profession. Some of the diverse motivations for joining the teacher profession are indicated in the following responses:

I applied to work as a pupil teacher and realized I enjoyed the work.

I was encouraged by a family relation.

A minister or religious leader encouraged me.

My husband was a teacher and I admired him.

My mother was a teacher and I admired her.

I started as a Kindergarten teacher and worked without pay for sometime before being hired as a pupil teacher.

Self motivated and had the required results.

I liked children.

I saw no other female professions beside teaching.

I wanted to be a secretary but developed an interest after teacher training college.

(Casely-Hayford with Wilson 2001)

The reasons why female teachers found themselves in very poor rural areas were equally diverse and often contradictory. The untrained teachers, for example, appeared to have had little choice about where they were posted since they were often recruited primarily for the purpose of serving in a rural area. Those who were trained were posted by District Education Officers. Our interviews suggested that these officers took account of the marital status and location of the husband of newly trained teachers as well as their background (e.g. training college, ethnicity, parent's socio-economic status) when choosing a posting for them. They also took account of the distance of the school from the district capital and accessibility to town centres (e.g. along a main road and near a 'junction') and whether the community had a reasonable level of social services. The study also indicated that in order not to 'scare them' (newly trained female teachers) away from teaching, careful consideration was also made of the newly trained teachers' ability 'to cope with difficult circumstances'. One senior education officer in Sene district stated that 'if you are posted outside the district, you are dead'.

Most District Education Officers took it upon themselves to 'protect' the newly trained female teachers from some of the communities being posted to remote rural areas. East Gonja District Senior Education Officers stated that they looked upon female teachers as 'their own daughters' and therefore did not post women to areas where they would be 'handicapped or fall victim to local chiefs or rich farmers who wanted to take them as their second wife'. The image they presented was that women were seen as having such a 'weak moral character' that they were likely to feel lonely and therefore become vulnerable to 'an unwanted marriage' with such local men. There was also the danger that they might marry local men from a lower socio-economic category. This was seen as a severe handicap for a young woman who had just completed tertiary education since it meant she would fall back into village life – getting married to a 'local man could detract from her hard earned status'. Although none of the newly trained rural female teachers we interviewed were married, most of them aspired to find a partner in the near future. Several long serving female teachers had married 'local men' during their initial years of teaching, most marrying farmers, cocoa purchasing clerks or local sub-chiefs. These female teachers were spoken of as 'being no different from the locals' – an image that contributed to their low respect from parents, and female students in their communities (see below).

However our research also suggested that if married rural female teachers were to follow social conventions of the day, then there was a danger that they would follow their husbands and eventually move away from the area. As one Girls' Education Officer in the Northern Region told us:

> One of our major problems up here in the North is our female teachers follow their husbands; if the husband is posted to the village, the female will go – if he is not, she will not go. It is our culture that the woman should be near the man.

Some Manpower Officers and District Directors of Education were therefore keenly aware that they might start an exodus of newly trained female teachers out of the district and possibly the teaching profession by forcing them to teach in a rural area against their will. As one District Education Director explained: 'There is an unofficial policy to place female teachers to the towns in order to facilitate marriage. We want them to get proper husbands or their whole future is at stake' (October 2000).

Given these views, all six-study districts adopted an unofficial policy of posting newly trained female teachers mainly into towns. The long serving female teachers already residing in towns and travelling to the rural schools each day were happy to remain living in the urban setting. One long serving female teacher residing in a poor rural community remarked that if 'the government lets me be like the town lady teachers, I will stay'. Most of the sample of rural female teachers we interviewed were interested in taking up postings in more urbanised areas. They perceived their town counterparts as living a much easier life and having access to a number of benefits that were not available in rural areas such as: credit, markets, better social services and access to income generating activities, electricity and potable water.

Several interviews with newly trained female teachers confirmed that they did not feel they had the strength or willingness to serve in rural areas for an unlimited time – they set their own personal limits on how long they would remain before seeking a transfer or leaving the profession all together. Interviews with staff at the Manpower Division in the headquarters of the Ghana Education

Service confirmed that very few women were willing to serve in the Western Region and Northern Regions of Ghana and most women often drifted 'back to headquarters saying that it was too difficult (Field notes, Female Teacher Study)'. The following vignettes highlight the experiences of two newly trained female teachers who had to cope with difficult aspects of their posting.[5]

Abena was a newly trained female teacher and sat cooking her stew while we interviewed her. She explained how difficult it had been to bring her personal items to the district. She was a 'Ga' from Labone (Accra) and trained at Foso (Central Region). She and another friend had been posted to the Western Region since they thought it would be 'an experience'. She arrived after eight hours of uncomfortable travel from Accra, which cost approximately 80,000 cedis in order to reach the district capital. Her colleague Kate was posted about seven miles away from the district capital – Assankragua – but did not last one week before she asked for a transfer. Kate decided to leave and find another posting in another town (Winneba) closer to her home (Volta Region). Abena was left behind to endure in this remote district. Abena's only regret was there was no computer school in the district capital since she wanted to learn how to operate a computer and further her studies. One other male colleague from the same training college was also posted to the same town and was helping her adjust to life in the District Capital. She talked about her inability to find accommodation and the inconvenience of having to live with the education officers before securing accommodation.

Esther was another newly trained teacher posted to the Western Region. She explained that she was from Kete Krachi in the Volta Region but she attended Holy Child Training College in Takoradi. She was posted to a very deprived rural area by the religious unit. The research team visited one Friday and found her teaching alone at a school with over 100 pupils while her male colleagues had all found reasons not to attend school, such as poor health and the need to go to town to collect their salary. Esther was inspired to serve in a rural area partly as a result of her religious conviction – she hoped that she could make a difference to people's lives in the area. Her brother had accompanied her on her first visit to the community (Pisasso) when she spoke to the Chief and the community members. They were very happy to have a female teacher especially one heading up the school. They promised to do everything possible to make her stay comfortable. She was given a bungalow and the community supplied her with foodstuffs until she was settled. But the community itself had a severe water problem (onchocerciasis) and she was not taking precautions by boiling the water.

Esther was happy serving the community, and helped organise the people in order to improve the school structure and facilities; one of the JSS girls told her that she would go into teaching after completing the SSS. She was facing some difficulties with the male teachers at this school since she was the Head and much younger than the other three men who were all untrained teachers.

In Abena's case, there was a distinct sense that she had tried to adjust to living in a remote area with her friend but eventually found herself 'left behind' in what was a particularly difficult setting. Esther's case in contrast suggested that she had strongly engaged in community life and had discovered a 'mission'. Out of the sample of female teachers whom we interviewed, she and one other female teacher in East Gonja were the only teachers who had a strong service ethic. Esther was not thinking of her own comfort in taking up the post but was more concerned about what it meant to offer a service to the community, what impact a newly trained teacher could make on a community and what leadership, community relations and organisational skills were needed to mobilise the community and assist the school. She was also concerned about the girls in the village and attempted to act as a good role model for them.

Adjusting to community life in a remote rural area

If you feel proud you will face problems but if you get into a community and are friendly you will have no problem with them. For example, the previous teacher had to leave due to a poor relationship with the community.

(Female teacher in rural Ghana, field notes)

The Ghana Female Teacher Study found that the most important quality of a newly trained female teacher was her ability to develop good community–school relations. These were essential for both male and female teachers so that they were able to function in a comfortable and effective manner. Without a good relationship with the community, some of the female teachers who had been serving for over ten years in the same district were unable to get help to undertake a simple construction and repair job for their school, despite numerous attempts. This sometimes resulted in bad feeling between the teacher and the community and led to teacher absenteeism until the school building was repaired.

Several newly trained female teachers we interviewed were not well adjusted to their new communities. They spoke of loneliness and did not see themselves as potential change agents or role models. They were also very sure that they would have to leave the community within a short period. Two years appeared to be the longest time they could consider committing themselves to living in a particular community. Most spoke of their plans to pursue higher education at the University of Winneba or Cape Coast. Unlike the newly trained female teachers who were often from urban centres outside the district in which they were teaching, most of the long serving female teachers were from rural areas themselves and had family living in nearby communities. This made their adaptation to the community in which they were teaching much easier

The problems experienced by female teachers living in rural areas were compounded by their low socio-economic status in the community. Untrained female teachers received 160,000 to 180,000 cedis net salary (approximately 45 US dollars per month) and, in some cases, were found to use teaching as a supplementary source of income to their primary activity of hairdressing and/or trading. In contrast, trained female teachers received a salary of between 270,000 and 320,000 cedis depending on the female teacher's rank. Not surprisingly, longer serving teachers reported that they could not survive on the salary provided by the Ghana Education Service (GES). All teachers interviewed in the study complained that their salary was low in comparison to women working in the health sector and those working in other occupations who were serving in rural areas and receiving extra allowances, accommodation and other benefits. They also worried that as much as 5–10 per cent of their salary had to be used to travel to the district capital to collect their salary at the end of each month. These monthly trips also took them away from their school duties since they had to travel during the week when banks were open.

Most of the female teachers interviewed were also involved in activities to supplement their teaching salary with farm and off-farm work. Urban-based female teachers had a great advantage compared with their rural counterparts in being able to earn extra income. In some cases, however, such supplementary income-generating activities contributed to the low status of the teacher in the community. District education officers gave examples of how female teachers were found carrying out degrading tasks such as selling ice water in the evening at the local lorry station. Rural-based female teachers spoke of their inability to engage in these petty trading activities (such as selling of ice water and ready-made food) compared to their urban counterparts.

Rural-based female teachers also compared themselves to their urban counterparts who had been able to build their own homes, purchase bicycles, clothing and purchase televisions and other consumer items on credit. Rural-based teachers were also at a great disadvantage since they did not have access to credit or a large market to sell items. No one in the rural area was willing to give building materials on credit and therefore they found it difficult to build and maintain their homes. Most of the rural female teachers interviewed were engaged in farming activities for both consumption and market purposes. There were also reports that their children would assist them with farm activities during the school hours. One community, in the Western Region had agreed that instead of the community providing food stuffs for the teachers – the children could farm for the teachers on Fridays. The school used the children on a rotational basis and farming activities became a main source of income, which supplemented the teachers' salary and food supply.

Teachers' personal and professional lives

The interconnections between female teachers' professional and personal lives took many forms and were clearly gendered. The main factors highlighted during the literature review and pre-fieldwork interviews of the Ghana Female

Teacher Study point to the socio-cultural factors and family/home constraints facing women in the teaching profession (Casely-Hayford with Wilson 2001). Female teachers in Ghana were found to make a range of adjustments in order to meet the demands of their professional life while maintaining their family and home life. Several changes in a female teachers' working life such as marriage, childbearing and child rearing roles have a tremendous impact on their professional performance and ability to cope. Studies in Ghana point to the complex and multiple roles Ghanaian women balance, managing their home and working lives (Nikoi 1998; Ardayfio-Schandorf 1994; Oppong and Abu 1987).

Their responsibilities as mothers and wives played a major part in the difficulties rural women teachers faced. For example, one of the most important dilemmas they identified working in rural areas was the problem of how to educate their own children, particularly given the quality of the local schooling. Female teachers who were posted to rural areas made it clear that they would not live in remote areas over extended periods because of the poor quality of education available to their children. In some districts, this meant that they would only accept postings to schools near a major town or circuit centre where they could access private schooling. Only two out of 18 female teachers (with children) had their own children attending the school they were posted to (Nyankontre and Bissaso). Both these schools had a large teaching force and were considered to be better developed since they provided both primary and JSS education. The other communities had only 'village schools' often with only three classrooms and one teacher. The majority of female teachers put their children in private schools outside the community in which they taught (Ningoor, Nketrakura). Both trained and untrained teachers spoke of being unable to support their children beyond the JSS level because of their limited income from teaching.

Female teachers in several rural communities (particularly in East Gonja districts of Bankamba and Kojobonikope) also indicated that, because they were unable to supplement their salary with other income generating activities, they were unable to support their children at senior secondary or tertiary level institutions. These women were often solely responsible for the payment of the child's education since their husbands were farmers and solely responsible for providing food for the family. Other studies in Ghana reflect this trend (Casely-Hayford 2000).

Another gendered issue was whether female rural teachers had any opportunity to develop their careers. The majority of female teachers we interviewed in the study districts did not have any way of upgrading their professional knowledge. We found that many untrained female teachers serving in rural areas did not purchase newspapers or books, nor receive any regular in-service or special training or incentives from GES programmes since these were only open to 'trained teachers'. This left untrained 'pupil' teachers at a severe disadvantage – many of them worrying about their job security and happy to maintain a low profile in the teaching service. Interviews with both District Education Officers and other teachers revealed some of the problems of retraining and upgrading female teachers already in the system. Education officers spoke of long serving female teachers as 'untrainable' since many had lost their basic literacy skills and most were seen as alienated from the teaching profession and more likely to see themselves not as teachers but caregivers to children.

Male teachers' perceptions of female teachers were particularly discouraging. Negative male perceptions of female teachers have been highlighted in several studies. Male teachers are reported to believe that female teachers do not spend as much time in the classroom and do not prepare for classroom teaching in the same way they do because of their domestic responsibilities and reproductive role in the family. Female teachers are accused of being lazy, bringing their babies into the school when they are still nursing and often of being late (Avotri *et al.* 1999). They are also seen as engaged in 'unhelpful conversation during school hours' (GES/DAE 1995). Male teachers were recorded as having the following views:

> men are more resourceful, they quarrel less, are more helpful, are more energetic, have more leadership qualities, are smarter; women have mood swings, they are gossips, are bossy, cause confusion because male teachers may express an interest in them.
>
> (GES/DAE 1995: 30)

Both men and women thought that women were absent from work more than men because of childcare responsibilities and health problems caused by child-bearing and lactation (GES/DAE 1995). Despite this, women are believed by community members to make better teachers, particularly at the kindergarten and primary levels, since they are thought to be more patient, more sensitive, less strict and more trustworthy particularly concerning financial matters. At the same time, community members felt that women did not make good school inspectors.

The effects of the 'poor supply' of female teachers on girls' education

The Ghana Female Teacher Study uncovered a crisis with respect to rural education in Ghana, particularly in light of the poor supply of trained female teachers and the lack of interest of female teachers to serve in rural communities. The study further confirmed findings from previous studies revealing that a cycle of deprivation prevents most rural communities in Ghana from using their basic education system as a means to human development (Casely-Hayford 2000). Here there is a vicious circle that links the lack of female teachers with girls' low educational performance, under-achievement and deepening poverty at the community level.

The problem of female teacher supply is directly related to a number of factors. First, the entrance and retention of female candidates at the teacher training institutions may be very low, not least because of the poor performance of female students at basic and secondary levels of education. Most of the 20 communities involved in the Ghana Female Teacher Study experienced very low levels of enrolment and high dropout rates among girls, particularly at upper primary and JSS level. Interviews with parents and head teachers revealed a lack of parental interest in education particularly related to the aspirations of female pupils despite intensive campaigns around girls' education. Most parents were frustrated with the poor performance of teachers in their schools (especially compared with the town schools). They lacked evidence that their children were learning and would be able to achieve higher levels of education after attending the local school.

Girls' low educational performance and underachievement has been associated in turn with the lack of female teachers in their schools. Croft (2000), for example, found girls' low self-esteem in the basic core courses such as maths and English prevents them from attaining higher academic levels. Poor science and maths results of girls, particularly from rural areas were recorded throughout the basic and secondary levels of education in Ghana (Sutherland-Addy 2002; FAWE 1999). High academic requirements for entry into teacher training colleges then prevents girls from entering the teaching profession (Sutherland-Addy 2002; Casely-Hayford with Wilson 2001). However, the lack of female teachers as role models for girls in school as well as the lack of gender sensitive approaches arguably contributes to this cycle of underachievement. Gaynor's diagram best illustrates this dynamic (see Figure 10.1).

The Ghana Female Teacher Study confirmed Gaynor's analysis and uncovered a range of other gender and socio-cultural factors contributing to this cycle. Out of the 87 female senior secondary school (SSS) students interviewed only 11 said they would like to go into the teaching profession (12.6 per cent). Very few of these SSS3 girls knew the secondary school courses required for entry into teacher training college – none of the girls had received career coun-

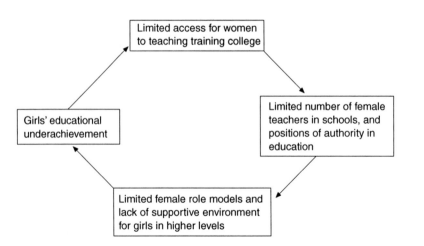

Figure 10.1 Cycle of girls' underachievement and limited female teacher participation (source: Gaynor 1997).

selling or knew how to pursue their career choices. The majority of girls were taking programmes in business and vocational areas that would not qualify them for entry into a teacher training college and many explained that they feared maths and science subjects and opted for vocational and secretarial programmes that did not require the same level of intensity.

The most significant findings from our interviews and observations of female teachers within the six districts was the lack of positive female role models in the teaching profession for girls even within districts where there were female teachers. There was a danger, which most long serving female teachers appeared to be concerned about, that they would become 'too much like the locals' and that their students could not see a difference between the female teachers and the other villagers (newly trained teachers were exceptions to this rule). Many female teachers were not able to act or behave as good role models and they were acutely aware of this dilemma. Their own presentation, their social distance from the community, the location of their residences were all critical factors in maintaining a level of respect from community members.

Most importantly, female teachers' adaptability and respect for rural life, their performance and attitude towards their work as a service to the community, was critical to their acceptance by the community. There was also a strong perceived link between their income level and their social standing. Interviews with both senior secondary school students and community members revealed that, in their view, the social status of the teacher was associated with what status symbols they could demonstrate to the community. When we asked SSS girls why they did not choose to enter the teaching profession, they explained that teachers had to walk to school while their own pupils were driving around in cars. Several teachers spoke of their inability to buy suitable clothing for school because of their lack of access to ready-made garments, which were only available in the large towns. 'The female teachers look the same as the community members – no decent clothing to wear to school' (female teacher, Sene District). Several teachers mentioned that they felt embarrassed when walking to their farms in shabby clothing on the same path as their own pupils. Newly trained female teachers serving in rural areas kept their image up in the village by always dressing properly for school. However there was a significant difference between the quality of school uniforms worn by rural- and urban-based teachers.

Another indicator of the teachers' low socio-economic status was their inability to support their own children through higher levels of education. This was also the main reason that female teachers gave for not encouraging their own children to enter the teaching profession. Discussions with SSS3 female students in Kintampo and East Gonja revealed that these factors had a significant impact on their perceptions of the teaching profession.

Where teachers had prospered economically, they appeared to attract a higher level of respect. For instance, in the Western Region of Ghana, some female teachers and their families had done extremely well in supplementing their income from cocoa farming activities and plantain cultivation. These teachers offered positive role models in terms of being successful farmers and as a result had achieved a level of respect from the community. The social status of the female teacher was also affected by their role in the community. Where female teachers had married into the village, they were treated the same way as other local women – often with disrespect. Some of the female teachers in the community described how male pupils at primary and JSS level called them names and made fun of them in the community (Kojobonikope, East Gonja). In contrast, those female teachers who had maintained some social distance from the community and had demonstrated leadership capacities seemed to be able to establish a higher social status for themselves. They were still confronted with discrimination and derogatory remarks by elders and men but were able to contain these and wield some level of respect because of their community leadership roles.

However, the most important factor that affected the social status of the female teacher in the community was the perception of the community about her professional ability and performance at school. Newly trained female teachers commanded some respect and could maintain this, especially if they kept some social distance from the community. They usually remained astute and careful about interacting too closely with the community until they had established their position. Some took an active role in assisting communities improve the school but this required experience in community mobilisation, which most newly trained teachers were lacking. The interviews with men and women's groups across the 20 communities revealed that community members kept a watchful eye on their female teachers.

Our interviews with the Girls' Education Officers and female teachers themselves gave some indication of what characteristics were associated with their perceptions of 'good female role models in such communities' – these included:

- proper dress;
- proper relations with men in the community (married or staying with one partner);
- humility and good relations with the community;
- a willingness to take up responsibility in the community;
- a basic level of proficiency in their teaching duties.

We found that very few long serving and newly trained female teachers exhibited these qualities. Most female teachers felt they were victims of the environment in which they were living, and instead of attempting to change their conditions they fell into negative patterns of behaviour.

Conclusions

The Ghana Female Teacher Study indicates that the strategies required to improve the supply and retention of female teachers in areas of rural poverty depend on improving the status of the teacher in general in Ghana. The current status of teaching is so low that several teachers reported dissuading their own children from entering the profession. Women are particularly vulnerable to this low status since they already occupy a low social status within Ghanaian society (Nikoi 1998; Ardayfio-Schandorf 1994) and are not likely to be attracted to, or remain in, professions that further handicap them.

The Ghana Female Teacher Study revealed the critical need to improve the skills of rural teachers, in order to avoid further polarising the problems of teaching and learning in these areas. Simple communication and community development techniques are needed in order to prepare men and women to serve as teachers. Teachers should also be better oriented and informed about the context of rural education, motivated to serve and make a difference to the lives of children in these areas: currently there is no course at the teacher training or university level that orients teachers to the harsh realities of rural education and the context of learning in resource deprived areas. Instead most trained teachers emerge with an attitude of 'doing time' in these areas and leave immediately after their two-year posting.

More research is needed to study the characteristics of female teachers at training college level. This would assist in the design of courses, which help teacher trainees adjust themselves to rural life. Only a few trained teachers married to local men remain teaching in the rural areas or large circuit centres where socio-economic conditions are better. The Ghana Female Teacher Study also reveals a tremendous need to raise the female teachers' self-image through closer dialogue, encouragement and training by the government of Ghana and the District Education Offices in particular. Untrained teachers should be included when in-service programmes are offered in the districts. Most importantly, teachers should be trained and oriented as change agents in the communities they serve. This attitudinal shift will only come about with the introduction of more contextually oriented courses at training college and district levels.

The Ghana Female Teacher Study suggests that attracting more female teachers to serve in rural areas will depend largely on a change of attitudes among newly trained teachers particularly if they are to become effective role models for girls in future. Strategies, which ensure that female children from rural areas are mentored, supported and sponsored, appear to be long-term solutions to the problem. In the short term, female teachers from around the country could be encouraged, oriented and prepared to serve for at least two years after completing training college in poor rural areas.

Rural girls need to be mentored and financially supported in order to ensure that they attain higher levels of education. Rural Education Centres have been suggested as a key strategy for assisting rural girls in disadvantaged districts of the country in order to break the poverty cycle, which is compounded through poor educational quality and lack of parental care. Governments will have to support education for rural girls in order to produce the type of female teachers they so desperately need.

Notes

1 The full title of the study is *How the poor get poorer: an exploration into the participation, quality and needs of female teachers in deprived rural areas of Ghana*. It was funded by the Ministry of Education and the World Bank in 2000.
2 Three main sites were identified in six districts cutting across three ecological and socio-culturally diverse areas of Ghana (i.e. Northern Region, predominantly Muslim, Western Region cocoa growing and Christian and Brong Ahafo Region, transition zone and ethnically mixed).
3 The Ghana Female Teacher study resulted in a typology for identification of different levels of deprivation in rural Ghana. Three main categories were identified based on socio-economic infrastructure, location, number of schools and population strength. The categorisation included: less deprived areas, deprived and extremely deprived areas within the study districts.
4 During the fieldwork I succumbed to malaria and infections the last week of the study and could not find any pharmacy in the district capital with antibiotics to treat the problem; the team had to travel out of the district nearly 50 kms to find a hospital and obtain the necessary medication.
5 These vignettes were adapted from field notes based on in-depth interviews and translated from the local language Twi.

References

Ardayfio-Schandorf, E. (1994) *Family and Development in Ghana*, Accra: Ghana University Press.

Avotri, R., Owusu-Darko, L., Eghan, H. and Ocansey, S. (October, 1999) *Gender and Primary Schooling in Ghana*, Brighton: University of Sussex. IDS publication and FAWE sponsored.

Brock, C. and Cammish, N. (1997a) *Factors Affecting Female Participation in Education in Seven Developing Countries*. Second Edition. Serial no 9, London: DfID Publication.

Brock, C. and Cammish, N. (1997b) 'Gender, Education and Development: A partially annotated and selected bibliography'. Serial No 19, London: DfID Publication.

Casely-Hayford, L. (2000) 'Education, Culture and Development in Northern Ghana: Micro Realities and Macro Context: Implications for Policy and Practice', Unpublished DPhil Thesis, University of Sussex, UK.

Casely-Hayford, L. (2002a) 'Ghana Education Sector Review: General Education, Gender and the Disadvantaged', Accra: Ministry of Education.

Casely-Hayford, L. (2002b) 'Situational Analysis of Gender Issues in Education: from Literate Girls to Educated Women', Accra: Education Sector Review Report, Ministry of Education.

Casely-Hayford, L. with Wilson, S. (2001) 'How the Poor Get Poorer. Investigation of the Needs of Females in Rural Deprived Areas', Accra: Girls' Education Unit, Ministry of Education.

Croft, A. (2000) 'Gender Gaps in Primary Schools and Colleges: Can teacher education policy improve gender equity?' Muster Discussion Paper 14, University of Sussex Muster Project, UK.

Foundation of African Women Educationalists (FAWE) (1999) 'Highlighting Partnership Building with Stakeholders and Presentation on Teenage Pregnancy and Attrition Rates Among Girls at the Basic Education Level in Ghana', Report on 2nd Network Forum, Accra, Ghana.

Gaynor, C. (1997) *The Supply, Condition and Professional Development of Women Teachers. The Management of Teachers*, Paris: IIEP.

Ghana Education Service (GES/DAE) and UNICEF (1995) 'A Study of Teacher Motivation and Conditions of Service for Teachers in Ghana', Accra: Ministry of Education.

King, E.M. and Hill, M.A. (1993) Education of Females and Economic Development, Washington: World Bank Discussion Paper.

Nikoi, G. (1998) *Gender and Development*, Accra, Ghana: University of Cape Coast.

Oppong, C. and Abu, K. (1987) 'The Seven Roles of Women: Impacts of Education, Migration and Employment and Ghanaian Mothers', Geneva: International Labour Organisation Series No. 13 Women Work and Development.

Rugh, A. (2000) 'Starting Now: Strategies for Helping Girls Complete Primary School', Washington, DC: Academy for Educational Development.

Sutherland-Addy, E. (2002) 'Impact Assessment Study of the Girls' Education Programme in Ghana', UNICEF Ghana.

UNESCO (2003) *EFA Global Monitoring Report 2003/4: Gender and Education for All – The Leap to Equality*, Paris: UNESCO. Available online at: www.portal.unesco. org/education/en/ev.php.

World University Service of Canada (WUSC) (2000) 'Improving Girls' Self Esteem: The Role of the Teacher: An Action Research Project' (Pilot Study).

Part III

(Re)defining global equality agendas

11 Globalising the school curriculum

Gender, EFA and global citizenship education

Harriet Marshall and Madeleine Arnot

This chapter aims to bring the school curriculum into the analysis of gender, education and development. There is a marked absence of discussion both in the academic field of development studies and in the political domain of educational policy making around Education for All about what is required of the school curriculum so that it could help promote gender equality. All too often national school curricula reproduce gender inequalities in the public and private sphere and sustain hegemonic male regimes on a national and global scale (Arnot 2002). Curriculum research, however, can challenge these social messages embedded in curricular formations as well as raise deeper questions about whose forms of knowledge should be transmitted through official forms of schooling. Critical sociological research, for example, recognises the importance of the rules governing the access and redistribution of knowledge, and also the politics behind the selection, organisation and evaluation of legitimate knowledge through formal national educational institutions within developing economies and the impact these have on indigenous social stratifications. It can also critically assess new global interventions into the school curriculum whether in the name of economic progress, human rights or social justice. These global developments are controversial not least because of the challenge they represent to what has been considered the prerogative of national governments – to transmit its own selection of educational knowledge to its citizens, using its own contextualised pedagogic style. The study of national curricula therefore offers the possibility of exploring the equity dimensions of global–national and local educational interfaces and policy agendas.

This chapter has limited but hopefully valuable ambitions. It aims to initiate discussion of the curriculum in relation to gender, education and development by exploring the global significance of recent interventions on gender, and in particular girls' education. The first section briefly considers the implications of globalisation as a transformative process on the development of educational knowledge and queries whether the school curricula could address persistent worldwide gender disparities, inequalities and female subjugation. In the second section, we focus specifically on whether new global declarations around gender equality such as those analysed in the UNESCO Education for All *Global Monitoring Reports* (see Chapter 4, this volume) imply certain roles for the school curriculum. The final section addresses the possibilities for gender equality implied by recent interest global citizenship education – a new curriculum subject and approach that promises much. We consider in a preliminary way whether these new developments represent a move towards forms of educational knowledge that are critical rather than legitimating and 'normalising' in relation to gender inequalities.

This chapter draws upon our own work[1] and the insights offered by Western feminists and critical sociologists on these new global curricular initiatives. As such, the analysis we offer is only temporary, waiting to be disturbed and enriched by post-colonial cultural critiques (Smith 1999). In the long run, critical curriculum theorising must involve *localised* investigations into the gender politics of national school curricula in non-Western environments, linking such analyses to the material and socio-cultural conditions of gender relations in these societies. Western critical analyses of educational knowledge with their emphasis upon liberal education, illusions of neutrality and hierarchies of knowledge expertise, are insufficient analytic frameworks for the study of such local cultural-curricular formations.

The gender politics of the curriculum

Sociology of the curriculum in the 1970s and 1980s in Western European countries demonstrated the ways in which the school curriculum was a political arrangement and social construction, where what counts as knowledge is 'selected' and prioritised and where inevitably some knowledge is excluded or marginalised. Sociologists of education, following Bernstein (1977: 85), saw that the way 'a society selects, classifies, distributes, transmits and evaluates the educational knowledge it considers to be public', is central to any power structure. The distribution of power and principles of social control shapes the relationship between school knowledge, everyday local or regional knowledge and creates the conditions for the reproduction of social inequality nationally. Arguably these principles also play a part in shaping the impact of global economic agendas on national social stratification and educational systems.

Curriculum theorists, however, such as Goodson (1997) argue that if we look inside the curriculum, we will find forces that are both stabilising and destabilising. It has the potential both to empower and disempower women as well as men. Curriculum theorists in the West have demonstrated this in relation to inequalities in race, class, sexuality and gender. These inequalities can be reproduced (albeit in transfigured form) through *overt* curricular knowledge as well as through what came to be known as the *hidden curriculum* of schooling (teachers' values, school rituals etc.). Gender, class, sexual and ethnic identities were also calibrated, resisted, reworked and celebrated through peer group subcultures, classroom resistances and multiple alliances and allegiances. There is no simple equation, for example, between the representation of women in the curriculum and girls' definitions of femininity (cf. Arnot and Mac an Ghaill 2006).

Whilst feminist analyses of the curriculum moved from its own intellectual roots in liberal democracy towards post-structuralist and postmodern understandings of the performances and multiplicities of gender identities in contemporary Western societies (ibid.), it has never lost sight of the significance of political praxis – of teachers, researchers and youth. Critical pedagogues in developed nations aim to create dialogue, engagement and ownership amongst those disadvantaged by the social biases and negative representations found in school texts, teaching materials and teaching strategies. The aim of much critical pedagogy is to make clear to students that the curriculum is a site of meaning-making and that the social construction of knowledge opens up possibilities of including their knowledge. Increasingly the voices and lived experiences of male and female youth have been drawn into the curriculum arena challenging dominant 'expert' and hierarchical organised knowledge forms. Teachers' gendered assumptions are seen as critical mediators of official knowledge – linking textual messages to teaching practice. The story of cultural and social reproduction through the curriculum is therefore now recognised as highly complex as well as a deeply significant part of educational achievement. Schools are understood to be 'productive' institutions that create both agency *and* social stratification through their knowledge-producing work.

Some capability theorists have recognised this productive element of the curriculum in development contexts. Walker (2006: 175), for example, points to the importance of providing girls with 'access to subject knowledge which will enable them to make future career choices, or simply enjoy this knowledge as an intrinsic good'. The access of girls to the more powerful subjects in schools (such as science and mathematics) becomes, from this perspective, central not marginal to an economic development agenda and a programme of gender justice. The curriculum represents a core development capability if made gender sensitive, offering girls' agency and autonomy, aspiration and voice. Walker summarises this view:

> Schools contribute, for many people quite substantially, to the formation of their capabilities to function. Ideally schools ought to equip people with the capabilities to pursue opportunities they value. How valued and valuable opportunities and capabilities are distributed through formal education to whom, and how this maps over structures of race, gender, class, able-bodiedness, religion, and so on is then a matter of social justice in education and hence for education policy.
>
> (ibid.: 181)

The study of the school curriculum within a development framework, however, needs to consider the context in which national curricula are being revised – that of globalisation and new global educational agendas associated with Education for All. These contexts, although linked, are not necessarily compatible. As a result there is considerable ambivalence, as we briefly indicate below, about the egalitarian potential of a curriculum that has been reshaped by globalisation – what we might call a *globalised curriculum*. Below we consider a number of different globalising influences on educational knowledge that might shape such a curriculum.

Globalisation, gender and educational knowledge

Schooling historically was a very national affair and consequently curriculum theorists developed conceptual frameworks almost entirely within this national context. As Meyer (1999) points out, most critical sociological analyses have focused first on equality in access and achievement and, second, on the function of education in relation to the national societies that manage it. This has resulted in the field being:

> inattentive to the actual curricular content of education (because the func-
> tionality of this is assumed), and also to the curricular changes that go on in
> response to rapid globalisation in the world (because the local or national
> character of schooling is assumed).
>
> (ibid.: 3)

Meyer argues for an analysis of how globalisation reconstructs national educational curricula and, in particular, how the school curriculum conceptualises 'an imagined world society'. His attention is captured by the possibility that an ideal knowledge base for a global education could be found in a mixture of human rights, scientisation, rationality and natural law (Meyer 1999, 2006) and by the standardised world visions proposed by such global agencies as UNESCO and the World Bank. Recently these world visions, especially around Education for All, have placed gender equality at the centre of their recommendations.

Globalisation is associated with increased economic international exchanges between countries and linked to these changes are transformations in social consciousness about the involvement of future citizens in the world society (Meyer 2006). Three globalising curricular ambitions can be identified within many transnational initiatives. Here we focus on three global contexts: first, the global movement for *gender equality* (exemplified in the UN Millennium Development Goals); second the movement for *global citizenship education* (exemplified by the work of some international and national non-governmental organisations); and third the agenda associated with the global *economic outcomes* of schooling. Economic globalisation demands a highly skilled, mobile, economically literate and flexible male and female workforce. However, the values and motivations associated with this globalising thrust are sometimes in stark contrast to any notions of global equality of opportunity and social justice for all implied by the first two goals.

Burbules and Torres (2000) describe the complex educational scenario that schools in developed as well as developing economies now face:

> new developments in cross-cultural education (for example, international education and global distance education); the impact of structural adjustment policies imposed by international agencies on developing countries in the name of creating a global economy; the rise of entrepreneurial universities in response to the pressures of globalisation; and attempts to reform primary and secondary curricula and teacher training in the name of globalisation, stressing the imperatives of flexible production required for international competitiveness.
>
> (ibid.: 41)

These elements, however, suggest that educational establishments will have to cope with more than vocational/economic liberalisation and marketisation. Clearly, educating the new global learner will be quite a challenge. In a globalised context:

> Crude moral codes or simple national identities ... look very dated and inappropriate but then so do the forms of educational knowledge in current curricula.... In the new social order, educational institutions would need to provide basic social and political rights and offer opportunities to develop an informational base; acquire the skills of preparedness for conflict, capacity for compromise, civic courage, curiosity, tolerance of ambiguity and the making of alliances. These forms of education ... have to stress the malleability of knowledge, the uncertainty of explanations and the relativity of perspective.... In such a future, it may make little sense to talk about knowledge as property or subject positions – rather reflexive modern individuals could be offered knowledge that was 'possibilistic, probabilistic and uncertain' ... In the future, learning is likely to be intense, at speed, with ranges of choice and opportunities for immediate decision-making.
>
> (Arnot 2006a: 5)

As Rizvi (2000) points out, such globalised curricula could provide the space for the 'production of the global imagination'. Whilst he recognises the fear that such new citizenship forms might represent unrestrained Westernisation, Rizvi argues that, in reality, a student's global imagination is a product of a range of factors: globalisation 'affects people and nations in a variety of different ways that are both asymmetrical and contingent' (ibid.: 222). For example when considering the perspectives of Malaysian students in Australian universities, Rizvi notices how, in contrast to colonialism, globalisation

> has a commercial dimension that makes it sensitive to the needs of both markets and clients. It is sensitive to difference and preaches the need to respond to local needs. It has a culturally interactive disposition, even to

the point of commodifying difference, constructing it so it can be sold in terms of language of diversity and multiculturalism.

(ibid.: 222)

These transpositional curricular spaces also offer opportunities for more radical educational approaches. The new global citizen could experience a curriculum that emphasises notions of mobility, multiculturalism, diversity and diaspora. It could also encourage 'critical literacies' (Kellner 2000) and offer an analysis of the more pejorative effects of globalisation. Rizvi (2007) has further identified the need to foster key 'epistemic virtues' of historicity, reflexivity, criticality and relationality in global citizenship education related projects.

From a gender perspective, such curricular opportunities need to be thought through carefully. Jill Blackmore (2000), for example, encourages feminists to at least consider whether globalisation (even though associated with unjust neoliberal agendas) could be a catalyst for the development of gender-equitable educational theory and practice. 'Women feel both the pain and the pleasure associated with seductive notions of choice', and they 'largely bear the responsibility as the competitive state withdraws from its social welfare obligations while reprivatizing women's productive labor' (ibid.: 135). Yet despite this, globalisation encourages a reconsideration of the gendered relationships between citizenship, education and the market:

> globalisation requires new understandings about citizenship vis-à-vis the nation-state in order to address the severe tensions between citizenship and the market, which pit materialism against spirituality, rationality against emotion, selfishness against altruism, atomism against solidarity, wants against needs, along gender lines.
>
> (ibid.: 150)

Globalisation has the potential to offer curricular space for women to consider what they want from citizenship and there is therefore a case for using the school to 'understand better how these new formations and relationships are gendered and to consider how we need to develop anti-imperialist curricula and transnational feminist practice' (ibid.: 151). Wright (2001) also reminds us not to accept international human rights goals without considering the complexities associated with their Euro-American and colonial roots. He argues for the importance of recognising that 'global history is a history of colonialism' and that 'those individuals who cannot recognise their own position within colonialism are often the most vociferous in their demands that human rights are the representation of universal values of freedom, equality and justice' (ibid.: 224–225).

These few tentative examples of global curriculum theorising cannot easily provide us with a conceptual framework, although they indicate the directions which such conceptual thinking might take. Empirical/conceptual research is needed to unpack the ways in which globalised educational knowledge relates to international and national power relations, stratifications and critical social movements for change. Below we offer our own analyses of first, the curricular implications of Education for All and, second, the promise of global citizenship education.

The curriculum of Education For All

The inclusion of a gender agenda within the development framework has been highly significant for the development of national curricula even if not initially appreciated as such. The UN naming of the International Year of Women (1975) and the Beijing Conference were especially important because of the explicit inclusion and recognition of the particularity of women's lives and their needs. The Millennium Development Goals (MDGs) and the 'Education for All' (EFA) campaign, initiated by UNESCO in 1990 and reframed in 2000, represented the most recent examples of international efforts to increase and improve girls' education. The involvement of the World Bank and its particular conceptual framework has been important for developing the quantitative, time-bound international targets. The EFA Dakar framework (UNESCO 2000) required each country to produce a National Action Plan that also incorporated six specific, time-bound goals: these goals concerned early childhood care and education, universal primary education, youth and adult learning, literacy, gender and quality.

Whilst women's rights movements have praised the centrality of gender equality in this development agenda, there has been some concern that they, 'sideline key gains made in Beijing, Cairo and other UN conferences, set a minimalist agenda and fail to integrate gender perspectives into all eight MDGs' and that they do not therefore address the fundamental causes of poverty and gender inequality such as 'power, distribution of resources, militarism, fundamentalisms and current economic orthodoxy' (Barton 2005: 1). As an example, it is significant that, although the *EFA Global Monitoring Reports* (UNESCO 2002b, 2003, 2004) include many educational and gender statistics, only the most recent report includes any data that relate to the curriculum. Below we offer the first tentative steps towards a curriculum analysis of these reports.

The curricular implications of EFA

The subtitle of this section is something of a misnomer because current documentation on EFA suggests that no such curriculum exists in an official sense. This is partly because the document recognises the rights of individual nation states to choose and administer their own school curriculum. Nevertheless, there is an implicit curriculum within the parameters of EFA that could well affect the form of this curricular provision in the longer term. The *EFA Global Monitoring Report* 2005 on the 'quality imperative' (UNESCO 2004) goes so far as to set a policy framework for determining curricular aims and content (Chapter 4, UNESCO 2004). Our own textual analysis of these documents has uncovered four interlinked messages about the role of the curriculum in gender equality embedded in these documents.

The first message concerns the need to include 'rights' within the curriculum. The 2003–2004 *EFA Global Monitoring Report* explores some of the reasons why girls are still held back in relation to education and equality. It identifies some of the obstacles and solutions by working with a framework drawn from a rights agenda. In particular it highlights the three aspects of gender equality that could be used to assess gender attributes of curriculum provision and the content of the curriculum. These are: 'individuals' rights *to* education and their rights *within* and *through* education' (UNESCO 2003: 116). In the section on 'rights within education' the report describes some of the gender-based violence preventing schools from being places of learning, growth and empowerment (especially for girls) and focuses on how teachers' attitudes and textbooks may help sustain the naturalness of such female subordination and male violence in everyday practice. It signals how 'getting the curriculum right is important, although extremely challenging' (ibid.: 145). If traditional gender values of the community are not taught in school (or they are challenged by schools), then girls may be prevented from coming to school:

> In some countries parents may not send daughters to school if they feel that the curriculum is promoting ideas that are at odds with prevailing social norms. In Guinea, parents perceived subjects such as home economics, childcare and sewing, gardening and handicrafts as important for girls, and criticised their absence from the schooling curriculum.
>
> (ibid.: 146)

The report points to the importance of silences and subtleties in the curriculum as much as observable sexism as significant for the endurance of gender inequalities.

The second message concerns the need to consider 'curriculum as opportunity'. The chapter 'Lessons from Good Practice' (Chapter 4, ibid.) heralds the role of the curriculum as essential for ensuring that girls should be given equal opportunities for 'success and advancement' whilst in school.

> The role of the curriculum in this process is crucial, in that it is a key source of pupils' knowledge about, and orientation within, the social world. This is widely acknowledged, and many countries have initiated reforms both to reduce biases in subject choices confronting girls and boys, and to remove any implications of gender stereotypes from textbooks and other teaching materials.
>
> (ibid.: 178)

However, it is not clear what criteria are being used to measure the success of these gender initiatives, and one of the few examples of textbook reform (i.e. in Cambodia) seemed to result in gender equality being 'expressed mainly in an evenly balanced number of male and female illustrations ... rather than in a way that would explicitly challenge cultural norms or traditions' (ibid.: 178).

The third message concerns the need to consider 'curriculum as reform'. The report suggests that there are eight aspects of education that gender equality policies should address. Six items on the list have identifiable links to curriculum change and reform (see Table 11.1). If these issues were addressed, it would have major implications for what should be taught. However, the UNESCO report offers little help to teachers to consider how they might deconstruct curricular materials, rethink teaching styles or redesign curricular offerings. Further, this list is strongly reminiscent of liberal feminist agendas in the UK in the 1970s that made no reference to any form of critical pedagogy or deconstruction of hegemonic male forms of knowledge (Arnot 2002).

All the UNESCO *EFA Global Monitoring Reports* were careful to emphasise that developing and changing the curriculum cannot be isolated from other efforts and reforms. For example, they emphasise the importance of simultaneously including gender awareness in teacher training.

The fourth message we found within the UNESCO *EFA Global Monitoring Reports* concerns the need to consider 'curriculum as a democratic tool'. This message is not widely discussed in the report – it tends to be inferred. The underlying emphasis is upon the need for a greater political commitment to EFA goals and it is strongly suggested that these goals will only be met in some of the countries concerned if there is greater decentralisation and democratisation, not just of educational institutions, but also of the curriculum.

The subsequent *EFA Global Monitoring Report* (UNESCO 2004) offers considerably more detail on the curriculum (although it still has limitations). Chapter 4 of this report is especially significant for placing curriculum policy and curriculum content more firmly on the EFA quality agenda. The 'inclusive learning environment' that is envisaged as an 'essential attribute of high-quality education' (ibid.: 143) is linked with effective teaching and learning. Teaching and learning is considered in relation to appropriate and relevant curriculum aims, curriculum content, educational policy and use of time. The report

Table 11.1 What approaches to gender equality in the classroom should address

1 Gender stereotypes, i.e. challenging stereotypical views such as girls being unable to benefit from secondary education or less able to succeed in maths or science
2 Sexual violence, abuse and harassment – raising awareness of these issues and using teachers to raise awareness of learners
3 Ideologies in the curriculum
4 Curriculum choices – e.g. encouraging girls to take mathematics, science and technology subjects
5 Teaching styles, including differential attention paid to boys and girls
6 Extramural activities – providing sporting opportunities for girls as well as boys;   • differential enrolment of boys and girls in school;   • school organisation and discipline – making schools more girl friendly

Source: adapted from UNESCO 2004: 177.

recognises that knowledge about educational quality is an issue often over-shadowed by issues of access, and indicates that better learning outcomes also relate to trying to 'encourage creativity, originality and intolerance of injustice – non-cognitive skills that can help people challenge and transform society's hier-archies rather than accept them' (ibid.: 226). It also gives an overview of some of the contextual world problems, such as those relating to health (especially HIV/AIDS), violence (especially against women) and conflict (and its effects on schooling) that ideally should be acknowledged in a school curriculum, and which in turn highlight the urgency for building values and attitudes that promote peace by developing the skills of communication in schools.

The 2004 report focuses on 'establishing appropriate goals for the curricu-lum, developing relevant content, using time well, ensuring that teaching styles are effective, carefully considering the language of instruction and developing a sound assessment policy' as well as supporting 'the supply, distribution and use of learning materials' and a 'secure, accessible physical environment with appro-priate facilities' (ibid.: 146). Crucially, however, it fails to problematise the school curriculum in relation to gender equity in education. For example, no gender and curricular differentiation is made in the statistical analyses. Thus, whilst the 2003–2004 *EFA Global Monitoring Report* places gender at the centre of the analysis but pays very little attention to the curriculum, the reverse is almost true with respect to school knowledge in the 2005 *EFA Global Moni-toring Report*.

The 2005 *EFA Global Monitoring Report* hints at an uncomfortable relation-ship between knowledge and skills necessary for economic and 'productive lives and livelihoods' on the one hand, and concerns for 'social and cultural values, human rights, greater equity and equality … good citizenship, democracy and world peace' (ibid.) on the other. Although this report acknowledges that most weight is usually given to the former, this implied relationship between know-ledge and values and societal power structures needed more in-depth considera-tion of gender. For example, one table (ibid.: Table 4.1, p. 147) outlines the policy choices in determining national curriculum goals (reflected, for example, in the UN Convention on the Rights of the Child) but does not address the potential differential value clash between *generic/global* cognitive skills and values development and *country/local* cognitive skills and values development, for boys and girls.

To summarise, the 2005 report rightly reminds readers of the difficulty of assessing outcomes in terms of quality or values in the EFA project but it does little more than describe the curricular situations and fails to offer any sugges-tions about further research (such as the critiquing of dominant curricular knowledge forms or critiquing the contradictory notions of citizenship advoc-ated in curricula). Once combined these reports create a vision of a gender fair/friendly curriculum but they do not offer a critically engaged intellectual challenge, on the grounds of gender, to national curricula. Perhaps this is an impossible task for a global report, especially given the diversity of national cur-ricular patterns. The principles of what might constitute a gender neutral curriculum were identified and suggestions were given in the later reports on how this might be developed through teacher quality and the organisation of learning. The difficulty here is that the impression might be given that such a gender neutral curriculum could be achieved without addressing gender power relations, especially those embedded in 'taken for granted' curricular knowledge. Had such a challenge to dominant knowledge forms been signalled, it might have pointed to the relevance of uncovering the relations of power that sustain particular gender distributions of knowledge, and particular gendered knowledge selections, modes of teaching, styles of academic performance and assessment. A key international curriculum target might then emerge that validated women's connected forms of knowledge and their life experiences, moral and political values, and civic virtues and their approaches to learning.

However, having said that, in more industrialised nations where educational priorities are not so focused upon access, global citizenship education appears to offer new 'potential' curriculum spaces in which gender equality can be positioned and discussed critically, The final section of this chapter therefore turns to this relatively new and not uncontroversial curriculum subject to consider whether it could be used to empower girls and women.

Global citizenship education, gender and the curriculum

Nearly half of all the countries that submitted data to UNESCO offer some form of citizenship education in schools. The possibility therefore exists that citizenship education could offer opportunities to engage critically with global gender concerns. Development or global education (comprising traditions such as human rights education, world studies, anti-racist education and peace education) can also provide relevant up to date sources of educational knowledge about gender. However, although the movement for global education in England is associated with a distinctive pupil-centred and participatory pedagogy (the affective dimension of global citizenship education being particularly important), its curricular implications are considerably more flexible and vague (Marshall 2005a). Global knowledge could, if developed, engage critically in an exploration of, for example, the relationship between North and South, and attitudes and values associated with global interdependence and global social justice.

Whilst the EFA agenda appears to be working with particular notions of the educated national citizen, the movement for global citizenship education in countries such as Canada, the USA, the UK, Germany and Australia has an explicit perspective of the student learner as potential 'global' and even the 'cosmopolitan' citizen. The latter goal encourages a critical engagement with the world, guided by a vision of global social justice. Thus whilst EFA and the Millennium Development Goals represent attempts to change the global gender context by setting targets to change national schooling, global citizenship education is an example of bringing the global gender context into the national agenda. Below we explore this latter agenda in more depth.

Global citizenship, cosmopolitanism and the globalised curriculum

Meyer argues that 'the real unifying principle underlying the emergent global society is the natural human person ... a human being with natural (rather than positive or associational) human rights' (1999: 13). This sort of depiction of the common and/or natural personhood and the rights associated with this may provide the 'cultural glue' to sustain a globalised curriculum. Here ethnocentric, nationalistic or patriarchal curricula would be replaced by discussion of issues relating, for example, to the wider world environment, a science that locates all humans in common (such as the universe beyond earth), international human rights (and abuses), and political institutions emphasising global solidarity and shared understanding.

The concept of a 'cosmopolitan citizenship' (often interchangeable with global citizenship) suggests an allegiance to a new form of global civil society and a new global consciousness that conceptualises a 'cosmopolitan order transcending state boundaries and focusing on the rights of individuals' (Carter 2001: 3). It addresses 'the global nature of threats posed to the survival of the human race and of the planet by nuclear and chemical weapons and environmental degradation, and on the trend towards a global economy' (ibid.: 3).

Cosmopolitan citizenship embodies an 'awareness of cultural diversity, respect for other cultures and a desire for peaceful coexistence' (ibid.: 2). As a school subject, it would involve a range of cognitive, affective and action dimensions, empowerment and existential dimensions, and a cyclical learning process (Hicks and Bord 2001). However, it is not self-evident that this new engagement with global social justice would necessarily challenge local/national gender (and other) power relations.

Significant curricular resources and initiatives (most notably through the work of NGOs) around global citizenship have emerged although not many specifically address gender issues. Gender inequality is often represented as a subsidiary issue to poverty or the Millennium Development Goals. Save the Children (UK, a member of the British Overseas Aid Group) has recently published *Young Lives, Global Goals* (Save the Children 2005) with sections that specifically address gender issues (in relation to poverty, education and health care). This represents one of the boldest attempts at getting hard-hitting global gender issues into schools. Save the Children also links schools on its website and through its resource catalogue to information packs on other global gender issues such as *Forgotten Casualties of War: Girls in Armed Conflict* (www.savethechildren.org.uk).

Assessing the impact or indeed the amount of use this sort of curricula resource receives in schools is difficult. A recent two-year DFID funded research project in the UK (Davies *et al.* 2005)[2] found that teachers, learners, teacher trainers and LEAs recognised the need to teach a range of global citizenship issues (such as religion, poverty and war) but again gender was not listed amongst them. Perhaps this lack of global gender issues related to the identified 'lack of confidence to teach current controversial issues' amongst teachers, teacher trainees and LEA personnel in the UK (ibid.: 145).

In contrast the gender profile in the Global-ITE (Initial Teacher Education) Project was more developed. This was a three-year project aimed at enabling trainee teachers in India, Kenya and England to 'link global and global social issues to each other, and relate them to the school curriculum; and to promote a global perspective on citizenship education' (Inbaraj *et al.* 2004: 83). The project researchers recognised the limitations of teaching controversial topics (such as social justice as a problem associated with class, gender, ethnicity, drug taking, violence) and endorsed a more gender sensitive 'global' citizenship education. They emphasised the importance of 'not assuming that individual women's personal choices will be consonant with Western feminism, or even international feminism' (ibid.: 84).

The project worked with teachers in all three countries. It encouraged debate about the nature and challenges of global citizenship education by considering issues of power and control. For example, it unearthed the contradictions between, on the one hand, Kenya's 'Social Ethics Education' that endorses the nuclear family and promotes the concept of marriage in which final authority rests with the husband, and, at the same time, endorses the Centres for Excellence Schools for Rescued Girls in Kenya that educate girls who were at risk of female genital mutilation and/or early marriage. The Indian research team encouraged teacher trainers to design exercises to sensitise children to their own stereotyped attitudes and beliefs as well as gender stereotyping in school textbooks. Interestingly, in this case study, many trainee teachers felt that a focus on gender inequality in the curriculum was outdated, believing that issues relating to the media or the environment were more important (revealed in UNESCO 2004). The study emphasised the need to 'take risks' within the curriculum, which might entail a more radical, participatory and empowering pedagogy than mainstream practice and the re-prioritisation of global knowledge. For example, global citizenship education in Kenya used drama and narrative, which dealt with issues 'ranging from the rights of ownership of one's body, to freedom from violation and pain, to human reproductive choice, and to independence of spirit' (Inbaraj *et al.* 2004: 88).

These global curricula initiatives promise a good deal and yet in practice they have yet to sustain a systematic gender critique of global or national citizenship frameworks. Their potential in relation to the goals of EFA is as yet unproven.

Some concluding remarks

In this chapter, we have identified some of the global visions of a gendersensitive school curriculum and have discussed a variety of ways in which a national curriculum can become 'globalised'. Global knowledge *can* be disempowering and global citizenship education can also be empowering but the reverse of both is also true. By excluding or marginalising knowledge about gender inequality, education may limit the potential of girls to foster voice and aspiration to increase their agency.

The curricular messages offered by UNESCO *EFA Global Monitoring*

Reports are somewhat problematic and contradictory but they have started at least to focus attention on the interconnections between 'quality' of education and gender messages of the curriculum. The curriculum is understood as both an opportunity for individual/group progress and as potentially transformative of some aspects of social relations. The underlying theme is that different, possibly new, notions of the learner citizen can be created through the curriculum. But this still begs the question about what constitutes the most appropriate forms of educational knowledge that are needed to sustain gender equality. Should that new citizen be an upholder of global human rights, or local and national rights and cultural values or should young women and men not both be taught to acquire the skills of reflexivity, individualisation, flexibility more appropriate to the global order? The required forms of competence in the future might be focused, for example, less on learning traditional school subjects and more about achieving, for example, communicative competence, courage, flexibility, risk taking, the ability to sustain alliances and negotiation skills (Arnot 2006a, b).

Gender equality amongst those Ulrich Beck and Elizabeth Beck-Gernsheim (2002) call 'Freedom's Children' would mean encouraging both young women and men to place themselves at the centre of their lives, to acquire knowledge that releases them from traditional social identities such as those of masculinity and femininity, ethnic, regional and local and national identifications. Gender equality in this context is less about matching male and female access to traditional hierarchical and linear curricula, about ensuring equal male and female representation in school textbooks and materials, or equal participation in classrooms: it is about creating individuated selves who know about lateral thinking, interdisciplinary knowledge forms, multiplicities of truths, narratives and relativities (Arnot 2006a, b).

A gender analysis of the national curricula within development contexts requires (a) in-depth historical and sociological unpacking of national curricular norms, (b) a recognition (if not deconstruction) of the various male and female forms of school knowledge and their representations in curricula, (c) an understanding of different types of gendered performances within different school subjects and, (d) a sensitivity to the changing gender relations brought about by globalisation and its significance in terms of female and male relationships to knowledge (Paechter and Head 1996; Paechter 2003). This sort of curricular analysis, which is relevant to the formation of the modern female learner citizen (as it is to the male learner citizen), is the next step in the promotion of gender equality in developing economies. Without such analyses, national gender regimes and male hegemonic power cannot be challenged – indeed many proposed curriculum reforms might well be what Nancy Fraser (1997) called affirmative rather than transformatory remedies, offering redistributive justice but not addressing recognition of cultural and gendered diversity (Arnot 2006b). From this more critical perspective, egalitarian policies that focus on gender parity solely in terms of access to the school curriculum or indeed solely on schooling will only scratch the surface of gender inequality.

The goal of creating gender equality globally has reminded us that the school curriculum has more than a functional significance (Meyer 1999). It has reignited the debate about the politics of educational knowledge in the twenty-first century.

Notes

1 This chapter draws on Arnot 2006a, 2006b, and Marshall 2005a, 2005b, 2007, and Marshall and Arnot 2007 (in press).
2 The qualitative study based in the West Midlands of England, which drew upon data from six primary and six secondary schools, three teacher training institutions and 13 Local Education Authorities.

Bibliography

Arnot, M. (2002) *Reproducing Gender: Essays on Educational Theory and Feminist Politics*, London: RoutledgeFalmer.

Arnot, M. (2006a) 'Freedom's children: a gender perspective on the education of the learner citizen', *International Review of Education*, Special Issue on Education and Social Justice, 52, 1: 67–87.

Arnot, M. (2006b) 'Gender equality, pedagogy and citizenship: affirmative and transformative approaches in the UK', *Theory and Research in Education*, 4, 2: 131–150.

Arnot, M. and Mac an Ghaill, M. (eds) (2006) *The RoutledgeFalmer Gender and Education Reader*, London: RoutledgeFalmer.

Barton, C. (2005) 'Women's movements and gender perspectives on the millennium development goals' in *Civil Society Perspectives on the Millennium Development Goals*, United Nations Development Project, available online at: www.choike.org/documentos/mdgs_cso_barton.pdf (accessed 20 April 2006).

Beck, U. and Beck-Gernsheim, E. (2002) *Individualisation: Institutionalised Individualism and Its Social and Political Consequences*, London: Sage.

Bernstein, B. (1977) *Class, Codes and Control: Volume III*, London: Routledge.

Blackmore, J. (2000) 'Globalisation: a useful concept for feminists rethinking theory and strategies in education?' in N. Burbules and C.A. Torres (eds) *Globalisation and Education: Critical Perspectives*, London: Routledge.

Burbules, N. and Torres, C.A. (eds) (2000) *Globalisation and Education: Critical Perspectives*, London: Routledge.

Carter, A. (2001) *Political Theory of Global Citizenship*, Florence, KY: Routledge.

Davies, L., Harber, C. and Yamashita, H. (2005) *Global Citizenship Education: The Needs of Teachers and Learners*, Birmingham: Centre for International Education and Research (CIER).

Fraser, N. (1997) *Justice Interruptus: Critical Reflections on the 'Post-socialist' Condition*, London: Routledge.

Goodson, I. (1997) *The Changing Curriculum: Studies of Social Construction*, New York: Peter Lang.

Hicks, D. and Bord, A. (2001) 'Learning about global issues: why most educators only make things worse', *Environmental Education Research*, 7, 4: 413–425.

Inbaraj, J., Kumar, S., Sambili, H. and Scott-Baumann, A. (2004) 'Women and citizenship in global teacher education: the Global-ITE Project' in S. Sweetman (ed.) *Gender, Development and Citizenship*, Oxford: Oxfam Development Education Programme.

Kellner, D. (2000) 'Globalization and New Social Movements: Lessons for Critical Theory and Pedagogy' in N. Burbules and C. Torres (eds) *Globalization and Education: Critical Perspectives*, London: Routledge.

Marshall, H. (2005a) *The Sociology of Global Education: Power, Pedagogy and Practice*, Unpublished doctoral thesis, Cambridge University.

Marshall, H. (2005b) 'Developing the global gaze in citizenship education: exploring the perspectives of global education NGO workers in England', *International Journal of Citizenship and Teacher Education*, 1, 2 (available online at: www.citized.info/ijcte).

Marshall, H. (2007) 'The global education terminology debate: exploring some of the issues' in M. Haydon, J. Thompson and J. Levy (eds) *A Handbook of Research in International Education*, London: Sage.

Marshall, H. and Arnot, M. (2007) 'The gender agenda: the limits and possibilities of global and national citizenship education', *World Studies in Education*, 7, 2: 81–106.

Meyer, J. (1999) *Globalisation and the Curriculum: Problems for Theory in the Sociology of Education*, paper presented at the International Symposium, University of Lisbon, November 1999.

Meyer, J. (2006) 'World models, national curricula, and the centrality of the individual' in A. Benavot and C. Braslavsky (eds) *School Curricula for Global Citizenship*, Hong Kong: University of Hong Kong.

Oxfam (2006) *Education for Global Citizenship in Schools: A Guide for Schools*, Oxford: Oxfam Development Education Programme (an earlier version of this document was published in 1997).

Paechter, C. (2003) 'Power/knowledge, gender and curriculum change', *Journal of Educational Change*, 4: 129–148.

Paechter, C. and Head, J. (1996) 'Gender, identity, status and the body: life in a marginal subject', *Gender and Education*, 8, 1: 21–29.

Rizvi, F. (2000) 'International education and the production of the global imagination' in N. Burbules and C.A. Torres (eds) *Globalisation and Education: Critical Perspectives*, London: Routledge.

Rizvi, F. (2007) 'Internationalization of curriculum: a critical perspective' in M. Haydon, J. Thompson and J. Levy (eds) *The Sage Handbook of Research in International Education*, London: Sage.

Save the Children (2005) *Young Lives, Global Goals*, London: Save the Children.

Smith, L.T. (1999) *Decolonising Methodologies: Research and Indigenous People*, London: Zed Books.

Walker, M. (2006) 'Towards a capability-based theory of social justice for education policy-making', *Journal of Education Policy*, 21, 2: 163–185.

Wright, S. (2001) *International Human Rights, Decolonisation and Globalisation: Becoming Human*, London: Routledge.

UNESCO (2000) *The Dakar Framework for Action: Education for All, Meeting our Collective Commitments*, Paris: UNESCO.

UNESCO (2002a) *An International Strategy for Putting the Dakar Framework for Action on Education for All into Operation*, Paris: UNESCO.

UNESCO (2002b) *Education for All: is the World on Track? EFA Global Monitoring Report 2002*, Paris: UNESCO.

UNESCO (2003) *Gender and Education for All – the Leap to Equality EFA Global Monitoring Report 2003/4*, Paris: UNESCO.

UNESCO (2004) *Education for All: the Quality Imperative EFA Global Monitoring Report 2005*, Paris: UNESCO.

12 Nationhood and the education of the female citizen in India

Nitya Mohan and Rosie Vaughan

The latter half of the twentieth century witnessed the emergence of an inter-national agenda to promote female education, most prominently seen in the Millennium Development Goals and the 'Education for All' campaign. Within these campaigns, the notion of 'progress' is largely based on a movement towards gender parity in statistical indicators such as enrolment figures, survival rates and examination achievements. However, these country-based statistics are merely the tip of the iceberg, as they represent major shifts in the politics and the processes of national educational policy making. A full understanding of progress in female education requires an in-depth reading of the socio-cultural and national policy contexts within which these statistical shifts occur.

This chapter argues that our understanding of both global and national understandings regarding girls' education policy requires a critical historical methodology that taps into national narratives around gender, education and development. Such an historical perspective would consider the shifting concep-tualisations of gender roles in relation not just to economic development, but also to nationhood. The evolution of the relationship between national identity and gender policy approaches is an especially important consideration in the path of female education reform (cf. Chapter 6, this volume). Such a focus can also contribute to an understanding of relations between national governments and international organisations in the field of education – where often gender inequality has become symbolic of westernisation and economic progress. Historical analyses of educational policy making also allow us to consider the agency of national governments rather than seeing them simply as recipients of international funding and agendas. As Goodson and Hargreaves (2006) point out, a deeper reading of the evolution of education policy reveals critical lacunae in the existing analytical literature; our understandings of national and international policy developments can be limited if we neglect the historical and longitudinal aspects of change.

In this chapter, we investigate gender and education within the Indian context. We employ three different lenses to explore the construction of girls' education as a policy concern in the last three decades. The first section consid-ers the relationship between Indian independence, the construction of the female citizen and the emergence of a feminist/women's movement in India.

The educational demands that emerged from this political constellation set the context, but not necessarily the reason for the ways in which educational policy makers in the Indian government tackle the issue of gender equality in education. The second section of the chapter draws upon textual analysis of various government reports to demonstrate complex shifts in the construction and reconstruction of the female citizen and her role in the newly independent nation state. In the final section, we briefly trace the interface between India and the international agendas around gender equality.[1] Here we discuss the criticisms that a number of Indian feminist scholars have made about the disadvantages to gender equality of certain of these global educational trends.

Female citizenship and nation building in colonial and post-colonial times

Gender identities and relations we know do not exist in a vacuum: they are inextricably linked to hierarchies of power and exploitation. The mutually constitutive identities of gender and nation position women and men in particular ways. For example, the national duties of men are to protect their faith/nation; women on the other hand, become the national embodiment and the bearers of 'tradition' (Moghadam 1994, quoted in Giles and Hydman 2004).[2] These identities, shaped by power relations, are transformed by shifts in gender politics and conceptions of nationhood. At the same time, gender-based power relations are at the centre of nationalist projects (Giles and Hydman 2004). The interactions between gender, nationality, class and caste therefore provide an important analytical device to understand the relationship between gender equality and national development. The discursive narratives of nationhood (or how we belong and how we identify) have important implications on the evolution of feminist cultural production. Using examples from secondary sources on the politics of colonial and post-colonial India, we can trace the genesis of the feminist movement and the construction of its political/reform agenda vis-à-vis girls' education.

Partha Chatterjee (1993) notes that, although nationalism is a process of affirmation of difference through the unifying discourse of 'the nation', it remains one within which differences in race, caste, class and gender are hardly unifying. A consideration of the ways in which women as a differentiated group are simultaneously co-opted into and oppressed by national movements can, however, offer important understandings into the ways in which agency and citizenship are constructed within a nation. Much of third world feminism owes its roots to the participation of women in nationalist struggles (Jayawardhena 1986: 23). In the Indian context, it is noticeable that the early resistance struggles and social reform movements for political independence and modernisation regarded the idea of women's emancipation through formal education as central to many of the reformist agendas (Kumar 2005: 112). Broadly speaking, these new visions of progressive society saw the role of women as 'professionalised housewives' who could also take responsibility for helping the less fortunate in their communities.[3]

In early and mid-nineteenth century India, questions regarding the position of women in society and the role of education had already become a key issue in the most controversial debates over social reform. However, such issues suddenly disappeared from public debate toward the start of the twentieth century. From then onwards, the 'women's question' was subsumed by an overtly political agenda concerning the politics of nationalism. Partha Chatterjee (1993: 120–121) argues that the 'nationalist resolution of the women's question' was achieved in terms of the 'preferred goals' of nationalism by 'situating the "women's question" in a inner domain of sovereignty far removed from the arena of political contest with the colonial state'. According to Chatterjee, Bengali nationalist discourse constructed the notions of 'woman and home' as symbolic of national tradition, separating the outer, material sphere (represented by the colonial state) and the inner domain (represented by Indian tradition). The inner sphere constitutes the spiritual-self and is embodied by the symbol of the 'traditional woman' associated within patriarchy with domestic space. The myth of the 'uncolonizable feminine domain of the community is vital to nation-building narratives because national communities define their inner coherence and outer boundary through the trope-laden female body' (Zacharias 2001: 32). Thus, the category of 'woman' was transformed into a cultural symbol rather than a material being with social, political or emotional needs (Mondal 2002: 914).

The 1920s and 1930s witnessed the first wave of the feminist movement in India. By this time, the notion of education for women had become more acceptable, particularly as it was no longer associated with a loss of national identity and as 'social progress' no longer appeared to be directly at odds with traditional feminine ideals. It is crucial to note that in the first wave of the feminist movement in India, women's organisations were able to draw both on the benefits of modernity as well as on the metaphor of 'Indianness' invoked by the nationalist discourse (Sen 2000: 57).

With the growth of the nationalist movement in the 1920s and 1930s, many Indian women activists found themselves torn between continuing to campaign explicitly for women's rights, or concentrating their efforts on the fight for independence. In the latter case, the goal was to establish concrete rights for women once India was free from colonial rule. Many chose the latter course, persuaded by male activists that their demands for equality would be realised on independence. One consequence was that the cause of women's rights was advanced but co-opted within the state-sponsored project of nation building in independent India. Moreover, nationalism endorsed 'new' patriarchal arrangements that subsumed feminist activists within the homogeneous cultural category of 'Indian' women Sen (2000: 57). In fact, from the 1930s, participation in the Indian nationalist movement meant that public roles for middle class women became more acceptable. Gandhian nationalistic discourse modified the earlier, more passive and idealised notions of Indian womanhood and repositioned women's agency in new, powerful ways that sanctioned the participation of large numbers of women in the nationalist movement (Kishwar 1985).

By the time India became independent in 1947, a number of educational institutions for women had been established all round the country that benefited the new generation of young women. During the struggle for independence, women had worked alongside men, playing equal but complementary roles. However, conflicts between the overarching nationalist agendas and the particular concerns of the women's movements posed significant challenges for feminist activists in post-independent India.[4] Women's concerns were no longer taken into account, nor were the various struggles they pursued, for example, their resistance to imperialism and fight for social and economic justice before and after independence was recognised (ibid.: 58).

After independence, the Indian Constitution's new objective was free and compulsory education for all girls up until the age of 14 (Government of India 1951). The provision of elementary education for all was now a matter of social justice (more than just economic growth). The state proceeded to outlaw many of the practices inhibiting female access to schooling – such as child marriage – and as a result official concern moved away from the role of social factors in inhibiting girls' schooling (Sen 2002: 199). At the same time, the optimism that came with freedom from colonial rule was associated with a strong belief that educational inequalities could largely be solved simply by providing more schools. Increased funds were diverted into education, and the 1950s saw the highest per capita investment of the post-independent period (Ramachandran 1998: 56).

The first decades of the new Indian nation provided women with equal legal rights and entitlements. However, in the educational area, a gender differentiated form of citizenship was sustained. The content and nature of girls' education, planning documents and government commissions in the early years of independence supported the notion that men and women had different roles. Gender equality in education was not seen as desirable nor beneficial at either a societal or individual level. The University Education Commission (1948–1949), for example, saw women's education as necessary, but concluded that the existing system was unsuitable for women because it was based upon men's needs, leaving women unable to cope with their specific problems of daily life.

Overall, a gendered notion of the modern Indian citizen pervaded; the definition of an essentialised Indian woman may have shifted to include an active life in the public sphere but the notion of different social roles was maintained (Chatterjee 1993: 129–130).[5] While all educational committees and commissions since independence suggested ways in which education could bring about change in Indian society, they did not recognise the pivotal role that women's subordination played in the maintenance of existing norms, nor the fact that education itself may be strengthening and sustaining these unequal roles (Mazumdar 1988: 27–28).

The place of female citizens within Indian society again came to the fore through a second wave of feminism, which focused on the divergent interests of women from different castes, classes and communities. Their collective national profile and presence, however, was one of commitment to fighting 'asymmetries and inequalities in gender relations' (Tharu and Niranjana 1996). The range of national campaigns engendered a cultural radicalism within which a wide range of issues and a multiplicity of voices could be accommodated (Sen 2000: 58). The category of 'gender' became central to deconstructing dominant patriarchal Indian narratives, raising the profile of women as well as incorporating them as humanist citizens of the nation (ibid.: 1996).

This second wave feminist movement in India was precipitated to some extent by the state's proactive stance on women's empowerment and international interest in gender (see below). It led to the development of a new construction women as 'citizen subjects'. Although the transition from the category of 'woman' as a subject of nationalist narratives to a citizen subject of the nation state had been made with the post-independence constitution, it was only fully realised in this later period (Zacharias 2001: 39). The redrafting of women's national citizenship began to place them 'not as the "sign of the nation" or embodiments of national tradition but as subjects of the developmental state: its legal, cultural and political apparatuses as well as its international affiliations' (ibid.: 39–40).

A key turning point in education came with the publication in 1975 of what came to be one of the founding texts of the women's movement, 'Towards Equality', the Report of the Committee on the Status of Women in India, produced by the Ministry of Education and Social Welfare. The report represented a significantly more radical conceptualisation both of the ideal position of women in society and of the role of education in redressing current imbalances in the status of girls and women. The report also had considerable impact on the women's movement and in particular on its educational agenda. Until this point, the women's movement in India had focused on legal rights and unjust social practices as a means of addressing women's low status and lack of economic independence. Now there was a new emphasis on using education to tackle the root causes of women's oppression. More radical solutions to remove the social barriers to female education began to be considered seriously, and a number of non-governmental organisations shifted the agenda from simple literacy classes towards programmes of self-help through which women could get gainful employment and financial independence.

Empowering women? The reconstruction of female citizenship through national education policy making

Of all areas of government reform, education policy in particular reflects predominant visions of the future of the nation, and the ideal role of citizens in bringing this about. Here we shift our attention to the ways in which Indian educational policy-makers reconstructed female citizen subjects. We trace, through a number of government reports and legislation in the last few decades of the twentieth century, two distinct phases in the construction of women as subjects in the developmental state. The first phase visualises a nation of transformed social relations and of women as subjects and agents contributing to this; and a later period in which women have been increasingly perceived as instrumental agents of poverty reduction and national economic development.

One of the key themes in the 1986 National Policy on Education (NPE) is the positioning of education as a tool for bringing the constitutional aim of social justice and equality (Government of India 1986, 1988b: 69, 75–76). In the section 'Education for Women's Equality', government policy was envisaged as playing a key role in transforming gender relationships in society. The revision of the content of education and the planned programme of research into pedagogic innovation involving a number of national educational institutions, for example, would ensure 'the development of new values through redesigned curricula, textbooks, the training and orientation of teachers' (Government of India 1986: 6). In this way, educational policy makers recognised the potentially transformative power of education in the gendering of identity and the redefinition of gender roles.

The reformed National Education System was to play 'a positive, interventionist role' and action was to be taken in favour of women in order to 'neutralise the accumulated distortions of the past', to be replaced with the 'new values'. As an extension of this, equal roles for men and women in society were envisaged, with the elimination of sex stereotyping and the promotion of women's participation in non-traditional occupations, and existing and emergent technologies. The NPE Programme of Action however went further. It highlighted for the first time, the aim of 'empowering' girls and women as a key policy goal and specifically defined the 'parameters of empowerment'. These are listed as: building a positive self-image; developing the ability to think critically; building up group cohesion and fostering decision making and action; ensuring equal participation in the process of bringing about social change; encouraging group action in order to bring about change in society; and providing the wherewithal for economic independence.

A direct outcome of this policy was the *Mahila Samakhya* programme for women's empowerment, which has been implemented across several states since 1989. Significantly, the title of this programme means 'woman speaking with equal voice'.[6] Its aims were ambitious: in order to change the status of rural women, it was agreed that education must help women to question rather than accept, to enable them to affirm their own potential and sustain processes that so that they could move from situations of passive acceptance to assertion and collective action. Women were to take control of their lives through the medium of independent and conscious collectives (*sanghas*) that would sustain social change processes.

With these ambitions, the 1986 NPE significantly altered the state approach to the education of girls and women. It offered a new construction of the female citizen. The policy was the product of a high level of cooperation and shared understanding between feminist academics and central government educational reformers that had developed after the publication of 'Towards Equality'. Previous government approaches had affirmed the constitutional aims of educational provision but had either remained ambiguous about the reasons for educating girls and women, or had largely referred to a need to improve their roles as wives and mothers. The 1986 NPE took an unprecedented step towards changing the position of women in Indian society; the policy text itself acknowledged this to be 'an act of faith and social engineering' (Government of India 1986: 5).

No equivalent comprehensive central government reform of education was undertaken until the 2001 introduction of the *Sarva Shiksha Abhiyan* (SSA), which was developed after a decade of participation in the international 'Education for All' campaign (cf. Ramachandran 2003). The SSA was conceived of as an umbrella programme for achieving universal elementary education across the entire country, making free and compulsory education to children of ages 6–14 a fundamental right mandated by the Constitution of India. Girls were identified as a target group, requiring particular attention as 'their participation in primary education has been far from desirable'; the framework clearly states that there will be efforts to mainstream gender concerns into all of the SSA activities.[7]

However, a subtle shift in the positioning of girls' education was now evident. In contrast to the detailed prescriptions in the NPE and Programme of Action, the SSA framework did little to acknowledge the transformative power of education in relation to gender patterns and identities in Indian society. The framing documents gave little detail in relation to curriculum or teacher training beyond stipulating that there should be a 'congenial learning environment' for girls in order to provide equitable learning opportunities, or that teacher training should include gender sensitive content.[8] Although throughout the 1990s, 'female empowerment' had continued to be a stated goal of female education, government documents increasingly used the concept only in relation to *Mahila Samakhya*, as opposed to a continued overall project of social change. The term is largely absent from the main SSA framework of 2001, appearing in relation to the National Programme for the Education of Girls at Elementary Level (NPEGEL) scheme for underprivileged girls, and in the 2004–2005 Ministry of Human Resource Development (MHRD) Annual Report, in the description of *Mahila Samakhya* (Government of India 2005a: 73). By 2005, there was a less-clearly defined notion of the empowered female citizen: instead of ascribing a role to women in breaking down pervasive unequal structures throughout society, more emphasis was placed on the role of empowerment in girls and women achieving equal educational participation.

The term empowerment increasingly lacks definition, and it is employed in scenarios that may not be conducive to the original meaning in the 1986 NPE. For example, a section of the recent MHRD Annual Report describes the midday meal scheme thus: 'it has been decided to empower mothers of 12,000,000 school children covered under the scheme to supervise the preparation and serving of the meal' (Government of India 2006: 7). The concept of empowerment has increasingly been used in relation to encouraging economic participation as opposed to transforming gender roles. Since 'empowerment' is only used in the SSA literature in the sections which focus on NPEGEL and *Mahila Samakhya*, it is possible that the concept is now only something considered applicable to women from poorer and disadvantaged sections of society. While the targeting of rural illiterate girls and women is undeniably important, it is interesting to note how this application of the concept of empowerment has come to represent a larger proportion of national campaigns for female education in India.

What might be the causes of this shift? Given the progressive nature of the 1986 NPE, it is possible that the stipulations about female empowerment and the reconstruction of gender relations were too radical to survive amongst the mainstream activities of the Ministry of Human Resource Development where those aspects relating to the transformation of gender roles were being quietly marginalised from the mainstream of education policy. While specific programmes such as *Mahila Samakhya* carried forth the original notions of female empowerment and gender change, these were not reflected in the central concerns of the state education sector (NCERT 2005b: 88–89).

This marginalisation of feminist concerns about gender inequality and identities and roles in Indian society is evident in the cursory reporting of the original text of the section on 'Education for Women's Equality' in Ministry of Human Resource Development Annual Reports. The entire section is reproduced up until 1989–1990. However, the text is then not quoted in subsequent reports. In the 2005–2006 report, part of the original NPE text reappears for the first time in nearly a decade, but some of the more powerful phrases are notably absent. Among the original sentences that have been removed are those that state that the National Education System will play a 'positive, interventionist role in the empowerment of women' and that it will lead to 'the development of new values'.

The spread of neo-liberal ideas since the early 1990s into the social policy sector may have encouraged a focus on the basic provision of education instead of these socially transformative aspects, particularly as social sector ministries have to operate within the constraints imposed by the Ministry of Finance (Jha 2005: 3677–3678; Patel 1996). As a result of this agenda, there is less discussion of policy outcomes in terms of social transformation and social equality – educational goals are increasingly those of educational enrolment and equality of educational opportunity. Despite the continued use of the term 'gender', specific references to equality are now replaced with phrases such as 'eliminating gender disparities', 'mainstreaming gender concerns' and 'gender analysis' (Government of India c.2004a: 1; Government of India c.2004b: 3).[9]

Changes in political leadership may also have contributed to the ongoing struggle between competing visions of women's role in the modern Indian state: between progressive feminist ideas on gender equality, and traditional visions of idealised Indian femininity within the upper and middle classes (Chatterjee 1993). Recently, differences were clearly apparent between the National Democratic Alliance (NDA) and United Progressive Alliance (UPA) governments' perspectives on girls' education, something particularly evident in their respective approaches to curriculum reform. Under the NDA government (1998–2004), a new curricular framework was introduced that attempted to grapple with the influence of westernisation and 'an alien technological ethos' and sought to impose a particular interpretation of Indian tradition through the school system (NCERT 2000). This included a traditional interpretation of women's role in society, maintaining the best qualities of Indian womanhood and an unproblematised view of gender relations. The new goal was to 'recognise and nurture the best features of each gender in the best Indian tradition' – one feminist author regarded this as 'without doubt a huge step backwards from the National Education Policy' (Bhog 2002; NCERT 2000: 9).

Recently, since the change in goverment to the Congress-led United Progressive Alliance in 2004, however, the tide has started to turn. New work by the National Council of Education Research and Training (NCERT) specifically emphasises the role of gender relations in maintaining unequal power structures (NCERT 2005a, 2005b). Observing that 'schooling actually reinforces the gendered inequality of socialisation and social control', it calls for an education that 'enables girls to challenge relations of power'. Significantly, for our purposes, NCERT argues that that there should be a collective transformation towards 'substantive citizenship' (NCERT 2005b: 8–10). The resulting National Curriculum Framework noted; the 'deep gender bias and pervasive patriarchal values in Indian society', that in school education 'values and culture get reinforced unless there is a variation in the experience' and that 'it is in the interest of all to liberate human beings from the existing inequalities of gender' (NCERT 2005a: 9, 66, 83). Further, the reconstituted Central Advisory Board of Education (CABE) recently published a report that stated that instrumentalist approaches to girls' education (i.e. which focus on fertility control, better health etc.) need to be 'vehemently opposed' and emphasised that education 'has a reformatory role to play' rather than passively responding to demand (Central Advisory Board on Education 2005: i–iv).[10] However, since the CABE is a relatively autonomous advisory body, there is some distance between these recommendations and actual policy formation.

In sum, the construction of female citizenship, the transformatory role of education in relation to gender relations and inequalities is embedded in complex ways within educational policy. Uncovering that political agenda is only the start. In the next section we consider how the political construction of female education and citizenship comes into play in the interface between India and her international allies.

Recalcitrance or caution? Indian responses to international agendas on gender and education

These national movements and state responses to the issue of gender education and education, whilst interconnected, are not independent influences. Education policy in India has had increasing contact with international agendas, only some of which are educationally focused. Since 1991 India has been involved in structural adjustment measures with international financial institutions. During the 1990s, the union and state governments have also joined with a number of international and bilateral agencies to create localised, innovative education projects such as the District Primary Education Project (DPEP), *Lok Jumbish* and *Mahila Samahkya*, involving the receipt of external funds, and participation in joint planning and review processes. Formal participation in the 'Education for All' and Millennium Development Goals' campaigns has also involved recognising and adopting international educational targets and goals, the preparation of National Plans of Action, progress reports, and attending and hosting international conferences.

Can any relationship be detected between changing understandings of gender, education and nationhood in India, and this involvement with international agendas? There are some similar trends, such as the increasingly less radical definition of equality in education, an increased focus on enrolment and attendance, and the use of strategies such as non-formal education, decentralisation and para-teachers, which have also characterised international campaigns. Shifts in the use of the term 'empowerment' are also evident in international policy circles, with some authors arguing that the concept has lost its original meaning (Cornwall and Brock 2006; Sen 2006: 138–141).

Alternatively, a longer term perspective also provides examples of policy dissonance and defence of policy autonomy. National goals have been kept distinct: for example, the national SSA target for the universal enrolment of girls is set at 2010, earlier than the EFA and MDG target of 2015, and it covers eight years of elementary education as opposed to the prioritising of primary schooling in international campaigns. The 1986 NPE itself was far more explicit in addressing gender power relations than the 1990 EFA campaign and later strategies that do not refer to patriarchal issues so prominently. In documentation produced as part of the Indian government's participation in the EFA campaign, selected sections of the 1986 NPE paragraphs on female education are reproduced to illustrate the Indian approach to female education (Government of India 2003: 47–48). Moreover, there are several examples of explicit resistance within the national government to external influence on education policy, as seen in debates within the CABE meetings in the early 1990s towards external funding for education.[11]

Despite an explicit emphasis on changing gender relations as a goal for female education policy, it is interesting to note an absence within Indian education policy documents of specific references to direct economic benefits.[12] The 1986 NPE contains no mention of social or economic benefits flowing from the education of girls and women. In contrast to often-made links between female education and fertility decline, the 1987–1988 MHRD report details a programme on 'population education' that is entirely separate to the education for women's equality section and does not specifically target girls as opposed to boys (Government of India 1988a: 8).

One of the main sites of debate in terms of the significance of interaction with external organisations concerns the spread of neo-liberal policies. The impact of liberalisation policies on education in India is unclear and highly contentious, and opinions are divided over the extent to which education reforms have been directly or indirectly driven by external agencies such as the World Bank and the IMF, particularly in relation to the process of structural adjustment from 1991 onwards.[13]

Some scholars argue that adjustment and related conditions led to a high level of external influence on education policy. Feminists have pointed to the inherent contradictions that underpin global policy imperatives, which may advocate pro-female policies within international education campaigns while working against them through market-led strategies (Chege *et al.* 2005; Leach 2000; Stromquist 1997). Some Indian scholars have even argued that neo-liberal policies are one cause of the dilution of the original 1986 NPE women's education agenda.[14] Sadgopal concludes that 'India unfortunately gave up its progressive policy on women's education in favour of the international framework that was guided more by the considerations of market than by women's socio-cultural and political rights' (Sadgopal 2003: 22).

Yet it is difficult to ascribe *direct* policy influence as there are no official conditionalities attached to being part of the EFA or MDG campaigns; and there is no publicly available evidence of conditions relating to World Bank education loans, or the wider process of structural adjustment.[15]

Conclusion

If we are concerned with achieving global improvements in female education, studies of national dynamics of policy development allow us to go beyond the narratives suggested by international campaigns and explore first the internal political dynamics between nation building and social movements, educational policy makers' responses and the synergies between national and international policy imperatives. In India, the second half of the twentieth century saw women's national citizenship redrafted, from women as embodiments of national tradition, to citizen subjects and agents of the development of the nation. Documentary analysis of education reforms in the last three decades reveals a subtle shift in the role of education policy and educational programmes in the construction of the female citizen. The 1986 NPE offered a more overtly critical view of education, in which schooling was to be reformulated, making girls and women active agents in a social transformation of gender roles, as part of a broader project towards social equality. This shifted in the 1990s to a more passive and unproblematic view of education and empowerment; in which the ideal female citizen enjoys equality of formal enrolment and retention, to enable participation in, and contribution to, the economic development of the nation.

In this chapter, we have used an historical account to suggest possible reasons for this shift, including the marginal position of education in the women's movement, increasing neo-liberal tendencies within social policy and changes in political leadership. Despite some notable similarities between this shift and characteristics of international campaigns, there is also evidence of defence of the sovereignty of national education agendas. Other methods and sources may shed further light on the causes of shifting conceptualisations. This chapter has examined national agendas using secondary and documentary sources. Interviews with past and present policy makers, as well as feminist activists, may infuse a more gender sensitive understanding into policy development. Although not currently accessible to researchers, internal documents relating to policy-forming processes will, in time, give further insights both at national and international level. It would also be interesting to look at the processes of accumulation of policy-related knowledge, such as the origin of research studies on female education, or the initiation of changes in the collection of gender-disaggregated educational statistics. It should not be forgotten that central policy in India tells us a limited amount about state or ground-level implementation, so further studies are necessary at local government levels. Moreover, education policy on gender is integral to wider shifts in development thinking, both at national level and in international development discourse.

Notes

1 Education policy in India is divided between the central and the state governments; this chapter is concerned only with central government policy.
2 See also Koontz (1986).
3 For example, the *Brahmo Samaj*, a Bengal-based reform society where women met to be taught religious lore, needlework and to discuss social issues (Forbes 1999).
4 In fact during the 1940s, the essentialist conception of 'Indian women' began to unravel. By independence, neither women's organisations nor the nationalists could claim to speak for women as a collectivity from a united platform.
5 Chatterjee charts the transformation of the idealised Indian woman from physical confines defined by *purdah* to a more flexible 'domain set by differences'.
6 *Mahila* (woman), *Sam* (equal), *akhya* (voice).
7 Government of India 2001: Section 5.1.1–2; Government of India 2005c: 58. Two programmes specifically target girls' schooling, the *Kasturba Gandhi Balika Vidyalaya* (KGBV) scheme establishing residential schools for girls from disadvantaged groups, and the National Programme for Education of Girls at Elementary Level (NPEGEL), providing additional components for underprivileged and disadvantaged girls of classes I–VII.
8 Government of India 2001: Section 5.1.2; Government of India 2005c: 62. However it should be remembered that SSA is specifically a framework for achieving and implementing universal elementary education (UEE) and does not necessarily supersede NPE.
9 The most recent papers from CABE make frequent references to gender equality in and through education; it remains to be seen what impact these will have on official policy (Central Advisory Board on Education 2005).
10 CABE is the highest advisory body to advise the central and state bodies in the field of education. Having been dissolved in 1994, it was reconstituted in July 2004.
11 At the 45th CABE meeting, concerns were raised that external funding for education should be considered 'with the utmost caution as there was a scope for infiltration of anti-national elements along with financial assistance'. After some debate, it was stipulated at the 46th meeting that external funding must be 'in total conformity with national priorities, strategies and programmes' and that 'project formulation should be the responsibility of the Central or State government, or other national agencies'

(Central Advisory Board on Education, 1989: 2, 6, 93; Central Advisory Board on Education 1991: 181).

12 Note that this covers only documents from the Department of Education; documents from projects with international agencies, or from other departments such as the Planning Commission may offer different perspectives.

13 This can be seen through the example of the District Primary Education Project (DPEP), which is alternately seen as part of the World Bank's adjustment policies in India, or an entirely 'homegrown' education policy of the Government of India (Ramachandran and Saihjee 2002: 1601).

14 In Sadgopal's view, the 1986 NPE provided the space for international funding agencies to exacerbate these trends.

15 It is also possible, however, that central government policy may be subject to indirect influence: government officials in India will have come into contact with external educational ideas through interactions with the World Bank and other educational aid projects over the course of the 1990s. There has also been a certain amount of movement of officials between external agencies and positions in the national government (Jha 2005).

References

Bhog, D. (2002) 'Gender and Curriculum', *Economic and Political Weekly*, 37: 1638–1642.

Central Advisory Board on Education (1989) *Proceedings, 45th Meeting*, New Delhi: Ministry of Human Resource Development.

Central Advisory Board on Education (1991) *Proceedings, 46th Meeting*, New Delhi: Ministry of Human Resource Development.

Central Advisory Board on Education (2005) *Report of the CABE Committee on Girls' Education and the Common School System*, New Delhi: Ministry of Human Resource Development.

Chatterjee, P. (1993) *The Nation and Its Fragments: Colonial and Postcolonial Histories*, Princeton: Princeton University Press.

Chege, F., Leach, F. and Stromquist, N.P. (2005) 'Review Symposium: Gender and Education for All: The Leap to Equality', *British Journal of Sociology of Education*, 26: 673–682.

Cornwall, A. and Brock, K. (2006) 'The new buzzwords' in P. Utting (ed.) *Reclaiming Development Agendas: Knowledge, Power and International Policy Making*, Basingstoke: Palgrave Macmillan, pp. 43–72.

Forbes, G. (1999) *Women in Modern India*, Cambridge: Cambridge University Press.

Giles, W. and Hydman, J. (2004) 'Introduction' in W. Giles and J. Hydman (eds) *Sites of Violence: Gender and Conflict Zones*, Berkeley and Los Angeles: University of California Press.

Goodson, I. and Hargreaves, A. (2006) 'Educational Change over Time? The Sustainability and Nonsustainability of Three Decades of Secondary School Change and Continuity', *Educational Administration Quarterly*, 42: 3–41.

Government of India (1951) *Women and Education in India*, New Delhi: Ministry of Human Resource Development.

Government of India (1986) *National Policy on Education*, New Delhi: Ministry of Human Resource Development.

Government of India (1988a) *Annual Report 1987–1988*, New Delhi: Ministry of Human Resource Development.

Government of India (1988b) *National Perspective Plan for Women*, New Delhi: Ministry of Human Resource Development.

Government of India (2001) *Sarva Shiksha Abhiyan: Framework for Implementation*, New Delhi: Ministry of Human Resource Development.

Government of India (2003) *Education for All: National Plan of Action, India*, New Delhi: Ministry of Human Resource Development.

Government of India (*c.*2004a) *Guidelines for Implementation of Kasturba Gandhi Balika Vidyalaya*, New Delhi: Ministry of Human Resource Development.

Government of India (*c.*2004b) *Guidelines for Implementation of the National Programme for the Education of Girls at Elementary Level as a Component of the Scheme of Sarva Shiksha Abhiyan*, New Delhi: Ministry of Human Resource Development.

Government of India (2005a) *Annual Report 2004–2005*, New Delhi: Ministry of Human Resource Development.

Government of India (2005c) *Sarva Shiksha Abhiyan: Manual for Planning and Appraisal*, New Delhi: Ministry of Human Resource Development.

Government of India (2006) *Annual Report 2005–2006*, New Delhi: Ministry of Human Resource Development.

Jayawardhena, K. (1986) *Feminism and Nationalism in the Third World*, London: Zed Books.

Jha, P. (2005) 'Withering Commitments and Weakening Progress: State and Education in the Era of Neoliberal Reforms', *Economic and Political Weekly*, 40: 3677–3684.

Kishwar, M. (1985) 'Gandhi on Women', *Economic and Political Weekly*, 20: 1691–1702.

Koontz, C. (1986) *Mothers of the Fatherland*, London: Jonathan Cape.

Kumar, K. (2005) *The Political Agenda of Education: A Study of Colonialist and Nationalist Ideas*, New Delhi: Sage.

Leach, F. (2000) 'Gender Implications of Development Agency Policies on Education and Training', *International Journal of Educational Development*, 20: 333–347.

Mazumdar, V. (1988) *National Specialised Agencies and Women's Equality: National Council of Educational Research and Training*, New Delhi: Centre for Women's Development Studies.

Mondal, A. (2002) 'The Emblematics of Gender and Sexuality in Indian Nationalist Discourse', *Modern Asian Studies*, 36: 913–936.

NCERT (2000) *National Curriculum Framework for School Education*, New Delhi.

NCERT (2005a) *National Curriculum Framework*, New Delhi.

NCERT (2005b) *Position Paper for the Focus Group on Gender Issues in Education (for NCERT National Curriculum Review)*.

Patel, I. (1996) 'India', *International Review of Education*, 42: 75–96.

Ramachandran, V. (1998) 'Promises, Promises', *Seminar*, 464: 54–59

Ramachandran, V. (2003) 'Gender Equality in Education (India): Progress in the Last Decade', Background paper, *UNESCO EFA Monitoring Report 2003–04.*

Ramachandran, V. and Saihjee, A. (2002) 'The New Segregation: Reflections on Gender and Equity in Primary Education', *Economic and Political Weekly*, 37: 1600–1613.

Sadgopal, A. (2003) 'Exclusion and Inequality in Education: The State Policy and Globalisation', *Contemporary India*, 2: 1–36.

Sen, G. (2006) 'The quest for gender equality' in P. Utting (ed.) *Reclaiming Development Agendas: Knowledge, Power and International Policy Making*, Basingstoke: Palgrave Macmillan, pp. 128–143.

Sen, S. (2000) 'Towards a Feminist Politics? The Indian Women's Movement in Historical Perspective', World Bank Policy Research Report on Gender and Development, Working Paper Series No. 9, Washington, DC: World Bank.

Sen, S. (2002) 'A father's duty: state, patriarchy and women's education' in S. Bhattacharya (ed.) *Education and the Disprivileged*, New Delhi: Orient Longman.

Stromquist, N. (1997) 'Gender Sensitive Educational Strategies and their Implementation', *International Journal of Educational Development*, 17: 205–214.

Tharu, S. and Niranjana, T. (1996) 'Problems for a contemporary theory of gender' in S. Amin and D. Chakrabarty (eds) *Subaltern Studies IX: Writings on South Asian History and Society*, New Delhi: Oxford University Press.

Zacharias, U. (2001) 'Trial by Fire: Gender, Power and Citizenship in Narratives of the Nation', *Social Text*, 69: 19.

13 Poverty reduction and gender parity in education

An alternative approach

Emefa Takyi-Amoako

For developing countries to reap benefits from female education and significantly reduce poverty, it is crucial that the attainment of gender parity in educational planning and management is not focused only on redressing the imbalance between female and male enrolment rates at the primary or basic education level. Gender inequality needs to be redressed in areas such as retention, completion, access to quality education and progression to higher levels. This is ever more important considering that donors and government sometimes provide short-term support and overlook girls' progression to the higher levels of education.

Studies that examine the interrelation between gender, education, poverty and development show that, while policies of International Financial Institutions (IFIs) prioritise female education, they ignore the harsh impact of structural adjustment especially on poor households where female education may not be of a high priority (Heward and Bunwaree 1999). Indeed poverty is a crucial element in female subordination due to its link with restricted domestic systems (Stromquist 1999). Advocacy efforts that have acknowledged the need to apply gendered models of economic development to developmental processes have emerged (Heward and Bunwaree 1999). Crucially, they emphasised that gender ought to assume a pivotal position in macroeconomic planning for an effective reduction of poverty (ibid.; Moser 1993). The fissure between the positive rhetoric of the international and national agents of education on the one hand, and the persistent deprivation and oppression in the lives of girls and women on the other, is of grave concern. There is rising anxiety over the growing divide between wealthy female populations and the poor ones both within and between nations. The continuous transformation of culture, politics and economy has profound implications for gender relations in education (Heward and Bunwaree 1999).

Although the liberal and humanist perspectives of global organisations such as the World Bank and UNICEF on gender education are valid, they fail to take into account the labyrinthine interplay of organisations, discourses and practices among the agents of educational aid delivery and reception (ibid.). In particular, it is crucial to examine the ways in which gender education and girls' education relate to major programmes of poverty reduction. To what extent can international agendas on education and gender equality influence national strategies for tackling poverty and by implication girls' education?

The chapter examines such questions through the framework of the IFIs' Poverty Reduction Strategy. It first makes the connection between gender and poverty by focusing on existing literature and the ways in which gender education, and girls' education in particular, is included in the World Bank/IFIs' current model for poverty reduction and equal access to education. The second half of the chapter focuses particularly on Ghana's response to this international agenda. It sets the poverty trends in Ghana within the African context, and shows how national poverty reduction strategies address international agendas and how efforts to attain gender parity in education are positioned in Ghana.

A close reading of the *Ghana Poverty Reduction Strategy 2003–2005* (GoG/NDPC 2003) shows that, despite the strategy's influence in shaping education sector policies, it fails to deal with the complex notion of gender disparity in education, which is crucial for reducing poverty in Ghana. Drawing on Alter and Hage's (1993) definition of *network performance principles* (comprehensiveness, accessibility and compatibility), I suggest that a holistic analysis of gender disparity can provide an alternative means of redressing gender imbalances in countries such as Ghana.

African poverty and international poverty reduction agendas

Growth rates in Africa had generally been low (Christiaensen *et al.* 2003) but the period between 2002 and 2004 witnessed a rapid growth of 7.3 per cent in Central Africa, 5.8 per cent in East Africa, 4.8 per cent in North Africa and 4.3 per cent in West Africa, which showed the lowest growth performance (Economic Commission for Africa 2005). The reasons for the general low growth are provided in Christiaensen *et al.* (2003). By 2000, the average per capita consumption in most African countries was at, or below, US$500 per annum; in the case of Ghana it was US$304. By the end of 1999, the percentage of people in poverty in Ghana was claimed to have fallen from 51.7 per cent to 39.5 per cent (ibid.; Coulombe and McKay 2003).

The poverty terrain of Ghana indicates significant variations within regions with less poor areas in very deprived northern regions and very poor areas in the coastal areas in the relatively rich south. There are higher poverty levels in the rural areas than in the urban regions. Poverty in Ghana is also gender related, with higher levels of poverty occurring among women and households that have high dependency ratios. In peri-urban areas growing landlessness is also engendering poverty. Most of the poor work in the agricultural sector as small-scale food crop farmers but some could also be found among producers of export crops such as cocoa (McKay and Aryeetey 2004).

Between 1991 and 1992 and 1998 and 1999, it was claimed that there was a sharp decline in poverty in Ghana from 36.5 per cent of the population to 26.8 per cent, which represented a reduction of 27 per cent over seven years (Fox

2002). However, considering the high economic status of Ghana in the initial years of independence of 1957 with a per capita income of £70, which was far higher than those of countries like India (£25), Nigeria (£29) and Egypt (£56), the gains were indeed very modest (McKay and Aryeetey 2004). High levels of poverty still remain and have consequences for gender equality as an educational goal. A microeconometric study on Ghana echoes the significance of education to poverty alleviation by indicating that income levels increased with educational attainment (Christiaensen *et al.* 2003). However, even though enrolment rates for both boys and girls are increasing, the disparity persists at the expense of girls (Chao 1999; NDPC 2005). Universal primary school enrolment was not attained in most countries, including Ghana, which had a net primary school enrolment rate of 82 per cent.

While Ghana is being praised for stabilising its economy, experiencing growth and reducing poverty by implementing Structural Adjustment Programmes (SAPs) and Economic Recovery Policies (ERPs) of the IFIs (namely, the International Monetary Fund and the World Bank), the social cost of these policies can not be underestimated. The move to adjustment in the 1980s from the poverty focus, paramount until the 1970s in a number of African countries, was due to the appearance of problems of balance of payment and debt crises (Hjertholm and White 1998). Adjustment lending that these external policies embodied was therefore not an answer to development problems or poverty but to debt crises and an effort to stave off financial crises in the developed world. In the 1980s, therefore, aid programmes and lending policies that African countries were compelled to adopt due to poor economic conditions arguably were more for the benefit of the donors than for the recipients (ibid.).

This led to critics repudiating the poverty focus. They gave voice to their views in two UNICEF reports of 1987 and 1990 entitled 'Adjustment with a Human Face' and 'State of the World's Children' respectively (ibid.). These reports argued that adjustment lending excluded the needs of the poor. By the late 1980s, these criticisms were having an effect. The World Bank began formulating a poverty policy that led to the 'New Poverty Agenda' in the 1990 World Development Report (ibid.). This publication marked the re-emergence of the 'poverty agenda in aid' (ibid.).

The concept of a poverty reduction strategy has now become the fashionable approach. This approach is driving the international agenda for development in most African countries including Ghana (Lewis 1996; Booth 2003). Fully introduced in 1999 by the international financial institutions with the support of other bilateral/multilateral donors, the poverty reduction strategy is used as a mechanism to help guarantee the efficient utilisation of debt relief under the so-called enhanced 'highly indebted poor countries facility'. It is also used as a condition for borrowing, and as aid eligibility in low-income countries (Booth 2003). Nevertheless, the question about the effectiveness of the current poverty reduction strategy approach in development still remains (Fraser 2005; WDM 2005; Stewart and Wang 2003).

Poverty Reduction Strategy Papers

As a condition for debt relief, loan and aid provision, the poverty reduction strategy process was initiated by the World Bank through the Interim Poverty Reduction Strategy Papers (I-PRSPs) designed by aid and loan recipient governments with the support of the IFIs (Booth 2003). In 1999, a Poverty Reduction Strategy Paper (PRSP) became one of the prerequisites for attaining their decision point when a country's eligibility to gain support under the Enhanced-Heavily Indebted Poor Country (HIPC2) programme is assessed. HIPC2 replaced the 1996 HIPC (HIPC1) initiative that failed dismally to reduce debt to sustainable levels (ibid.). The PRSPs are meant to ensure that funds accrued from debt relief are used to alleviate poverty and therefore they target government expenditure on poverty reduction measures (Panos 2002). The five principles behind the PRSPs are intended to boost national ownership of programmes through increased participation. These principles are that the processes must be country-driven, results oriented, comprehensive, partnership oriented and long term. The origin of these principles is the earlier Comprehensive Development Framework (CDF) designed by the World Bank. However, PRSPs have attracted criticism from development analysts who regard them as 'little more than classic structural adjustment', and their processes indicating 'little real change' because of the detrimental effect of similar structural adjustment programmes in the past (WDM 2005; Stewart and Wang 2003). The national 'ownership' claim is therefore seen as mere rhetoric.

According to a report published in September 2005 by anti-poverty campaigners of the World Development Movement (WDM), which analysed the PRSPs of about 50 countries, 90 per cent include privatisation conditions, 96 per cent abound with stringent fiscal policy, while more than 70 per cent contain trade liberalisation measures that undermine the economic independence and progress of these countries (WDM 2005; Stewart and Wang 2003). In fact, the PRSPs are understood in some quarters as a social technology of control of African national sovereignties by the uncomfortable alliance between non-governmental organisations (NGOs), donors and IFIs (Fraser 2005). Consequently, countries and their governments, although bearing the responsibility of leading the process, appear severely restricted particularly with regards to macro-policy and therefore are not necessarily empowered (Stewart and Wang 2003). Further, these poverty strategy papers appear not to recognise the impact of gender on poverty – an argument I explore below.

Gender in Poverty Reduction Strategy Papers

Criticism of these PRSPs has focused on the lack of consideration for the dispositional diversity of gender disparity, the simplistic policies and plans developed to achieve gender equality, and the partial monitoring and evaluative mechanisms put in place to track progress towards the Millennium Development Goal (MDG) for gender parity in education by 2005 (Febres 2005; Unterhalter

2005; Subrahmanian 2004).[1] Experiences from Tanzania, Bolivia, Vietnam and Mozambique indicate that there is an analytical dearth of the issues relating to gender inequality in the PRSPs of these countries (Bell 2003). Concerns have been expressed about how the PRSPs as a basic condition for debt relief, lending and aid provision in low-income countries seem to have failed the poor girls/women that they intended to support (Whitehead 2003; UNESCO 2003; Nightingale 2003). Analyses in most PRSPs seem to ignore the gendered features of poverty and fail to illustrate the different ways in which poverty affects boys/men and girls/women. Recommendations to devote a chapter to gender analysis have not been put into practice – the issues relating to gender are often examined in a fragmented and random fashion and the acknowledgement that macroeconomic policy and national budgets could be gendered is non-existent in most of these strategic documents (Whitehead 2003; UNESCO 2003; Nightingale 2003). Two aspects have been identified as undermining efforts to create gender-sensitive PRSPs. First, a dearth of insight into gender problems by the key players in these poverty reduction processes and, second, a lack of economic proficiency among civil society, and women's groups, that have an interest in gender issues (Whitehead 2003; UNESCO 2003; Nightingale 2003). A key recommendation, therefore, is that all major participants, such as the IFIs' representatives, national government officials and civil society groups obtain gender expertise. Equally important is the need for gender sensitive and expert groups, like ministries of women and other civil society groups with a gender stance, to undergo training in finance and economics procedures to enable them to have a more informed and a higher level of participation in the poverty reduction strategy processes (Whitehead 2003; UNESCO 2003; Nightingale 2003). Winter and Burnett (2002) show how female education is addressed under either gender issues or education and not under both sections, thus creating difficulties in converting gender plans into education strategies and actions. Even where female education is examined under gender or education, it is done in a very general manner (UNESCO 2003).

In light of this discussion, I use a gender lens to explore the particular context of the *Ghana Poverty Reduction Strategy 2003–2005 (GPRS I)* (GoG/NDPC 2003a) formally published in 2003, but which, as a process, began in 2001. I employ Alter and Hage's (1993) theoretical framework to identify the gender approach adopted by the Ghanaian government.

Ghana's response to poverty reduction and gender

In their analysis of inter-organisational networks of interactions or cooperation among organisations, Alter and Hage (1993) argue that within the process of cooperation between organisations, coordination takes place. Consequently, cooperation is seen as the extent to which the various elements in the service delivery system collaborate among themselves. Within the ecology of inter-organisational networks, this is classified as coordination among components – 'agencies, professions, client groups, and resource controllers – so that social services are delivered to clients' (ibid.: 88). Cooperation subsumes coordination, which is considered a performance objective – a programme goal of network or network performance (ibid.). In this process of cooperation where the performance goal is to achieve coordination, it is obligatory to ensure that these three network performance principles are met; *comprehensiveness*, *accessibility* and *compatibility*. They are cross-linked with the four fundamentals of service provision; programmes; resources, supplies/consumers and information (ibid.). Below, I start by using these latter distinctions to analyse both the actual representation of gender in the *GPRS I* (GoG/NDPC 2003a) and also its potential to promote gender equality. I begin with a textual analysis of the 2003 *GPRS* document.

Gender analysis in the Ghana Poverty Reduction Strategy 2003–2005[2]

Ghana had attempted to implement several poverty reduction frameworks in the past. However, the *Ghana Poverty Reduction Strategy 2003–2005* (*GPRS I* or as used in this analysis, the *GPRS*) (ibid.) is regarded as the prelude of the new national plan of action for alleviating poverty and delineating a strategy for tackling it (Driscoll and Christiansen 2004).[3] An analysis of the actors, participation and ownership in the *GPRS* process in Ghana revealed that the depth and quality of public involvement was heavily constrained by structural and cultural problems in the political economy of Ghana. According to Abugre (2001a), while the existing political culture perceived non-state actors as subsidiary to state actors, donors/lenders also seemed to put undue stress on the formality of participation and not on the quality of the participation process. Also the selection and inclusion criteria employed as far as non-state actors were concerned were unsystematic and less representative of the pro-poor (ibid.).

Nevertheless, the *GPRS* has been one of the major policy influences on the *Educational Strategic Plan 2003–2015* (*ESP*) that was developed in 2003 (GoG/MoE 2003a, b). Currently, it appears it is the latter document influenced by the *GPRS* that drives most of these Ministry of Education–donor organisation initiatives to focus on gender parity in education. Indeed, it is true that the development of a policy document is only the first step. What is crucial is continued interaction between donors and government and the ability of a country to marshal a plan into action.

In this analysis, the *GPRS* represents a solitary product that emerged from the production frame of the government–donor inter-organisational network of interactions that is also regarded as symbiotic cooperation (Amoako 2005; Alter and Hage 1993). The sections in the *GPRS* that address gender parity in education form part of the solitary product. The four tenets of service provision are:

- *programmes* (education policies and plans that aim to attain gender parity);
- *resources* (gender sensitive infrastructure, gender sensitive teaching and learning resources, conducive environment for all, especially girls/women etc.);

- *supplies/consumers* (enrolment, retention, completion, good quality education and post-basic education for both male and female pupils, students, teachers etc.);
- *information* (gender sensitive education curricula).

An effective coordination of the three performance principles with these four fundamentals of gender parity in education delivery might probably ensure the attainment of comprehensive, accessible and compatible gender parity in education in Ghana. The fact that the *GPRS* has influenced the *ESP* of the Ministry of Education symbolises an aspect of the Ministry of Education–donor agencies cooperation (GoG/MoE 2003a, b). The question however is: does the *GPRS* reveal a sophisticated analysis of gender disparity in education and does it indicate a complex approach to deal with it?

Although the *GPRS*, like other PRSPs, failed to devote a chapter to gender analysis and seemed to treat the subject in a somewhat fragmentary fashion, it nevertheless offered a brief gendered analysis of poverty. Had it embarked on a gender-blind poverty assessment it would have yielded a distorted notion of poverty and its dynamics. It thus highlighted the educational levels of people aged 15 years and above and discovered that, while 32 per cent had never been to school at all, nearly twice as many women as men (males 21 per cent and females 41 per cent) had never been. A rural–urban and regional analysis of education by gender revealed significant gender gaps between male and female school attendance. For instance, for every 100 girls that had never been to school, there were 45 and 65 boys in the urban and rural areas respectively. The higher dropout rate among girls was evident in the ratio of 100 girls to 201 and 417 boys in the urban and rural areas respectively that completed senior secondary school (SSS). Another instance also showed that, for every 100 girls who completed SSS, there were 833 boys, for example, in the Brong Ahafo Region, 600 boys in the Central Region, 460 boys in the Eastern Region, 440 in the Northern Region, 300 in the Western Region and 277 in the Volta Region, who also completed. Literacy rates also showed gender disparity in favour of men.

Despite these major disparities, the poverty diagnosis in the *GPRS* still seemed to exclude sophisticated empowerment and vulnerability frameworks (Abugre 2001b; Integrated Social Development Centre 2003). Hence the costing and finance part of the *GPRS* failed to reflect a gendered budget. Gender targets in education appeared non-existent, apart from setting enrolment target for girls from 71 per cent in 2000 to 80 per cent in 2004 and setting a reduced dropout rate target for girls from 30 per cent to 20 per cent and for boys from 20 per cent to 10 per cent at primary level. No gender targets were set for transition, literacy and numeracy rates at any level of education, not even the primary level (GoG/NDPC 2003a).

Thus while the 2002 draft of the *GPRS* (GoG/NDPC 2002) promoted gender parity in enrolment at the primary education level and set some targets to achieve it, the 2003 *GPRS* document fails as it neither set gender parity targets at the junior secondary, senior secondary and tertiary levels nor in non-formal education. There seem to be no targets that will enhance participation and retention of girls at either the basic level and/or other higher levels of education and in the non-formal sector (GoG/NDPC 2003a).

Again while the *GPRS* explored different approaches to reinforce institutions that protected the rights of girls and children, surprisingly it failed to address the serious concerns of female literacy that are critical to poverty reduction. Although the 2003 *GPRS* gender analysis of education included the senior secondary level, and looked at a share of boys and girls reaching mastery levels in English and mathematics, it still failed to set gender targets and explore comprehensively gender parity with regards to educational quality and outcomes, female participation at higher levels of education and the critical relationship between female literacy and poverty reduction. This showed an omission that reflected a lack of direction in the development and poverty reduction process, especially since it acknowledged the fact that 'poverty in Ghana has important gender dimensions and therefore requires focused public policy measures' (GoG/NDPC 2003a, b: 25).

Below, I suggest an alternative to the mainstream approach. This combines the three performance principles of *coordination* (*comprehensiveness, accessibility* and *compatibility*) outlined by Alter and Hage (1993) with regards to the four tenets of gender parity in education delivery.

An alternative approach to poverty reduction and gender

The three so-called network performance principles offer interesting insights into the nature of Ghana's poverty strategy but also its gender strategy. They are explained in more detail below, where I turn them towards gender issues.

Comprehensiveness here means that all levels and aspects of education that are plagued with gender disparity are addressed. This implies that the required resources and expertise are obtained for education policy interventions at all stages so that the expected parity of outcomes and equality of treatment of girls and boys, women and men can become a reality. Comprehensiveness can encapsulate the setting of gender parity targets in literacy and numeracy rates, in enrolment, retention and completion rates at all levels of education.

Accessibility in this context refers to the parameters of the *GPRS* ensuring that there are policies in place that repudiate exclusionary practices and enable any male or female pupil/student to gain access to every level of good quality education. It therefore incorporates the provision of appropriate infrastructure, gender-sensitive learning and teaching resources and a conducive environment to every male and female pupil/student who needs to access them. If the *GPRS* were to address gender disparity in education comprehensively, it probably would culminate in impartial access to (female) education. Thus the coordination process perhaps would engender universal access where every girl/woman and boy/man in the society can easily access the education service at any level without constraints. There is the need for gender parity attainment programmes in education to be all inclusive.

The third network performance principle is *compatibility*, which is indicative of the complementarity that exists between different parts of an education policy. This principle would encourage policies to aim at achieving holistic gender parity. It would engender education programmes, curricula and actions that complement each other in relationships of interdependence in the bid to attain gender parity in education. The *GPRS* is a macro-policy as well as a product of the donor–recipient cooperation, which has a significant bearing on the policies that are formulated in the education sector in Ghana. Yet it does not seem to reflect the compatibility of these elements in the service that are being delivered to the beneficiaries. It is important that the components complement and not contradict or undermine each other. However, because the first two principles have been violated, the goals of the resource providers (donors–Ministry of Education) fail to link harmoniously with the needs of the beneficiaries. For example, because the *GPRS* fails to set gender targets for retention and completion at the basic level as well as targets for gender parity at the higher levels of education, the progression of a girl from the basic to the higher level is already undermined. Again, because it does not set quality targets with regards to education at all levels, female education and even that of male education is weakened. For example, the *GPRS* rightly observes that:

> [t]he connection between education, female household heads and income earning capability is a good reason to worry about the fact that only 6% of females aged 15 and over had attained higher than secondary school education. Nearly 35% of all household heads are females. About 61% (53%) of female household heads in urban (rural) areas fall in the poorest 20% of the population. Most important of this statistics is that female poverty entails further deprivations that manifest in children's significant under nourishment and infant mortality.
>
> (GoG/NDPC 2003a: 25)

These comments acknowledge that women who achieve higher academic credentials are indispensable to the economic and physical well-being of their families, though it is the sort that Unterhalter (2000) referred to as the only parochial reason why women's education is seen as necessary. Nevertheless, the *GPRS* fails to indicate how it intends to boost the tiny number of women who attain higher levels of education. So there seems to be an incompatibility between the goals of the Ministry of Education–donor cooperation symbolised by the *GPRS*, and the needs of the female (and even male) pupil or student. Moreover, the fact that the findings of the brief gendered poverty analysis in the *GPRS* did not translate into the setting of the various gender parity targets and the costing/budgeting process also indicates an instance of incompatibility. Criticisms levelled against the simplistic approach of the *GPRS* (GoG/NDPC 2002) to gender and comments offered on various drafts of the *GPRS* for the period 2003 to 2005 about the need to address gender issues comprehensively did not seem to have had a great impact (Casely-Hayford 2002; GoG/NDPC

2003a, b). The current *Growth and Poverty Reduction Strategy 2006–2009*, also known as *GPRS II* (GoG/NDPC 2005) is another significant proof.

In sum, in those regards, the *GPRS* as an official product, is not a progressive document as far as addressing gender disparity in education is concerned. More attempts need to be made to transform and steer the *GPRS* towards a more gender oriented stance. Targets that guarantee parity in both areas of teaching and educational management are also essential (Casely-Hayford 2002). Gender parity targets need to transcend the basic level to the higher levels of the education system because there are gross gender imbalances at all levels of the social structure. These have to be redressed in order to transform literate girls into educated women. Without adequate provision for higher educational levels, the intellectual advancement that women need in order to bridge the gender inequality gap in society will remain elusive. While the 2003 Annual Progress Report of the *GPRS* showed some evidence of quality indicators and targets, these were restricted to the pupil teacher ratio and the pass rate for the Criterion Reference Test in Mathematics and English at the basic level. An indicator for the percentage of trained teachers in primary school was identified but no target was set for 2005, not even at the basic, let alone the higher levels (GoG/NDPC 2004).

A recent growth in repetition rates suggests that an increasing number of pupils and students are not academically ready to progress to the next stage in their schooling process (MoEYS 2004a). Recommending strategies to enhance "automatic progression", as indicated in the 2004 performance report of the education sector, might not be the answer (MoEYS 2004b: 48). Ghana's recent proposal for the Education for All/Fast-Track Initiative (EFA/FTI) indicates a broader perspective on quality issues but its focus is again only on primary education (GoG/MoEYs 2004b). Indeed, apart from the demand for GoG/MoE–donor organisations' symbiotic cooperation to produce policies that are comprehensive and address the education sector holistically, there also seems to be a need for a serious and sincere recommitment from the GoG/MoE to gender parity goals in the entire education sector and the other sectors of society (Amoako 2005). Policy and practice processes in the education sector need to reflect this recommitment. There is the danger that efforts to achieve gender parity in basic education will be undermined and will not yield the outcomes that will reduce poverty if post-basic education is neglected, for the latter is dynamically linked to the former (King 2005).

Conclusion

International poverty agendas such as the present poverty alleviation strategy have been slow in addressing gender inequality in education. This chapter illustrates how the *GPRS* has inadequately addressed gender inequality in education in Ghana despite the laudatory remarks it won from some development analysts (Sachs 2005). The strategy tends to tackle gender disparity in education in a piecemeal fashion. While the alternative approach is by no means absolute, it would be productive if the *GPRS* considers these three elements in its attempt to analyse gender disparity in education. Further, recent studies have shown that focus on universal primary education (UPE) alone at the expense of the other levels of education will fail to produce the permanent poverty alleviation results that appear to be the main objective of the *GPRS* and international development cooperation (Palmer 2005; King 2005; Wedgewood 2005; Hayman 2005; Akoojee and McGrath 2005; Tilak 2005). It is obvious that the scope of the Millennium Development Goals (MDGs) is limited and the inability to transcend them in education delivery, management and planning in Ghana will probably undermine their attainment.

In order to achieve a holistic gender parity that is comprehensive and permeates access, quality, outcomes, management in education and all levels within the educational system, gender disparity analysis in the *GPRS* may need to reflect Alter and Hage's three performance principles of *comprehensiveness, accessibility* and *compatibility*. It is important that recommendations for getting more gender experts, who are also proficient in finance and economics on board the poverty reduction strategies process wagon, are given due consideration. Also crucial is the need for the IFIs, multi/bilateral donors and recipient countries to work together in a manner that transcends the rhetoric of the poverty reduction strategies as country led and partnership oriented. In this regard, certain compromises and concessions have to be made by those who possess the economic clout and design PRSP frameworks.

One might ask whether it is possible to adopt such a sophisticated analysis and holistic approach for attaining gender parity, if the financial strength of a country is not assured. Is it possible if policy makers do not believe in, and therefore are not committed to, the gender parity agenda? Even if this alternative approach is adopted in the theoretical analysis of gender disparity in the *GPRS*, does this guarantee that the same approach will be actually implemented? In other words, how do we translate rhetoric into real practice? These questions persist. Adopting a more complex theoretical analysis of gender disparity in education does not automatically redress gender imbalance in education in the real world. Nevertheless, it offers at least the opportunity to reconceptualise gender disparity in a more complex and efficient manner that offers a credible picture of the state of affairs. This allows for more informed gender advocates who keep all stakeholders, especially national governments and international donors, on their toes to design more efficient implementation plans and make greater moral and financial commitments to attain gender parity in education. Ghana has taken the initial step and established a Girls' Education Unit. Such an initiative needs broadening in order to include the educational needs of the women that the girls will one day become. Indeed, the heavy cost implications for implementing the three principles to achieve holistic gender parity in education can never be underestimated. However, Ghana has already made the first brave attempt to institute the Ghana Education Trust Fund (GETFund), an alternative funding source to international aid. Imaginative identification of other sources for the generation of funds through local/national initiatives is required in both public and private sectors.

While not sounding unduly prescriptive, this analysis offers some lessons. The analytic framework of the three network principles can help analyse existing policy declarations and policies, and describe alternative approaches in more sophisticated ways. It can be regarded as a new analytic framework for policy analysis because it has the potential to ensure holistic approach to policy formulation and implementation. While the distinction between the three principles is convenient for this analysis, they are not mutually exclusive and thus engage in a ceaseless dialectic that ensures more sophisticated and holistic approaches to policy. This is the added value.

Notes

1 A review of 19 Interim Poverty Reduction Strategy Papers (I-PRSPs) and four completed PRSPs designed by the World Bank showed a dearth of holistic gender analysis in the main essentials and divisions (Subrahmanian 2004). For gender significance to transcend the rhetoric and emerge as a practical reality demands rigorous efforts to ensure that the sophisticated character of gender inequality permeates entire levels of policy and practice (ibid.). See also the evaluation report, 'Gender in the PRSPs: A Stocktaking' (2001) by the World Bank Poverty Reduction and Economic Management Network-Gender and Development Group.
2 This analysis was based on the previous GoG/NDPC 2003a and 2003b. The ideas for this chapter were conceived and drafted long before the current, *Growth and Poverty Reduction Strategy 2006–2009 (GPRS II)* was published (NDPC 2005). Another reason why *GPRS II* has not been the main focus of this analysis is that its treatment of gender disparity in education is no different and even less comprehensive than that of *GPRS I*. Although among its main educational priorities, *GPRS II* aims to close gender gaps in access to education in all districts and promote science and technology education with focus on encouraging more female participation, it fails to set specific targets and indicate convincingly how these priorities will be achieved. Note that the phrase 'the *GPRS*' used in this analysis refers largely to *GPRS I*.
3 A complete PRSP, which in Ghana's case is the *GPRS*, accompanied by other 'triggers' was a requirement for HIPC2 completion.

References

Abugre, C. (2001a) 'Participation in the PRSP process in Ghana. Actors, participation and ownership', ISODEC Papers. Available online at: www.isodec.org.gh/Papers/-participation-in-prsp-process-in-ghana.pdf (accessed 6 October 2005).

Abugre, C. (2001b) 'PRSP monitoring and information in Ghana'. Available online at: www.isodec.org.gh/Papers/prsp-monitoring-in-ghana.pdf (accessed 6 October 2005).

Akoojee, S. and McGrath, S. (2005) 'Post-basic education and training and poverty reduction in South Africa: progress to 2004 and vision to 2014' (Draft), Post-Basic Education and Working Paper Series No. 2. University of Edinburgh: CAS.

Alter, C. and Hage, J. (1993) *Organizations Working Together*, Newbury Park: CA: Sage Publications Inc.

Amoako, E.J.A. (2005) 'Inter-organisational network of interactions: efforts to attain gender parity in basic education in Ghana', Paper presented at the 8th UKFIET International Conference on Education and Development: Learning and Livelihood, Oxford, September 2005.

Bell, E. (2003) 'Gender and PRSPs: with experiences from Tanzania, Bolivia, Vietnam and Mozambique', Prepared for the Ministry of Foreign Affairs, Denmark.

Booth, D. (2003) 'Introduction and overview', *Development Policy Review: Are PRSPs Making a Difference? The African Experience*, 21, 2: 131–159.

Casely-Hayford, L. (2002) *Situational Analysis of Gender Issues in Education: from Literate Girls to Educated Women*, Accra, Ghana: Ministry of Education.

Chao, S. (1999) 'Ghana: gender analysis and policymaking for development', World Bank Discussion Paper 403.

Christiaensen, L., Demery, L. and Paternostro, S. (2003). 'Macro and micro perspectives of growth and poverty in Africa', *The World Bank Economic Review*, 17, 3: 317–347.

Coulombe, H. and McKay, A. (2003). 'Selective poverty reduction in a slow growth environment: Ghana in the 1990s'. Available online at: www.isser.org/Selective%20Poverty%20Reduction.pdf (accessed 8 July 2006).

Driscoll, R. and Christiansen, K. (2004) *The PRSP Approach: A Basic Guide for CARE International*, London: ODI.

Economic Commission for Africa (2005) 'Economic Report on Africa 2005: Meeting the Challenges of Unemployment and Poverty in Africa', Addis Ababa: Economic Commission for Africa. Available online at: www.uneca.org/era2005/overview.pdf (accessed 28 October 2006).

Febres, G. (2005) 'Gender issues in the CIS-7 countries' PRSPs', Uzbekistan: WBI.

Fox, J. (2002) 'Poverty in Ghana, 1991 to 1999. A country case study', Technical report submitted to USAID/Washington, DC. Available online at: www.pdf.usaid.gov/pdf_docs/PNACR804.pdf (accessed 8 August 2006).

Fraser, A. (2005) 'PRSPs: now who calls the shots', *Review of African Political Economy*, 32, 104: 317–340.

Government of Ghana/Ministry of Education (GoG/MoE) (2003a) *Education Strategic Plan 2003 to 2015 Volume 1: Policies, Targets and Strategies*, Accra: Ministry of Education.

Government of Ghana/Ministry of Education (GoG/MoE) (2003b) *Education Strategic Plan 2003 to 2015 Volume 2: Work Programme*, Accra: Ministry of Education.

Government of Ghana/Ministry of Education, Youth and Sports (GoG/MoEYS) (2004a) 'Education Strategic Plan implementation progress report – May 2003–June 2004 (draft)', Accra: MoEYS.

Government of Ghana/Ministry of Education, Youth and Sports (2004b) 'Ghana proposal for inclusion in Education For All fast track initiative', Accra: MoEYS.

Government of Ghana/National Development Planning Commission (GoG/NDPC) (2002) *Ghana Poverty Reduction Strategy 2002–2004: An Agenda for Growth and Prosperity. Analysis and Policy Statement*, Accra: GoG/NDPC.

Government of Ghana/National Development Planning Commission (GoG/NDPC) (2003a) *Ghana Poverty Reduction Strategy 2003–2005: An Agenda for Growth and Prosperity Volume 1. Analysis and Policy Statement*, Accra: NDPC.

Government of Ghana/National Development Planning Commission (GoG/NDPC) (2003b) *Ghana Poverty Reduction Strategy 2003–2005: An Agenda for Growth and Prosperity Volume II. Costing and Financing of Programmes and Projects*, Accra: NDPC.

Government of Ghana/National Development Planning Commission (GoG/NDPC) (2004) *Implementation of the Ghana Poverty Reduction Strategy. 2003 Annual Progress Report*, Accra: GoG/NDPC.

Government of Ghana/National Development Planning Commission (GoG/NDPC) (2005) *Growth and Poverty Reduction Strategy: The Coordinated Programme for the Economic and Social Development of Ghana (GPRS II)*, Accra: NDPC.

Hayman, R. (2005) 'The contribution of post-basic education and training (PBET) to poverty reduction in Rwanda: balancing short-term goals and long-term visions in the face of capacity constraints', Post-Basic Education and Working Paper Series No. 3. University of Edinburgh: CAS.

Heward, C. and Bunwaree, S. (1999) *Gender, Education and Development: Beyond Access to Empowerment*, London: Zed Books.

Hjertholm, P. and White, H. (1998) 'Survey of foreign aid: history, trends and allocation', Discussion Papers. Copenhagen: Institute of Economics, University of Copenhagen.

Integrated Social Development Centre (ISODEC) (2003) 'The Ghana Poverty Reduction Strategy. ISODEC's Position Paper'. Available online at: www.isodec.org.gh/Papers/GPRSpositionpaper.PDF (accessed 1 September 2005).

King, K. (2005) 'Post-basic education and training for growth and poverty reduction. Towards a sector-wide, multi-sector study of Kenya', Post-Basic Education and Working Paper Series No. 5. University of Edinburgh: CAS.

Lewis, P. (1996) 'Economic reform and political transition in Africa. The quest for a politics of development', *World Politics*, 49, 1: 92–129.

McKay, A. and Aryeetey, E. (2004) 'Operationalising pro-poor growth, a joint initiative of AFD, BMZ (GTZ, KFW Development Bank), DFID and the World Bank. A country case study on Ghana'. Available online at: www.dfid.gov.uk/pubs/files/oppg-ghana.pdf#search=%22mackay%20and%20aryeetey%22 (accessed 8 July 2006).

Ministry of Education, Youth and Sports (MoEYS) (2004a) 'Girls' education in Ghana: trends, initiatives and the way forward', Accra: MoE.

Ministry of Education, Youth and Sports (MoEYS) (2004b) 'Preliminary Education Sector Performance Report 2004', Accra: MoEYS.

Moser, C. (1993) *Gender Planning and Development. Theory, Practice and Training*, London: Routledge.

Nightingale, K. (2003) 'Failing women, sustaining poverty (a look at Anne Whitehead's Report)'. Available online at: www.bond.org.uk/networker/2003/sept03/gender-prsp.htm (accessed 13 October 2005).

Palmer, R. (2005) 'Beyond the basics: post-basic education, training and poverty reduction in Ghana', Post-Basic Education and Working Paper Series No. 4. University of Edinburgh: CAS.

Panos (2002) *Reducing Poverty: Is the World Bank Strategy Working?* Panos Report No. 45, UK: Panos Ltd.

Sachs, J.D. (2005) *The End of Poverty: Economic Possibilities for Our Time*, New York: Penguin Press.

Stewart, F. and Wang, M. (2003) 'Do PRSPs empower poor countries and disempower the World Bank, or is it the other way round?', QEH Working Paper Series-QEHWP 108, Oxford University: Queen Elizabeth House.

Stromquist, N. (1999) 'The impact of structural adjustment programmes in Africa and Latin America', in C. Heward and S.S. Bunwaree (eds) *Gender, Education and Development: Beyond Access to Empowerment*, London: Zed Books, pp. 17–32.

Subrahmanian, R. (2004) 'Promoting gender equality' in R. Black and H. White (eds) *Targeting Development: Critical Perspectives on the Millennium Development Goals*, Oxford: Routledge, pp. 184–208.

Tilak, J.B.G. (2005) 'Post-elementary education and training in India', Post-Basic Education and Working Paper Series No. 6. University of Edinburgh: CAS.

UNESCO (2003) *Gender and Education for All. The Leap to Equality*, Paris: UNESCO Publishing.

Unterhalter, E. (2000) 'Transnational visions of the 1990s. Contrasting views of women, education and citizenship' in M. Arnot and J. Dillabough, *Challenging Democracy. International Perspectives on Gender, Education and Citizenship*, London, New York: RoutledgeFalmer, pp. 87–102.

—— (2005) 'Global inequality, capabilities, social justice: the millennium development goal for gender equality in education', *International Journal of Educational Development*, 25: 111–122.

Wedgwood, R. (2005) 'Post basic education and poverty in Tanzania', Post-Basic Education and Working Paper Series No. 1. University of Edinburgh: CAS.

Whitehead, A. (2003) *Failing Women, Sustaining Poverty: Gender in Poverty Reduction Strategy Papers*, London: UK Gender and Development Network.

Winter, C. and Burnett, N. (2002) 'Advancing gender equity in education: a critical MDG. Clarifying the role and effectiveness of PRSPs'. A PowerPoint Presentation for DfID.

World Bank (2001) 'Gender in the PRSPs: a stocktaking by the World Bank Poverty Reduction and Economic Management Network-Gender and Development Group', Washington, DC: World Bank.

World Development Movement (WDM) (2005) '9 out of 10 World Bank Poverty Reduction Programmes Demand Privatisation'. Available online at: www.globalpolicy.org/socecon/bwi-wto/wbank/2005/0919ipocri.htm (accessed 18 October 2005).

14 Adult learning and the politics of change

Feminist organization and educational action in Latin America

Nelly P. Stromquist

The task of transforming society's gender beliefs and practices in the direction of equality and democracy is immensely complex. The formal educational system can emerge as an important means to achieve social transformation because it serves an increasingly larger sector of the population, which is staying longer in educational institutions. There is strong evidence that education is beneficial for women, as educated women are able to have better lives for themselves and for their children, as reflected in lower rates of fertility and child mortality, and higher rates of political participation and access to the labour market.[1] Yet, while positive outcomes can be linked to education, key asymmetries in society remain. Women's access to a full citizenship remains limited, as many civil and economic rights do not reach them. Not only do two-thirds of the world's illiterates continue to be women (UNESCO 2006), but most countries do not grant women crucial inheritance, property and divorce rights, a situation that is worse in African and Middle Eastern countries and better in Latin America and former socialist countries in Asia (Lloyd 2005). Moreover, men's sense of entitlement permeates many cultures at macro and micro levels, contributing to create polarized conceptions of masculinity and femininity.

In addition to formal schooling, one needs to consider the learning that occurs *outside* formal educational settings with adult women. This type of learning is critical because it serves persons who, because of their age, have accumulated numerous personal, labour and community experiences in which the gendered nature of society has been felt. These women, therefore, must be seen as important targets for efforts to alter the relations of gender. Further, learning opportunities outside formal structures offer them the possibility of thinking in political terms and designing ways of organizing shared objectives. Researching feminist NGOs in the provision of knowledge provides insights on alternative ways to produce change in the social relations of gender. These organizations represent the concrete and institutional form of the women's movements and their examination enables us to probe actions and strategies pursued away from the surveillance of state agencies and male control but within safe spaces. In those settings, women can produce knowledge and develop the strategies they need to engage in transformative action.

Feminist NGOs are increasingly taken as objects of analysis and much effort is placed on the relations they have with the state, the extent to which they foster new forms of democracy and the tensions they face in promoting social change. However, there is much less recognition of the means by which they accomplish their objectives. As entities of civil society that rely mostly on persuasion for social change, NGO educational activity is a key vehicle for the creation of new identities, the diffusion of counterhegemonic knowledge and the development of assertive individuals. Feminist NGOs therefore carry out a crucial, if little visible, function in their respective communities. The concept of *empowerment*, defined as a process by which oppressed persons gain some control over their lives, has been crucial in the debates seeking to transform gender in society and is a process firmly fostered through non-traditional forms of learning. Feminist NGOs vary in structure and objectives, but what unites them is the use of both *non-formal education* and *informal learning* to provide knowledge otherwise not provided by the state.

This chapter explores the ways in which both non-formal education and informal learning, sponsored and led by NGOs in Latin America, have promoted women's empowerment. It considers how research into this world of learning outside conventional educational structures has much to offer the study of gender, education and development. Although often recognized as important contributors, particularly to poverty alleviation, these NGOs are often outside the terrain defined by educational research and are seen as insignificant (especially if female) agents alongside nation state and international policy making bodies. This chapter demonstrates how researching such NGOs' educational interventions can throw light on the prevalence and modes of challenge to gender power/relations.

Alternative education for social transformation

Given that formal education encounters severe limits in efforts at social transformation, education *outside* the strictures, norms and practices of schooling becomes an important alternative. In these days of intense competition for employment and the allocation of the best jobs to persons with educational credentials, it is unlikely that schooling will continue to provide any knowledge that is not practical and does not provide immediate economic returns. That leaves the possibility of any significant alternative education open only to adult forms of education and to informal learning. Such education is provided by, among others, groups that advocate the improvement of women's rights. Its present coverage is limited but its consequences are worth examining. Schooling exists within regulating structures that heavily monitor its performance and tend to restrain actions that go against the status quo; besides, schools serve young populations whose experience of inequality is limited by their age. But these strictures do not apply to non-formal education that functions outside the boundaries of academic credentials and degrees, examinations and student selection. Non-formal education (that which functions outside public schools, has a flexible curriculum and generally serves adult populations) and informal learning (that which occurs as subjects engage in new practices – in this case for cultural transformation) emerge as fundamental practices that feminist organizations employ to promote individual and collective change.

By their very nature, subordinate populations comprise individuals who exist on the margins of established power, and thus their access to effective centres of decision making is limited. If new power is to be created for them, therefore, it must come from outside the official political structures. In this context, knowledge plays a key role. Even though women are often excluded as social actors, they can create power for themselves through collective efforts around, first, the acquisition, creation and integration of knowledge, and, second, by its distribution through the establishment of tangible networks mobilized around a common plan of action (Stromquist 2006). Outside the state's gaze, gathering in a friendly and supportive environment, women benefit from non-formal education programmes provided by women's and feminist non-governmental organizations (NGOs). These organizations can create settings where new ideas may be expressed and an agenda for action may be established without opposition by those most negatively affected.

These organizations recognize the gender perspective but some of their members may see gender as less useful politically than the concept of women's rights; for example:

> What gender are we talking about? There are people who say we should be working with men. As far as I am concerned, I don't have the least interest in doing so. In a conservative country, we must pursue the strategy of equality for men and women. Feminism is a political project for women. Gender is not. There are people in government who still do not understand the concept of gender. We have, therefore, to use political concepts such as discrimination, exclusion, equality – which are elements of humankind's patrimony for democracy. Parity is a feminist concept, based on equality.
>
> (CIPAF director in interview)

One question in this panorama of social transformation concerns the methods that have been used to facilitate change in the social relations of gender. In the existing literature, it has generally been the practice to focus on the proposals and attainments of the women's movement rather than to consider the organizational forms that have helped lead to their implementation. It has also been common to ignore the educational nature of actions taken by women and feminists. In this chapter I consider the kinds of issues that comprise the knowledge production and diffusion of feminist NGOs. How are these issues identified? What social impacts can be linked to the women's new knowledge? What are essential elements that enable concrete feminist action?

Researching feminist NGOs

Below I use such questions to examine the work of three NGOs in Latin America. I describe their educational activities and consider how knowledge is transmitted and used for the purposes of establishing a new consciousness around issues of gender. The NGOs chosen for examination were the Research Centre for Feminine Action (*Centro de Investigaciones para la Acción Femenina*; CIPAF)[2] in the Dominican Republic, and the Flora Tristán Center (FT from now on) and the Manuela Ramos Movement (MR) in Peru. They were selected because of their national and international reputation, and their long existence (more than 20 years) – which enables us to trace strategies and trajectories over time. These three NGOs define themselves as 'feminist' in the sense that sought concrete ways to improve the conditions and status of women while transforming social perceptions of feminine and masculine identities. They seek this both through personal change and state action. Their work is fairly typical of the kinds of activities similar NGOs conduct in the Latin American region.

The study was designed so that it explored: (a) how educational forms and strategies were used by these NGOs; (b) what specific kinds of knowledge were produced and transmitted by them; (c) what impacts can be attributed to NGO action and (d) their organizational forms. In each case, I conducted semi-structured interviews with a wide array of each NGO's staff, spending about two months in each organization per year over a three-year period. I also interviewed individuals in other NGOs and government agencies that had either observed or benefited from their work; and conducted documentary analysis of various plans, internal reports and other documents (for a detailed treatment, see Stromquist 2006).

The alternative knowledge of non-formal education

In helping poor women, who have little time and energy to attend educational programmes, feminist NGOs have learned to be creative in the design of educational interventions, giving them special appeal and short duration but with tangible impact. The most common form of intervention has been the workshops or *talleres* – short-term activities usually having a practical character and addressing a particular issue. Other forms of non-formal education, in Latin America, have included the *jornadas* (one-day meetings to examine a set of interrelated themes) and courses (recurrent sessions that follow the conventional format of regular meetings over the course of several months). Such themes as domestic violence, women's right to land ownership, reproductive and sexual rights, and political participation have typically been chosen to transmit information and knowledge on gender issues. These themes have required conceptual and theoretical discussion on women's everyday subordination, an understanding of the interrelation between ideological forces and material conditions, and an understanding of the interaction between gender, class and ethnicity. In some cases, explicit use has been made of feminist theory. Often, the new knowledge has been accompanied by the provision of services, particularly in health, legal assistance and, in the case of MR, the provision of small loans so that women may set up their own enterprises. This work, conducted mostly in urban areas, has served low- and middle-class women, most of whom were literate.

Courses have been used to address central aspects of problematic conditions of women in reproductive health, literacy and education, family and conjugal relations, income and access to land. The skills provided by feminist NGOs have also addressed personal development, organizing skills, leadership and lobbying techniques, and have served to address some of the concrete problems that women face in workers' unions, political parties and community organizations. It is important to recognize that the type of knowledge afforded by feminist NGOs is not provided by formal education institutions such as the high schools or universities. In this manner, feminist NGOs function to frame new discourses, create strong feminist identities and pressure key levels of government. For much of the work with adult women, feminist NGOs have utilized objectives and methodologies developed by popular education. Since many of the activists working within feminist NGOs had not originally received formal training in pedagogical methodologies, these women have sought the assistance of institutions with long trajectories in popular education, such as the Adult Education Council for Latin American and the Caribbean, but made substantial modifications to include gender issues.

Non-formal education is sensitive to situated knowledge, as participants in the learning process learn to trust others in order to widen their experiences as well as to gain a better reading of their own personal experiences. Popular educators consider that the creation of horizontal relations and a constant dialogue among those who are seeking to learn, creates an environment that promotes new questions to explore (Freire 1970). Those who uphold critical theory consider that a safe space under the guidance *of organic intellectuals* – i.e. those committed to the cause of a marginalized group – provides the most favourable conditions to foster the systematic analysis of existing social inequalities. Critical theory acknowledges the value of re-enacting previous life experiences so new knowledge, attitudes, skills and behaviours may be constructed. Consequently, educational action by the feminist NGOs acquires a broader meaning and usually begins by incorporating the reality of women's lives (their social, emotional, political and intellectual aspects) as a point of departure.

The educational strategies followed by women-led NGOs evince a careful balance between the work of developing a new identity and the pressuring of the state for corrective action. These strategies show an interesting combination of both following a predetermined curriculum and responding strictly to local demands expressed by the groups of women with which the NGOs seek to work. All three NGOs in the present study made contacts with groups of women, offering them a means of improving their situation by providing them with a strong sense of feminist knowledge through workshops, short-term courses and events. At the same time, they have responded to requests to attend to priorities felt in households, such as access to credit, health services and even access to food. CIPAF responded not by offering these specific services but by referring the women to other institutions that could do so. MR does have programmes that provide medical attention (on a limited scale) and information on reproductive and sexual health. Both FT and MR offer legal services, especially on issues of domestic violence and paternal financial support for minor children.

Their predetermined educational agendas have emphasized topics such as 'women's subordination' and 'feminist theory'. This content has been considered essential to shape the creation of new identities that while, on the one hand, continue to recognize the specificity of being a woman or a man, but on the other hand, aim to offer more flexible roles to men and women. According to one of the women in CIPAF: 'We discuss certain terms of our collaboration, the types of courses that we offer, the schedules, the teaching methodologies, but we do not negotiate our feminist content.' This position of having a certain knowledge that is not negotiable has also characterized the Peruvian NGOs.

Through their multiple and recurrent activities in non-formal education, feminist NGOs not only foster the acquisition of a positive language among the participants but also provide them with a concrete understanding of the beliefs, processes and institutions that affect economic and social life and, in particular, how these dynamics affect the conditions in which women and men function. The educational objectives seek to present and examine the problematic situations between men and women so that once these issues have been understood, women will seek to change them through collective action.

The emergence of informal learning

Working in such organisations represents a first step outside the isolation of the private sphere for many women. It also means acting in systematic ways and learning to distinguish between effective and ineffective strategies. To be placed in charge of all responsibilities of their own organization leads women to develop the capacity to act collectively – a new social experience for them because the confining nature of existing cultural patterns, ranging from family life to professional performance, generally forces women to narrow their sense of the collective to their family and to do so mostly through individual action and self-sacrifice. Informal learning as used here is defined as the set of skills and knowledge one gains through collective action for social change (Foley 2001). It comprises the behaviours, attitudes and the set of messages that are employed to convey information and knowledge.

The NGOs in the study evinced a wide range of informal learning activities. The running of a formal institution, by assuming daily functions that go from policy making to accounting, generates crucial skills and capacities among women working in these institutions. The importance of written communication through monthly newspapers, bulletins, books and posters to raise women's consciousness is unquestionable. In the Dominican Republic, CIPAF made constant and widespread use of its monthly newspaper *Quehaceres* to transmit feminist information that ultimately created an appreciation of the effectiveness of feminist action not only in the Dominican Republic but also in other countries in the region. This newspaper had become one of the most stable publications in the country. The two feminist NGOs in Peru experimented with various publications, from *fotonovelas*[3] to magazines to feminist almanacs; each has been used at different times of their history. MR and FT, together with four similar institutions, established a radio station they called 'Radio Milenia' to broadcast programmes whose topics ranged from health to political analysis. For the past five years, a TV programme ('*Barra de Mujeres*') produced by MR has been providing a weekly hour to link women's issues to ongoing national developments.

An extremely creative and effective activity of CIPAF has been the production of campaigns. These activities, executed about three to four times per year, have been carried out to give more visibility to a social issue under public discussion or meriting such discussion. With the simultaneous use of posters, a special issue of *Quehaceres*, radio spots, paid spaces in major newspapers and the use of powerful slogans, these campaigns – usually a week in duration – brought a substantial national consciousness to the selected issues. Slogans such as 'He who loves doesn't kill' and 'If someone raises his hand, may it be to salute you' (to counter domestic violence), and 'Stop the silence' (protesting the illegality of abortion that causes maternal deaths) served to transmit basic feminist principles and to create counter-messages and supportive symbols. The uses of posters, with women in assertive postures, served to convey oppositional discourse to the image of women as passive and obedient. The two Peruvian NGOs have also engaged in the production of campaigns, primarily on domestic violence, sexual abuse and political participation. Some of these campaigns have been accompanied by marches with the use of musical groups and demonstrations in front of major public buildings. Feminist organizations played an active role in the public protests that brought about the fall of President Alberto Fujimori in his unconstitutional attempt to be re-elected for the third time.

An important form of learning also takes place through the commemoration of special days. Sociologists recognize the observance of these historic events and designations as critical both for recognizing issues of importance to society as well as to introduce new concepts. The NGOs have been active in organizing events for such days as 8 March to honour the International Day of Women, 25 November to celebrate the International Day for the Elimination of Violence Against Women and 26 May to commemorate Women's Health Day. The idea of a day to remind society of the principle of non-violence against women, originally proposed by CIPAF in 1981, was adopted by the United Nations in 1999 as an international day. These events help create spaces where certain issues may be publicly debated and demands made. On these occasions, several events are carried out in visible spaces such as parks and sports arenas and involve the use of artistic forms such as songs, poetry, popular theatre, dances and the display of posters and banners, which call the audience's attention to the problems women face as well as provide a physical area in which women can engage proactively, such as by speaking and acting in the public sphere, and disseminating information to the passers-by. Participation in the activities of such days gives women a sense of citizenship and gives both men and women a sense of the importance of gender issues. These symbolic demonstrations are powerful in themselves because on a longer-term basis they contribute to the creation of new social representations. They also legitimate gender concerns internationally because they are celebrated by many governments throughout the world.

In addition, the feminist NGOs have engaged in substantial research activities and systematization of experiences that have resulted in the publication of books and the establishment of libraries within their buildings. Each of the three NGOs has produced a large number of publications, many of them based on their own research, which suggests the importance of new knowledge in the process of social change. By 2003, the empirical and theoretical production of the two Peruvian NGOs had increased considerably to the point that the feminist institutions had reached publication rates comparable to those in the social sciences of a large university. The book publications by FT are well known in the entire Latin American region.

While the feminist NGOs in the study had deployed strategies concerning non-formal education and informal learning, their interventions regarding formal schooling have been quite modest. Only in the case of CIPAF could one find a questioning of the school and advocacy of intervention strategies to affect the regular educational system, elaborated in a ten-year plan and training for teachers, counsellors, school principals and students. In the case of MR and FT, there is agreement that their preoccupation with formal education has been limited to the production of teachers' guides for sex education. The fact that the Peruvian NGOs have dealt only with sex education materials and not the entire formal educational system suggests a limited acknowledgement of the considerable gender socialization power that schooling wields, or their trepidation to attack it or concern about the consequences of entanglement with such an established and probably hostile institution.

The explanation provided by both MR and FT for their low involvement with formal education is that they began their feminist activities in order to solve the concrete problematic situation of adult women and this in turn took them to problems linked to this age group, problems associated with democracy, health, human rights and income generation. Formal education is also a terrain where the influence of the opposition by the Catholic Church is strong. In both Peru and the Dominican Republic, the hierarchy of the Catholic Church has acted promptly in the matter of sex education; to delete text it found controversial, to prevent any discussion of families or personal identities not based on heterosexual relations and to present motherhood as the true calling of women.[4]

The impact of feminist action

The accumulated work of feminist NGOs has resulted in important changes in cultural perceptions as well as in new legislation. At the individual level, women participating in the workshops offered by the NGOs report substantive personal change.

> We use the knowledge (acquired in the workshops) in our private lives. Before, we used to think that a person was only a woman or a man. In our family life, we were beasts of burden – taking care of husband, children. Our husbands' fear [of transformation] has not changed. He does not fix coffee. His mind is still closed, he says he doesn't know how to and refuses to learn. But with our children it is different. Today I don't have to iron [my son's] shirt. He irons his own; he even irons mine.
>
> (Woman from an agricultural union served by CIPAF)

> Yes, we have made progress. We now can talk about domestic violence. My husband does not say 'I washed the dishes'. He does so with making a comment about it. There have been improvements in domestic life but there have been also many ruptures. The cost is high. There are now shared domestic work especially among young couples. The division of tasks at home has changed.
>
> (Woman from a popular sector, now an urban leader served by MR)

In the Dominican Republic, in response to eight years of women's pressure, the government created a Women's State Secretariat in 1999 and gave it its own operating budget, personnel and equipment. The government also passed legislation to modify the agrarian law to give women access to land distributed under the agrarian reform, and rights to credit and technical training. It also passed legislation against intra-family violence, which established several penalties for perpetrators and enabled women to seek medical attention, and a law to protect minors and establish a mandate for child support by fathers not living with their children.

A Women's Ministry[5] existed in Peru shortly after 1995. It was created by former President Fujimori in an attempt to appear democratic (he was the only president attending the Fourth Women's World Conference and made the announcement for the creation of such ministry at this venue). From its inception, however, this ministry was given a large social agenda that included not only women's issues but sports, orphan children, resettlement operations, among others, but very little funding for gender issues per se. Nonetheless, Peru registers several advances in gender legislation, which include protection against sexual harassment, legislation in favour of domestic workers and measures to determine paternity and to secure fathers' support for children out of wedlock. An important victory has been the implementation of electoral quotas for political parties in municipal and congressional elections. These quotas (to include no less than 30 per cent of either sex among the candidates) have facilitated the increase of women in political office, particularly in municipal and regional government. In the 2006 presidential elections, a woman – Lourdes Flores of *Unión Nacional*, a conservative party – ran for president and obtained the third highest number of votes among several candidates. The 2006–2011 Peruvian National Congress is 30 per cent female. The presence of women in public decision making is an important development, and the greater participation by women in local and regional governments is considered to have 'changed the dynamics and the cultural symbols throughout the country' (Miloslavich 2006). As Guzmán (2003) observes, to attain gender equality requires going beyond equal *opportunity* and makes mandatory the participation of women through transformed basic rules, hierarchies and practices of public institutions. Women, therefore, must be present in public spaces, where debates about new and more democratic forms of governance can be created.

In Peru, feminist work succeeded in the establishment of a Women's Unit when the national Ombudsman's Office was created. It also succeeded in creating local offices to defend the rights of children and adolescents against violence (DEMUNAs), which receive complaints about family violence and forward them to relevant public offices. The DEMUNAs create an important space for the protection of both women and their children because violence against children is often accompanied by violence against women. Through those local offices, women are enabled to bring charges against abusive partners. Even though these offices are weakly funded, the fact that they exist points to an explicit effort by the state to combat violence against children. Through feminist action, there have been modifications to various pieces of legislation on issues of rape, family violence and sexual harassment, and new legislation on issues such as the creation of women's police posts, the mandated use of blood tests to determine paternity and the right of mothers to determine the last name of their children.

A major realization among NGOs is that, while legislation may be passed, implementation may fall substantially behind, in part because some state branches may not support the legislation (e.g. judges not applying the punishment mandated by law) or government officials may not understand several gender issues (e.g. the understanding of domestic violence by police). Aware of these types of obstacles, feminist NGOs have renewed efforts to engage in monitoring of state action and have endorsed the concept of accountability.

The feminist NGOs were led by middle-class women, mostly with university education. The awareness raising and training courses they provided served most often popular women (low-income women). They also served middle-class women, particularly those seeking or already in political office and those attending university (through enrolment in gender studies). Upper-class women were simply out of the equation, as they did not seek involvement in any of these activities.

The role of feminist organization

The examination of the educational and political work carried out by feminist NGOs reveals the crucial need for such work to be embedded in the development of stable organizations. The configuration of formal structures is important to develop an explicit sense of purpose, engage in focused action, and learn from one's success and failures through the development of an organizational memory. The existence of an organization also enables feminist action to take place in a deliberate way, where strategies can be designed and a repertoire of effective means be developed both to convey new knowledge and to persuade others to change. The accumulated experience and the social recognition earned over time further enables these NGOs to act as important representatives of women's demands and thus act as significant interlocutors with the state.

These feminist NGOs are led by middle-class women, all with higher education and with expertise in specific disciplines. They are also women convinced of the need to act politically. Their collective identity as women does not imply suppression of the recognition of differences that exist in terms of their positions toward abortion, degree of collaboration with the state and sexual orientation. The leadership of the feminist NGOs has varied in the degree to which there was rotation of persons in executive positions, with CIPAF evincing the least turnover and FT the greatest circulation. The NGOs also placed different emphasis in the work they conducted, often to match the professional composition of their staff members. But all engage in forms of non-formal education and informal learning as the key mechanism to bring about changes in the national imagery, in women's human rights and in their political power.

Some scholars fear that the creation of stable feminist organizations have negative consequences; thus, Alvarez states:

> The NGOization and transnationalization of the Latin American feminist field appeared to have led increasing numbers of feminists to privilege some spaces of feminist politics, such as the state and the international policy arenas, over efforts to transform prevailing representations of gender, emphasize changes in consciousness, and promote cultural transformation through local, grassroots-oriented organizing and mobilization activities.
>
> (1998: 315)

The charge is that important categories such as citizenship, development, the family and gender are not being adequately discussed (ibid.) and that 'the street and/or creative mobilizations [which were] innovative and daring and which marked the feminist existence and visibility in previous decades were lost' (Ungo 1998: 196). To this, a founding member of FT replies that new times call for new strategies and that a crucial realization today is that women's rights can exist only in the context of a wider democratic society.

In the face of a state behaviour which, while officially recognizing the need to improve the conditions of women, in reality lags well behind its action either to address women's needs or to alter the relations of gender, the work of feminist NGOs is fundamental to create a crucial point of entry to public policy. Sometimes this means engaging in action from below – through the education of women for a more proactive citizenship – and sometimes action from above – putting pressure on the state and influencing it to pass adequate legislation. At the same time, to become an actor of weight vis-à-vis the state, feminist institutions need to position themselves as organizations with knowledge, expertise and the ability to mobilize others. To act only as a movement, i.e. the confluence of forces around a given interest, gives women little leverage and fewer opportunities to develop the capacity to question the state as pertinent.

Conclusions

Overall, the contribution of feminist NGOs in the area of education presents features that are socially transformative: the knowledge conveyed aims at providing a critical understanding of how society functions and how changes can be introduced to modify people's mentalities about what it means to be female or male. The messages go beyond the mere attainment of numerical parity between men and women and seek to provide the grounds for a reconstituted social order. Through both cognitive and material means, women participating in the NGOs have been able to acquire considerable empowerment over their lives and secure recognition and redistribution in the process – two crucial elements recognized in the gender transformational literature (e.g. Fraser and Honneth 2003).

For these women, the term *feminist* is used with pride and signifies a strong commitment to social justice. Their NGOs address human rights, a wider definition of citizenship, access to concrete goods such as property, credit, sexuality and reproductive rights, the body not only as an intimate place but also as a political space, the rights to be free of violence and to secure benefits for one's children, and the need for a secular state. At times, the agenda is daunting, yet the multiple needs it comprises must be addressed, especially considering that some of the issues are avoided by the state or touched upon in very superficial manner. NGOs operating in poor societies – as in the case of Peru and the Dominican Republic – must further negotiate a delicate and difficult balance between attending the basic needs of low-income women and moving these women as well as others in higher social classes toward a theoretical understanding of gender issues. The demands derived from the pressing national needs and those from strategic action often conflict with one another; resolutions are not easy and sometimes one prevails over the other. In all, their contribution exceeds what might be expected given their size and financial resources. More feminist organizations for women, rising from subjection away from government resistance and control, and in spaces where new consensuses might be reached, seem imperative. The good news is that NGOs addressing women's rights in Latin America number about 600 and that those conducting research on women are about 120 (FLACSO-Chile 1995, cited in Henríquez 2003: 90).

Within the feminist movement, many strategies may be used to link the state and civil society. Education, however, emerges as a solid core in the production of counter-hegemonic knowledge and practice. Both streams of education – formal and non-formal – are needed. But it is important to recognize feminist NGO action as a crucial if not always visible way to educate women and others in the basic dimensions of gender in society. While these NGOs reach directly only a small number of women, their indirect impact is much wider and touches key formal institutions. As legitimate interlocutors in the process of gender transformation, they should be accepted at consultation tables in international forums and at negotiation tables formulating national agreements. In a context of weak policy-making institutions at higher levels, including the presence of global policies such as the Millennium Development Goals (United Nations 2000), which do not foster sufficiently the autonomous advancement of women, solutions will have to come from outside as well as from inside traditional political institutions.

Notes

1 For comprehensive reviews of studies that examine the impact of women's education on a long list of outcomes, see Herz and Sperling (2003) and King and Hill (1993).
2 At the time of founding CIPAF, *feminine* and not *feminist* action was chosen to avoid rejection of its work.
3 A literary genre that uses photographs to present the protagonists and plots of a story.
4 For a historical account of the family in Latin America, see Dore (1997).
5 Initially this ministry was called PROMUDEH (Ministry for the Promotion of Women and Human Development). After 2003, with a new administration, it was renamed MIMDES (Ministry for Women and Human Development).

References

Alvarez, S. (1998) 'Latin American feminisms "go global": trends of the 1990s and challenges for the new millennium' in S. Alvarez, E. Dagnino and A. Escobar (eds) *Cultures of Politics. Politics of Cultures. Re-visioning Latin American Social Movements*, Boulder, CO: Westview Press, pp. 293–324.

Dore, E. (ed.) (1997) *Gender Politics in Latin America: Debates in Theory and Practice*, New York: Monthly Review Press.

Foley, G. (2001) *Strategic Learning. Understanding and Facilitating Organisational Change*, Sydney: Center for Popular Education.

Fraser, N. and Honneth, A. (2003) *Redistribution or Recognition? A Political–Philosophical Exchange*, London: Verso.

Freire, P. (1970) *Pedagogy of the Oppressed*, New York: Herder and Herder.

Guzmán, V. (2003) Gobernabilidad Democrática y Género, una Articulación Posible, Santiago: Unidad Mujer y Desarrollo, UN Economic and Social Commission, October, manuscript.

Henríquez, N. (2003) *Ciudadanía y Derechos en una Nueva Era: Los Derechos Económicos y Sociales de las Mujeres como Desafío*, Lima: Comité de América Latina y el Caribe para la Defensa de los Derechos de la Mujer.

Herz, B. and Sperling, G. (2003) 'What works in girls' education'. Working draft, Available online at: www.savethechildren.net/nepal.key_issues/girls_education.doc. (accessed 18 February 2005).

King, E. and Hill, A. (eds) (1993) *Women's Education in Developing Countries: Barriers, Benefits, and Policies*, Baltimore, MA: Johns Hopkins University Press.

Lloyd, C. (ed.) (2005) *Growing Up Global. The Changing Transitions to Adulthood in Developing Countries*, Washington, DC: The National Academies Press.

Miloslavich, D. (2006) 'Ministerio de la Mujer ha sido un desastre para las mujeres', *Expreso*, 2 January.

Stromquist, N. (2006) *Feminist Organizations and Social Transformation in Latin America*, Boulder, CO: Paradigm Publishers.

UNESCO (2006) *EFA Monitoring Report. Literacy for Life*, Paris: UNESCO.

Ungo, U. (1998) 'Dilemas del pensamiento feminista: Del nudo a la paradoja' in C. Olea Mauleón (ed.) *Encuentros (Des)Encuentros y Búsquedas. El Movimiento Feminista en América Latina*, Lima: Flora Tristan, pp. 173–207.

United Nations (2000) *Millennium Development Goals*, New York: United Nations.

Index

Lightning Source UK Ltd.
Milton Keynes UK
29 May 2010

154874UK00003B/72/P